MODE
ELEMENTARY
LEVEL

revised edition
G. Windfuhr

Gernot Windfuhr
and
Hassan Tehranisa

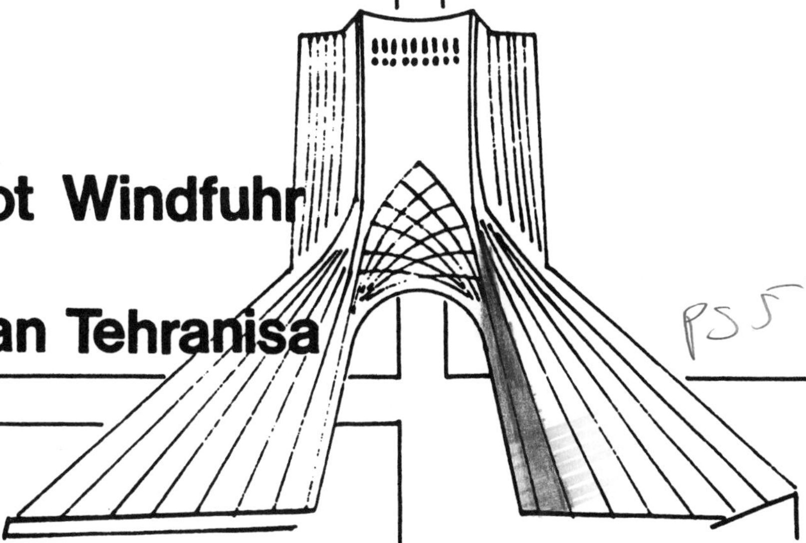

**Department of
Near Eastern
Studies
University of
Michigan
Ann Arbor, Michigan
1981**

[handwritten annotations:]

PS 59 - urd

81, 65, 53

fill in the blanks

translations
PS 65, 76,

scrambled sentences
here too pps 81, 71, 66

pp 32-82

lesson 3-5

to

Holger and Kirsten Windfuhr

and

Mahin Tehranisa

TABLE OF CONTENTS

ACKNOWLEDGEMENTS

The grammar of this textbook was written by Gernot L. Windfuhr; the remainder was composed jointly by the same and Seyed Hassan Tehranisa, a doctoral student of linguistics and teaching assistant of Persian in the Department of Near Eastern Studies at the University of Michigan.

The typing of the Persian text along with considerable editorial advice was done by Mr. Hossein Keshtkar, who also provided the cover design. Much thanks too goes to the patient efforts of Ms. Amy Van Voorhis, Ms. Diana Malouf, Mr. David Schoenbach, Ms. Jeanine Bugh, Ms. Sarah Dwight, and Ms. Kelly Kinney in typing the English text. Ms. Jane Hansen ably handled much of the day-to-day administrative and financial work for the project.

We thank the students of our Persian classes for their enthusiasm in being the 'testing ground' for the grammatical explanations and the didactic approach taken during the last few years.

Finally, we owe thanks to the Department of Near Eastern Studies for its support in producing this outline.

Gernot L. Windfuhr

The University of Michigan

Ann Arbor, Michigan

August, 1979

FOREWORD

This study is conceived of as an introduction to Persian grammar and as a basic reference guide.

It presents an outline of the grammatical structure of contemporary formal Persian including certain structures which have recently become acceptable in formal Persian. The structure of formal Persian is essentially identical with that of its colloquial variant. Hints at the latter are given in Appendix V.

Persian is an Indo-European language at a stage roughly the same as English. In both the former complex morphology is considerably reduced. Thus, syntax and semantics become more readily and more immediately the focus of attention. These are the aspects which continue to present problems to the learner.

Many important insights into the syntactic-semantic structure of Persian are quite recent, few of them have found their way into grammars and textbooks. This outline has benefitted from such insights.[1] In presenting them, an attempt was made to reformulate the technical observations in a linguistically accurate, yet intelligible language.

---

[1] The immediate basis of the grammatical discussion are G. L. Windfuhr: _Persian Grammar, History and State of Its Study, Part One_ = _Trends in Linguistics. State-of-the-Art Reports_ #12. The Hague-Paris (1979) and G. L. Windfuhr. _Persian Grammar. An Introductory Outline_. Ann Arbor, Michigan, 1978. Those books as well as this textbook benefitted, among others, from studies by Kh. Farshidvard,, Ch. A Ferguson, G. Hincha, C. T. Hodge, J. Meyer-Ingwersen, Parviz N. Khanlari, G. Lazard, Wolfgang Lentz, C. MacKinnon, J. A. Moyne, Gertrude Nye, L. Pejsikov, David Peterson, Ju. Rubinčik, Ali Ashraf Sadeqi.

If there can be said to be a guiding philosophy behind the conception of this volume it is that of the "middle way", seeking to serve the needs and interests of the wide variety of students studying Persian today, and seeking to accommodate the diverse philosophies of teaching Persian found throughout the major universities of the world.

A second guiding philosophy in this course is the continuing emphasis on the "four skills" approach, involving speaking, comprehension, reading and writing. Ideally, students completing this volume should be able to read most simple texts independently with the aid of a dictionary, carry on simple conversations, understand the substance of simple discourse, and write in simple narrative style.

The authors of this volume see students of Persian today as falling into several major groups, all with widely different concerns. The smallest group of students studying Persian are those who intend pursuing a career exclusively devoted to the study of Persian language and literature; despite its small size, this group is a most dedicated and demanding one. On the other hand, perhaps the largest group of Persian students today come from the social sciences and to a lesser extent the humanities and wish to pursue topics for graduate dissertations for which they need Persian as a field language, or a tool for library or documentary research. Another sizable group of students consists of persons who need or want to learn Persian for personal or business reasons.

Among instructors of Persian, there is a similar range of philosophies and predilections. In general, this volume has been designed considering instructors who are not themselves linguists or language teaching specialists, and who therefore have neither the time nor the inclination to engage in the intensive design of original instructional materials. Nevertheless, it is hoped that those instructors of Persian who have been actively engaged in linguistic research, or who have themselves written elementary texts, will find this material of interest as well.

It is assumed that the reader is an English speaking adult, and that learning a second language at that stage in life will initially involve 'translation', i.e. the comparison between the English and the Persian structures. Accordingly, the didactic approach taken is a version of contrastive grammar.

Appealing not only to the learning ability of adults but also their intelligence is likely to help in the learning process. Skills initially learned consciously and systematically are easier to internalize and automatize. Based on this assumption, the linguistic 'logic' inherent in Persian grammar, including the 'logic' of the interdependence of the grammatical phenomena - 'how they hang together' - is hinted at as much as such is possible at all. Inevitably a good part of those observations is didactic more than linguistic.

This study is an _outline_ of Persian grammar. Only the essential points are discussed, without an attempt at detail.

However, the coverage is fairly comprehensive[2].

As indicated above, this presentation focuses on the syntactic-semantic aspects of grammar. As such it differs from other textbooks of Persian; it is hoped that the reader may find that focus useful for the understanding of the peculiarities of Persian grammar[3].

The sequence of presentation is nominal morpho-syntax, clause syntax, verbal syntax, and the syntax of complex sentences. Included are observations on topicalization ('focusing') in various parts of grammar and the interaction of subordination and the verb system.

The main part is preceded by an outline of the pronunciation and the writing system and is followed by five appendices, presenting briefly main points on the orthography of the glottal stop, Arabic in Persian, handwriting, additional notes on pronunciation and stress, and formal to informal Persian.

It has been felt that students should develop all four principal language skills: speaking, comprehension, reading and writing throughout the year. Consequently, dialogues, readings and drills have been designed with this in mind. An attempt has been made to use "real" texts, especially in the later lessons, rather than constructed readings. To aid in comprehension, all reading texts and dialogues have been recorded for use in the language laboratory.

[2] Among the topics not included are participial clauses (literary Persian only), participial attributes, the gerundive and verbal noun phrases.

[3] Among topics of particular import is the Persian verb system. Its aspectual nature (completed-incomplete) and the existence of reported vs. narrated speech has only recently been recognized by this author.

The basic unit of this textbook is the Lesson. Rather than adhering to a uniform structure, each lesson has its own individual structure, so as to provide variety and, hopefully, continuous challenge.

The materials in this volume have been designed for flexible classroom usage. Many instructors may find it useful to have students memorize the dialogues given. Actual role-playing using the dialogues as "scripts" has often been found very effective as a teaching technique. Although most drills are conceived as "in-class" exercises with little or no outside preparation necessary, many can usefully be done as written exercises as well.

The lexicon presented includes approximately 1200 items. An attempt was made to provide lists of items belonging to the same contextual-topical area rather than relying only on the rather haphazard co-occurrence of items of any given text. In addition, a good number of readings and dialogues are designed to function both as reading and speaking practice and lexical-grammatical drills.

Most drills were composed with the objective of presenting a challenge to the student, including questions as to the reason for the use of particular grammatical constructions, in preference over mechanical drills.

In conclusion, we feel that this textbook presents the elements of Persian in a fresh and intellectually challenging way, in a way, we hope, which makes learning Persian at least a little bit more pleasant.

Notes on the Revised Edition

This textbook, first published in 1979, has enjoyed an increasing distribution. For the present third printing a good number of revisions, rearrangements of material, several additions and corrections have been made, and pictures added.

I thank Mrs. Jane Hansen and Mr. Sahba La'l for their skillful typing, and my students, and some colleagues, for their many suggestions.

The new texts and dialogs, and the revised texts, were taped by Mr. John Green and Mr. Sahba La'l.

A textbook is hardly ever perfect; moreover, didactic attitudes and students' interests keep changing. Yet I hope that even in this imperfect shape with all its limitations and biases, this revised edition of the textbook will continue to make the learning of Persian enjoyable.

Gernot L. Windfuhr
The University of Michigan
Ann Arbor, Michigan
October 1981

Tapes for the texts in this textbook are available from:

Ms. Peggy Thomas
Michigan Tape Duplication
University of Michigan
400-416 South Fourth Street
Ann Arbor, MI   48109
U.S.A.

L E S S O N 1
دَرسِ یِک

T H E   A L P H A B E T
اَلِفبا

1) General observations, 2) shapes, 3) the groups of letters, 4) the letters in alphabetical order, 5) different letters pronounced alike; 6) vowel signs, 7) five more diacritics

---

Note: Lessons 1 and 2 describe the writing and sound systems which require 'ancillary' skills different from the skills for producing texts, i.e. conversation and composition, the main objective, which begins with lesson 3. You should begin with lesson 3 even if reading and pronouncing have not been fully mastered; that will come with practice as you procede steadily and carefully.

1) GENERAL OBSERVATIONS

Persian words are written from right to left (just as books begin from the 'back'). The <u>shapes</u> of the Persian (Arabic) alphabet and of the Latin alphabet are remotely related. The most obvious similarity is between the letters 'L' in Arabic and Latin which are the inverse of each other: ل - L.

Differences

In Persian there are:

1) no capital letters vs. small letters as in English;

2) no 'printed,' i.e. unconnected, letters vs. 'handwritten' connected letters; also :

3) each letter has one, and only one, basic pronunciation (except for ی و ا: either /v-y-ʔ/ or /u-i-ā/; see p. 17).

1

2) <u>SHAPES</u>

    a) <u>Base line and 'bands'</u>

       English letters are written on a base line and extend

       over three 'bands'; most letters extend over either

       the upper two or lower two bands, some are written

       in the middle 'band' only.

       Similarly, in Persian the letters are written on a

       base line, but they extend over <u>four</u> 'bands': two narrow

       bands framed by two wider bands. Some letters fill just

       the lower central band, some both central bands, some the

       upper three bands, some the lower two bands. For example:

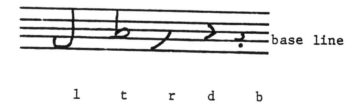

b) <u>Diacritics</u>

Each letter of the Latin alphabet has a different shape,
for example b:p / t:d / k:g. In Persian many distinctions
are not made by difference of shape but by diacritic dots,
e.g.:

Thus, there are 'pairs' of letters sharing the same basic
shape but having a different number of dots.

c) <u>Final arabesques</u>

In final position, most letters (basic shapes) end in an
arabesque (mostly either a long stretch to the left, or a
semicircle), e.g.:

d) <u>Connecting stroke</u>

Most Persian letters always <u>have to be connected</u> to
the following letters on their left by a 'linking stroke,'
in the central band, for example:

            db   d   b

Only four letter shapes must <u>never connect</u> to the left.
(see below)

3) <u>THE GROUPS OF LETTERS</u>

One way of learning the letters is to learn them in alphabetical
order. However, it may be easier to learn them as shape-groups
defined on the basis of the similarities of their shapes. The
criteria for this grouping are:

1) the basic shape shared by those letters which are distinguished
only by diacritic dots;

2) the shape of the final arabesque; and

3) whether the letters can be connected to the left,

    i.e. in the direction of the flow of writing, or not.

The pattern of practicing: The letters will be practiced as
follows: First, the letters in each group will be practiced
alone, then in combination with each other, finally in
combination with preceding groups.

Practice sheets

Writing could be practiced on paper with single lines or
even no lines. However, in order to get a better feel for the
relative sizes of the letters, it is preferable to use
copies of the attached page with the 'musical' staves.

Note

These writing practices are basically silent practices.
Persian pronunciation is practiced in the next section.
In order to avoid total silence, so to speak, all words of
this writing practice are also sounded on tape. Please
listen to the tape and try to repeat as a first step
towards listening and pronunciation practice.

					خورشید
					کوه
					ماهی
					گاو

PERSIAN WRITING PRACTICE SHEET

'Print' letters carefully ('smoother' handwriting should
be practiced later, see pp. 355-359).

All assignments should indicate your name, the date,
the number of the lesson, and the page of the textbook.

a) <u>Group A: letters always unconnected to the left</u>

There are four letter-shapes which do not connect

left; they are all contained within the word (which

you should memorize):

d   r   ?   v   ←

=vāred 'entering'

Copy:

دو ــ وارد ــ دار ــ دَر ــ رود ــ ورود ــ دارد ــ راد ــ دارا ــ دور #2
far (name) strong/ has entrance river door frame
           persistent

روا ــ داور ــ رد ــ داد ــ دُرد ــ رو
face ache ache rejection referee
                 failer

LISTEN TO THE TAPE

FOR INTONATION AND STRESS SEE PP. 361-366

The following letters are distinguished from two of

the letters above by dots only. They likewise do not

connect to the left:

ž   z   r   . z   d

Copy:

دزد ــ زود ــ زور ــ دراز ــ روز ــ زر ــ درز ــ زد ــ زار ــ زاد ــ ارز
currency born crying hit seam gold day tall strength thief
                                                    force

راز ــ زور ــ درازا
length secret

FOR THE COMPLETE ALPHABET SEE p. 15

The following groups:

1) all connect to the left;

2) all, except Group G, have an arabesque when in final position;

3) Groups E and F have special shapes a) when connected from the right in middle positions, and b) when standing alone, i.e. unconnected on either side.

b) Group B: letters with a left-stretch in final position

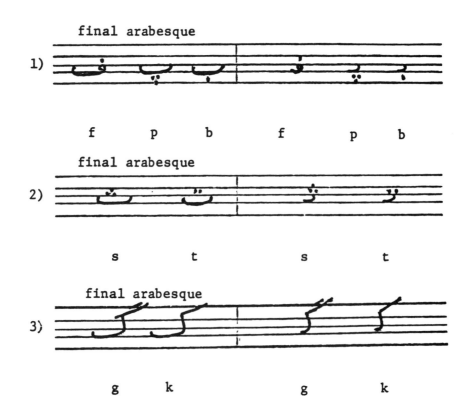

These letters are connected with a small linking stroke on the base line.

Copy:

تب ـ کف ـ تک ـ کت ـ پف ـ تف

coat   alone   bubble   fever
floor

These letters can also be connected to the letters of Group A., i.e., while the letters of Group A cannot be connected with following letters, these must be connected with preceding letters other than Group A.

Copy: (Combination of Group A and Group B)

ـ بابا ـ بازار ـ دا را ب ـ بد ـ بر ـ ببر ـ بز ـ باز ـ بار ـ پا ـ

foot   load   open   goat tiger over bad
(paw)

پارو ـ پدر ـ پر ـ پر ـ توپ ـ تا ـ تار ـ تبر ـ ببر ـ وفا ت ـ برف ـ تو

you snow death ~~death~~ axe string to/till ball   shovel

کدو ـ کر ـ کرد ـ کود ـ کفر ـ کور ـ بزک ـ ترک ـ برکت ـ پا کت ـ

paw cat battycat turk bzak koor aatheistic fertilizer elect squash

تگرگ ـ برگ ـ بگو ـ گاو ـ با زرگا ن ـ فرد ـ ژرف

gov   birg   tager
cow

c) Group C: letters with a left-downward swing in final
   position

final arabesque

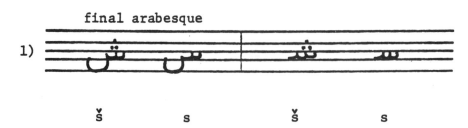

1)

   š   s   š   s

Copy: (Combination of Group A, B and C)

سر ــ سد ــ سگ ــ بس ــ داس ــ کس ــ فارس ــ کشور ــ کشاورز ــ رسا

رشک ــ کشو ــ پاساژ ــ پسر ــ سار ــ ساگن ــ شاد ــ شام

شاگرد

final arabesque

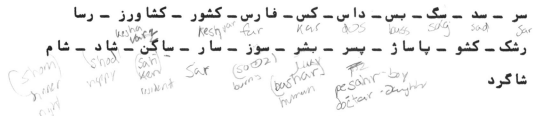

2)

   z   s   z   s

Copy: (Combination of Group A, B and C)

ضد ــ تمادف ــ صدف ــ فرض ــ وصف ــ وضو ــ صف ــ ماف ــ صدا ــ صد ــ

ضرورت ــ ضرب ــ ضرر ــ صبر ــ صدر ــ صفا ــ صورت

final arabesque

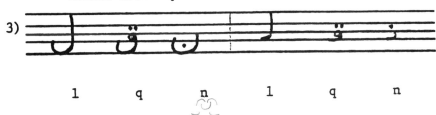

3)

l   q   n   l   q   n

Copy: (Combination of Group A, B and C)

نو ـ نور ـ نر ـ سن ـ لوكس ـ لاك ـ لگد ـ بلور ـ بلوار ـ گل ـ

گلاب ـ قفل ـ رقص ـ قصر ـ شال ـ بشقاب ـ قاب ـ قشنگ ـ قبول ـ

لباس ـ لذت ـ نادان ـ نانوا ـ ناشی

d) **Group D:** one letter with the simplest, one with the most

elegant arabesque

final arabesque

y   m   y   m

Copy: (Combination of Group A, B, C and D)

مد ـ مادر ـ مرد ـ مگس ـ من ـ كم ـ كردم ـ كردی ـ كرد ـ كرديم

كرديد ـ كردند ـ سی ـ بلی ـ ميكنم ـ ميكنی ـ ميكند ـ ميكنيم

ميكنيد ـ ميكنند ـ ماست ـ مال ـ مبل ـ ياددا شت ـ يكديگر ـ يكسان

e) <u>Group E: letters with inward swing in final position</u>

final arabesque

1)

x   h   c   j   x   h   ch   j

Copy: (Combination of Group A, B, C, D and E)

جا ــ چون ــ کج ــ محمد ــ کچل ــ رنج ــ حسن ــ پنج ــ لحاف ــ جشن

چشم ــ چمن ــ حل ــ حق ــ ناخن ــ خال ــ نخ ــ مخ ــ بخت ــ تخت ــ

سخت ــ کج ــ جوب ــ چوب ــ جواد ــ نجار ــ بخاری ــ خر ــ چرم ــ

جسور ــ جاوید ــ جام

arabesque

2)   alone   final   connected from right   initial

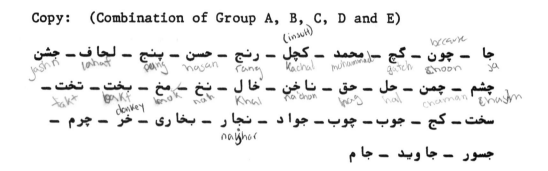

q   ?   q   ?   q   ?   q   ?

Copy: (Combination of group A, B, C, D and E)

علم ــ دعا ــ باغ ــ ربع ــ بغل ــ بعد ــ علی ــ عجیب ــ عقب ــ عاقبت ــ

بغداد ــ بعضی ــ عقاید ــ تعمیر ــ عاج ــ عابر ــ عادل ــ عاشق ــ عالم

عالی ــ عدد ــ غایب ــ غاز ــ غروب ــ غلط ــ غیبگو ــ غنچه ــ غم

f) Group F: the letter called the 'two-eyed /h/' because

of its initial shape

alone	final	connected from right	initial
h	h	h	h

Copy: (Combination of Group A, B, C, D, E and F)

هر ــ هم ــ بها ــ هندوستان ــ چهار ــ تنها ــ سه ــ به ــ چه ــ که ــ

هفت ــ پانزده ــ ده ــ عقیده ــ بقیه ــ همین ــ نه ــ نهر ــ هشت

ژاله ــ هنوز ــ هدف ــ هدیه ــ هرگز ــ هزار ــ هلو ــ هنرمند ــ هوا

g) Group G: two letters without final arabesque

z   t

Copy: (Combination of Group A, B, C, D, E, F and G)

فقط ــ ظهر ــ نظر ــ طرف ــ طاهره ــ طالبی ــ طاعون ــ طبیب ــ

ناظر ــ منظره ــ مطلب ــ ظن ــ مظنون ــ طرفدار ــ طبقه ــ طرح ــ

طعنه ــ طناب ــ طلب ــ طوطی ــ ظرف ــ ظاهرا ــ ظریف ــ ظالم ــ ظرفیت

4) <u>The letters in alphabetical order</u>

Up to here, the letters have been introduced according to
their shapes. The actual alphabetical sequence of the letters
is given in the accompanying chart. Note that most letters
have the same shape in initial position and in middle
position. Also, most letters have the same shape in final
position whether connected or not. Only two letter
shapes have special connected forms (boxed in on the chart).

The letters in
alphabetical
order

(A = letters
occuring mostly
in Arabic
loanwords;
P = letters
found in
Persian only.)

ALONE	END	MIDDLE	INITIAL			NAME
ا	ا	ا	ا	?		alef
ب	ب	ب	ب	b		be
پ	پ	پ	پ	p	P	pe
ت	ت	ت	ت	t		te
ث	ث	ث	ث	s	A	se-ye senokte
ج	ج	ج	ج	j		jim
چ	چ	چ	چ	c	P	ce che
ح	ح	ح	ح	h	A	he-ye jimi
خ	خ	خ	خ	x		xe
د	د	د	د	d		dāl
ذ	ذ	ذ	ذ	z	A	zāl
ر	ر	ر	ر	r		re
ز	ز	ز	ز	z		ze
ژ	ژ	ژ	ژ	ž	P	že
س	س	س	س	s		sin
ش	ش	ش	ش	š		šin
ص	ص	ص	ص	s^	A	sād
ض	ض	ض	ض	z	A	zād
ط	ط	ط	ط	t	A	tā
ظ	ظ	ظ	ظ	z	A	zā
ع	ع	ع	ع	?	(A)	?eyn
غ	غ	غ	غ	q		qeyn rein
ف	ف	ف	ف	f		fe
ق	ق	ق	ق	q		qāf
ک	ک	ک	ک	k		kāf
گ	گ	گ	گ	g	P	gāf
ل	ل	ل	ل	l		lām
م	م	م	م	m		mim
ن	ن	ن	ن	n		nun
و	و	و	و	v	○	vāv
ه	ه	ه	ه	h		he-ye docašm
ى	ى	ى	ى	y	ℛ	yā
ء	ء	ئأؤ	أ	?		hamze

5) <u>DIFFERENT LETTERS PRONOUNCED ALIKE:</u>

You have noticed that a number of letters of different shapes symbolize the same phoneme. This is because Persian has loaned many words from Arabic, where those letters do in fact represent different phonemes. But the Persians did not make those distinctions and assimilated the Arabic phonemes to the more similar Persian ones. (Just like Germans would pronounce 'what is this?' in German fashion as: vot iss ziss?)

The letters pronounced alike in Persian are:

four letters are pronounced /z/:	ظ	ض	ذ	ز
three letters are pronounced /s/:		ث	ص	س
two letters are pronounced /h/:			ح	ه
two letters are pronounced /t/:			ط	ت
two letters are pronounced /q/:			غ	ق
two letters are pronounced /ʔ/:			ع	ا/ء

The boxed-in letters are the ones to be used when writing your names.

Practice Names:

سوزان ـ نانسی ـ اسکات ـ اسپانیا ـ تهران ـ ایتالیا ـ قاهره

هایده ـ اهواز ـ زاهدان ـ فرانسه ـ هلند ـ پاکستان ـ تبریز

Note: written /nb/ نب is pronounced /mb/.

6) VOWEL SIGNS

a) Vowels are represented as follows:

1. The long vowels /ā-i-u/ are <u>always</u> represented by

   the letters / ا - ی - و /;

2. The short vowels /a-e-o/ <u>may</u> be represented by diacritic

   signs added over or under the preceding consonant

   letter as follows:

long		short	
/dir/	دیر	دِراز	/derāz/
/dur/	دور	دُر	/dorr/
/dār/	دار	دَر	/dar/

Practice:

1) Vowel /u/   ۱) کور ـ تور ـ نور ـ سوز ـ زور ـ شور ـ دور

2) Vowel /i/   ۲) بیست ـ تیر ـ نیست ـ سیب ـ نیم ـ سیم ـ سیمین

3) Vowel /ā/   ۳) کلاس ـ کار ـ ماشین ـ دهان ـ سال ـ مداد ـ تمام

Practice:

1) Vowel /a/   ۱) مادَر ـ تَبَر ـ فَقَط ـ ساعَت ـ دَفتَر ـ خَبَر ـ

                                حَسَن

2) Vowel /e/   ۲) پادِشاه ـ صادِق ـ کِرم ـ قِرمِز ـ نارِنْجی ـ

                                زاهِدان ـ چِشْمِه

3) Vowel /o/   ۳) بُزُرگ ـ تُعارُف ـ ناخُن ـ اَنگُشت ـ طُرق ـ اَنبَر ـ

                                شُتُر

<u>Note</u>: Many words end in a final consonant. This is <u>not</u> indicated by

     the silent sign ° (see section 7 of this lesson).

b) **Initial vowels**

When a word begins with a vowel, this vowel is in fact preceded by a slight glottal stop (as in English, e.g. ?utterly, at-?all, etc.). In Persian, this glottal stop is **always** represented by /alef/ as follows:

long	short
/?in/ این	اِسم /?esm/
/?u/ او	اُتوبوس /?otobus/
/?ān/ آن	اَبر /?abr/

Note that initial /?ā/ has a tilde (~) on it: آ .
This letter is actually a contraction of /alef/ representing the glottal stop and a second /alef/ representing
long /ā/; thus: اآ ── آ .

Practice: Initial short vowels:

۱) اَبْر ــ اَحْمَد ــ اَسْب ــ اَسْت ــ اَصْل

۲) اِسْم ــ اِمْتِحان ــ اِمْروز ــ اِنْشاء ــ اِضافه

۳) اُتوبوس ــ اُسْتاد ــ اُرْدو ــ الگو ــ امید

Practice: Initial long vowels:

۱) آب ــ آن ــ آمد ــ آثار ــ آزاد

۲) این ــ ایران ــ ایمان ــ ایده ــ ایرَج

۳) او ــ اور

c) <u>Final vowels</u>

Long vowels in final position are represented as elsewhere, i.e. by ا – ی – و . Final short vowels are represented as follows:

long		short	
/ki/	کی	بِه	/be/
/ku/	کو	تو	/to/
/tā/	تا	نَه	/na/

Note: The letter ـه representing final /e/ and /a/
is only an orthographic device; it is <u>not</u> to be mistaken
for the sound /h/, and is not pronounced.

Practice: Final short vowels:

۱) نه

۲) نا مه – خا نه – پُخْته – میوه – بَچه – سا ده

۳) مو – تو – شو – جو – دو

Practice: Final long vowels:

۱) اینْجا – آنْجا – تَماشا – پا – بابا – بالا – هَوا

۲) کی – با زی – مَعْنی – قا لی – تا کْسی

۳) با زو – با نو – پا رو – جا رو – زانو – یا رو – بو

DRILL:
Add vowel signs to the words on pp. 7-13 following their pronunciation on the tape.

d) <u>Diphthongs</u>

The two diphthongs /ey/ and /ow/ are represented as follows:

initial		medial		final	
/eyvān/	أَيْوان	/deyr/	دَيْر	/dey/	دَيْ
/owj/	أَوْج	/dowr/	دَوْر	/dow/	دَوْ

Practice:

1) /ey/

١) كَيْهان – حَيْوان – پَيْغَمْبَر – جَيْحون – پَيْدا

2) /ow/

٢) اينْطَوْر – حَوْله – حَوْمِلِه – تَوْهين – قَوْل – فَوْرًا

Practice: Initial diphthongs:

١) أَيْوان

٢) أَوْج – أَوْقات – أَوْلاد – أَوْصاف – أَوْلِيَا

Note that the diacritic is actually that for /a/, not those for /o/ or /e/ as one might have expected. The reason is that formerly the diphthongs were in fact pronounced /aw/ and /ay/, but later this /a/ assimilated to the following /w/ and /y/ respectively.

For reasons of clarity, even the long vowels can be identified by the vocalic signs and thus distinguished from other possible readings thus:

تَ تُو تُ تا تَيْ تِ تِي

ta   tow   to   tu   tā   tey   te   ti

Vowels Signs

	Initial	Middle	Final
ā	آن ān 'that'	ناف nāf 'navel'	تا tā 'till'
i	این in 'this'	تیم tim 'team'	کی ki 'who'
u	او u 'he/she'	تور tur 'tour'	تو tu 'inside'
a	اَبرو abru 'eye-brow'	پَر par 'feather'	نَه na 'no'
e	اِسم esm 'name'	دِل del 'heart'	خانِه xāne 'house'
o	اُردو ordu 'camp'	پُر por 'full'	تو to 'you'
ey	اَیوان eyvān 'portico'	کِیک keyk 'cake'	کِی key 'when'
ow	اَوج owj 'height	دَور dowr 'around'	نَو now 'new'

Note: except for ˉ in آ , the diacritic symbols are optional.

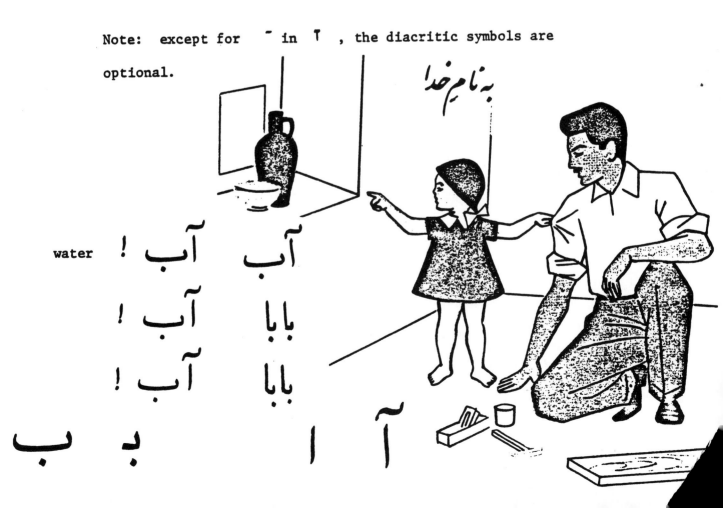

water ! آب آب

آب ! بابا

آب ! بابا

ب ب آ ا

DRILL: Try to read these words:

sponge	اِسْفَنْج *(esfang / esfakng)*		بازار
spinach	اِسْفِناج		شاه
pajamas	پِیْجا مه	sugar	شِکَر
pistachio	پِسْته	coffee	قَهْوه
woods	جَنْگَل	tea	چای
shawl	شال	orange	نارُنْج
khaki	خاکی	pepper	فلْفِل *(fel fel)*

Notes on و

a) <u>/o/ in European loanwords</u>

In loanwords such as /otobus/ 'bus'   the phoneme /o/ is represented by the letter و /v/ without diacritic, thus: اُتوبوس

b) In some Persian words /o/ is represented by و ; e.g.:

خود /xod/'self', خور /xor/ 'eat','sun', خوش /xoš/ 'well'
نخود /noxod/ 'pea'.

c) و after خ /x/ is silent in some words such as: خواب /xāb/
'sleep', خواه ‑ خواسْت /xāh-xāst/ 'wish, want', خوان /xān/
'read' and خواهَر /xāhar/ 'sister'.

(The 'irregularities' of c and d continue the orthography of an
earlier stage of Persian which had a complex phoneme /xw/. Later,
/w/ was lost before long vowels, but rounded a following short
/a/ to /o/; thus خود /xwad/ ➔ /xod/, خواب /xwāb/ ➔
/xāb/, etc.).

7) <u>FIVE MORE DIACRITICS</u>

Arabic has a few more diacritic symbols.

a) ° :سُكون (a small circle) indicates that there is <u>no</u>

vowel after the consonant; e.g. وَجْه /vajh/ 'way, means'.

b) اً :تَنْوین is the symbol for the (Arabic) adverbial ending

/-an/ (the equivalent of English '-ly'). The two dashes

are usually omitted, e.g.: فَوْراً = فَوْرا /fowran/ 'immed-

iately'.

c) ّ :تَشْدید is the symbol to indicate a double consonant,

e.g.: تَشَكُّر /tašakkor/ 'thanks', اَللّٰه /allāh/ 'Allah'.

Again, this symbol is usually omitted.

d) In some Arabic words a long 'ā' is not written, while

in others a written ی is pronounced /ā/. To indicate

the actual pronunciation of /ā/, an /alef/ may be written

on top of these words, e.g.:

اَللّٰه /allāh/; حَتّیٰ /hattā/

e) ص :وَصْله (resembling a small ص); it indicates that

the glottal stop of the Arabic definite article ال

is not pronounced; in Persian this is mostly found with

names such as عَبْدُاللّٰه 'Abdo-llah' instead of /ʔabdoʔallāh/.

The /l/ of this article assimilates to following dentals and

palatals, i.e. to /t, d, s, z, š, n/; e.g. نورُالدّین

'Nuro-ddin;.

This diacritic is usually omitted.

Drill: Try to read these English and French words which have entered Persian:

کِراوات	tie	ساندویچ	sand e vich / sandrich	اُتوبوس	bass
کُت	coat	سوپ	soap	تاکُسی	taxi
ژوپ	znore / skirt	سوس	sauce	ماشین	car
مینی ژوپ	miniskirt	سوسیس	sausage	ترن	train
پالتو	palto / jacket	سالاد	salad	پُمپِ بِنزین	gas station
بُلوز	blouse	ژامبون	salami	تِرافیک	traffic
پُلوور	pullover	هامبرگِر	hamburger	پارک	park
مایو	swimwear	بیفتِک	steak	پارکینگ	parking
پَتو	blanket	کُتلِت	cutlet	پُلیس	police
شوفاژ	A/c	اِشتِیک	steak	بانک	bank
وان	bath tub	اُملِت	omlet	پُست	post office
دوش	shower	ویسکی	whisky	تَمبر	stamp
کولر	cooler	وُدکا	vodka	تِلِفُن	telephone
مُبل	furniture	کوکا کولا	cocacola	تِلِگراف	telegraph
لامپ	lamp	پِپس پِپسی	pepsi	تِلِگرام	telegram
گاز	gas			تِلِکس	(telex)
		رادیو	radio	سینما	cinema
		تلویزیون	television	کافه	coffee
سانتر سانتیمتر	centimeter	گرام / گراموفون	gramophon	کافه تِریا	cafeteria
مِتر	meter	موسیقی	music	رِستوران	restaurant
کیلو	kilo	کُنسِرت	concert	گارسون	waiter
لیتر	liter	تآتر	theater	سوپرمارکت	supermarket
		آنتِراکت	intermission / Entract	هُتل	hotel
	thankyou	ویولون	violin	آسانسور	elevator
مِرسی		پیانو	piano		

LESSON TWO
درس دو

PRONUNCIATION
تَلَفُّظْ

1) Vowels, 2) consonants

The following pronunciation practices are basically oral. In order
to continue the practice of writing, all words are also written.
Please copy these words while practicing their pronunciation.

1) <u>VOWELS</u>

Singers practicing their pronunciation sometimes hold their
hand in front of their mouth and quickly pronounce short
syllables ending in various vowels <u>into</u> the palm of their hands.
That is how Persian vowels seem to be pronounced as compared to
English-American vowels. While this is not entirely true, the
practice of speaking into one's hand helps in the initial
phases of learning Persian.

beast-o-pany (25)

Persian has three pairs of vowels and one pair of diphthongs.
The most crucial pair is that of the two lower vowels, since
failure to distinguish between them results in misunderstanding.
The higher-mid pair of vowels has to be distinguished from the
two diphthongs in order to avoid misunderstanding (although
there are relatively few words where that could happen). The
pair of high vowels hardly ever leads to misunderstanding;
nevertheless, they too should be pronounced properly.

Generally speaking, the points of articulation of a Persian
vowel lies 'between' those of several English-American vowels or
variants of vowels. Moreover, all front vowels are somewhat
more fronted than English-American vowels.

a) <u>Lower pair /a:ā/</u>

/a/: lower than 'c<u>a</u>t'; higher and more fronted than
'c<u>u</u>t' and (American) 'c<u>o</u>p'

/ā/: further back than 'father'; similar to 'l<u>aw</u>' but
usually without rounding.

(/ā/ is always written by the letter /alef/, i.e. a long
vertical line; keeping this written length in mind is
helpful to observe the distinction in pronunciation.)

Practice:

1) Vowel /a/   ۱) سَر ـ فَرْدا ـ پَرْواز ـ سَگ ـ اَثَر ـ مُعَلِم ـ دَرْس

حَسَن ـ دَفْتَر ـ زَبان

2) Vowel /ā/   ۲) آب ـ آنْها ـ بالا ـ باهوش ـ آسان ـ رادیو

راحَت ـ راسْت ـ قاشِق و

b) <u>Higher-mid pair and diphthongs /e:o/ey:ow/</u>

/e/: lower than 'b<u>i</u>t'; higher and more fronted than

'b<u>e</u>t';

/o/: lower than 'f<u>oo</u>t'; similar to 'c<u>o</u>pe,' but without

rounding:

Practice:

1) Vowel /e/

۱) کِتاب ـ اِمْتِحان ـ مِداد ـ اِسْم ـ سِتارِه ـ اِمْشَب ـ دَرَخْت ـ زَرَنْگ

2) Vowel /o/

۲) پُر ـ پاسُخ ـ سُرْخ ـ مُعَلِّم ـ دو ـ دُخْتَر ـ تُند ـ بُزُرْگ ـ بُشْقاب

هُنَر

/e/ey/ /o/ow/: the position where English speakers most

regularly fail to distinguish between vowel and diphthong

is word-final position.

/ke/	'that, which'		/do/	'two'
/key/	'when'		/dow/	'the run'

In a way of speaking, then, /e,o/ are like the diphthongs

cut short, i.e. /ey/ and /ow/, like holding your breath

suddenly.

Practice:

1) Diphthong /ey/

۱) کَیْهان ـ حَیْوان ـ پَیْغَمْبَر ـ پَیْدا ـ جَیْحون

2) Diphthong /ow/

۲) کَوْکَب ـ دَوْ ـ جِلَوْ ـ چِطَوْر ـ حَوْصِلِه

ot /uw/.

Some American speakers tend to open their lips and unround
/u/. In Persian the lips must stay well rounded.

Practice:

Vowel /i/   بیمارِستان - جیلِهٍ - رُفتی - ایدِه - عَید

Vowel /u/   او - دور- کوه - طول - حوری

<u>Hint:</u> Whenever pronouncing /ā/ think you have a long match
vertically in your mouth. Whenever pronouncing /i/ the
match is horizontal. Whenever pronouncing /u/ pull your
lips as far forward as possible and sound them so that
there is just a tiny opening.

	front	back
high	i ← /siʃt/	/buvz/ → u
higher- mid	sit e ← set	foot → o /kowp/ ↗
	ey ← hey!	cope → ow
lower	cat a ← cut cop	law → ā father ↗

Approximate pronunciation

of Persian vowels.

صحنه‌ای از خیمه‌شب‌بازی

2) <u>CONSONANTS</u>

Most consonants are quite similar to English; some are
pronounced differently, a few are not found in English.

a) /c/ - <u>ch</u>ur<u>ch</u>; /j/ - '<u>G</u>eor<u>ge</u>,' '<u>J</u>ack';

/š/ - <u>sh</u>i<u>sh</u> kabob;

/ž/ - In English only found in 'azure.'

(often transcribed as <u>zh</u>).

Practice:

/c/ ۱) چراغ ــ چرا ــ چون ــ بچه ــ چین

[handwritten: mojve cheen, wrinkle, bache - child, chon - why, cherah, chē raag - lamp/light, neavse]

/j/ ۲) جام ــ جَمشید ــ أجداد ــ مَجلِس ــ مَسجِد

[handwritten: jam - goblet/cup, jamsheed, ajdod, mejlese]

/š/ ۳) شَمشیر ــ شاد ــ بَشَر ــ رِشته ــ تِمشک

[handwritten: tameshk, rashtery, reshte, basher, shad, sham sheer - word]

/ž/ ۴) ژالِه ــ ژُرف ــ ژیگولو ــ گاراژ ــ ژولیده

[handwritten: zholideh, garagh, zhegolo, zharf, zhale]

b) <u>/v/</u>

/v/ tends to approximate the pronunciation of /w/ before
back vowels, i.e. /ā-o-u/, e.g. /āword/ 'he brought,'
/tāwus/ 'peacock,' /āwāz/ 'song.'

Practice:

/v/ ۱) آوَرد ــ طاووس ــ آواز

[handwritten: avaz - song, tavoos]

۲) عَوَض ــ وَضْع ــ ویولُن

[handwritten: vee-o-lon, vaz, avaz - in return, vulin - situation]

c) **/l-r/**

In English these two are well rounded; in Persian they
are never rounded. The Persian pronunciation is approached
by pronouncing /l/ and /r/ with the lips spread to a grin
as wide as possible and moving the tip of the tongue
forward to the teeth. The Persian /r/ resembles the flip
heard when quickly pronouncing 'la**dd**er.'

Practice:

/l/ ۱) لازم ـ لوکس ـ گُل ـ کِلاس ـ قُفل

/r/ ۲) مَردُم ـ رِشتِه ـ رُئیس ـ رِضا ـ رَفت

Note: For the glottal stop as in رُئیس see Appendix I.

d) **/x/ (kh)**

Similar to the pairs of stop:fricative, /p:f/, /t:s/,
/č:š/ (<u>ch</u>:<u>sh</u>), there is also a fricative partner to /k/:
/k:x/. (This fricative is often transcribed in English
as <u>kh</u>). It is quite similar to the sound <u>ch</u> in German
'A<u>ch</u>tung!'

Practice:

/x/ ۱) خواهَر ـ خانُم ـ خواب ـ بُخاری ـ تَخت

e) **/h/x/**

Most students of Persian quickly learn to distinguish
between the stop /k/ and its fricative partner /x/ (kh).
But not a few overcompensate elsewhere; they tend to
pronounce /h/ like /x/, especially word-initial /h/.
Whenever pronouncing /h/, the less effort, the better!

Practice:

/h/
    ۱) اَحمَد ـ خواهَر ـ هَردو ـ مُهِم ـ مَحدود

f) **/q/ (gh)**

Similar to the pairs of voiceless:voiced fricatives
/f:v/, /s:z/, /š:ž/ (sh:zh), there is a voiced partner
to /x/:/x:q/. (/q/ is often transcribed as gh.)
For some learners, /q/ appears to be the most difficult
sound. In fact, it is quite easy to pronounce; it
approximates the sound of light snoring, and, of course,
French and German /r/ which is pronounced in the back
of the mouth. In Persian it is crucial to distinguish
/q/ from /r/ in order to avoid misunderstanding. Thus,
note:

         /r/   :   /q/

        front   back

(English /r/ unrounded)   (French, German /r/)

Mainly in word-initial position, /q/ tends to be
pronounced as an affricate, i.e., it is pronounced
with an onset; its articulation begins with a backed
/g/ before it is released as fricative: /^{g}q/.
This pronunciation is quite unique, but not difficult
to learn; it approximates the sound of the nasal
occlusion <u>interrupting a light snore</u> before it is
followed by the continuation of the light snore.
Never press or put too much effort into pronouncing
/q/. The less, the better.

Practice:

/q/

١) حُقوق ـ حَق ـ قُم ـ فَقَط ـ رَقْص

g) /ʔ/

/ʔ/ is the symbol for the glottal stop. In English this
is heard as the automatic click before vocalic onset,
as in 'utmost,' 'ever.' In Persian also the glottal
stop is heard before vocalic onset. But it also occurs
inside words. Unlike English, in Persian the glottal
stop is not an automatic sound but a consonant, more
specifically a glide and as such similar to /h/ and /y/.

Practice:

/ʔ/

١) مَسْئول ـ تَعْمیر ـ ساعَت ـ جُمعه

h) **Less effort on /h-?-y/**

These three consonants are glides, technically speaking.
In everyday speech, even rather formal speech, they
are usually just that. They are quite audible at the
beginning of words but much less so elsewhere. They
are pronounced very smoothly between vowels and consonants;
at the end of words /h/ and /?/ are, in fact, virtually
inaudible, i.e. dropped at the end of words, except in
very careful speech (see Appendix V). The less effort,
the better!

Practice:

/h/   ۱) صبْح ‪ـ‬ راه ‪ـ‬ نِه ‪ـ‬ دَه ‪ـ‬ کوه

/?/   ۲) جمْع ‪ـ‬ اِطلاع ‪ـ‬ مَمْنوع ‪ـ‬ سَریع ‪ـ‬ وُزَراء

/y/   ۳) چای ‪ـ‬ سَعْی ‪ـ‬ رَأی ‪ـ‬ نَهْی

(For stress, see Appendix IV .)

Table of Phonemes

Stops	fortis	p t c k
	lenis	b d j g
Fricatives	fortis	f s š x
	lenis	v z ž q
Nasals		m n
Liquids		l r
Glides		y h ?
Vowels	long	i ā u
	short	e a o
Diphthongs		ey ow

Note: 1) /c, j/ are actually affricates, 2) for further details see notes on pronunciation above and Appendix IV.

Drawing from an edition of Molla Nasroddin stories.

DRILL: Try to read these words:

(1)	(یِک)	lip	لَب *lab*		مادَر -mother
2	دو	brow	اَبْرو		پِدَر -father
3	سِه	navel	ناف		بَرادَر -brother
(4)	(چَهار)	foot	پا		دُختَر -daughter
5	پَنْج	tooth (dentist)	دَنْدان	grandchild (nephew)	نَوِه grandchild
6	شِش	no	نَه	man (mortal)	مَرْد man
7	هَفْت	name	نام	woman (gynaecologist)	زَن woman
8	هَشْت	new	نَوْ *dān*	I (cf. mine)	مَن I
9	نُه	door	دَر	you (thou)	تو you
10	دَه	mouse	مُوش	am	اَم am (verb)
		star	سِتاره	is	اَسْت ast

LESSON THREE

درسِ ســـــه

GETTING TO KNOW EACH OTHER

آشْنــائـی

1) Some expressions; drills; dialogue, 2) personal pronouns,

3) addressing and names; drills, 4) 'to be', 5) countries,

nationalities, languages; drills, 6) being someone or something,

7) asking questions, 8) وُ 'and'; vocabulary; drills

FOR INTONATION AND STRESS   SEE PP. 361-366

1) **SOME EXPRESSIONS**

very good	خِیْلی خوب
thank you	مِرْسی ممْنون
yes	بَلِه
no	نَخِیْر
that's right	دُرُسْت اَسْت
What is it in English?	بِه اِنْگِلیسی یَعْنی چِه ؟
What is it in Persian?	بِه فارْسی یَعْنی چِه ؟
Did you understand?	فَهْمیدید ؟
please (asking to do something) (I make a wish)	خواهِش میکنم
please (replying to thanks)	خواهِش میکنم
would you please? (polite for any request, e.g.	بِفَرْمائید

'have a seat,' the verb being implied by context.)

37

Some additional expressions

kindly   لطفاً

kindly listen ('make ear')   لطفا گوش کنید

kindly repeat (make repetition)   لطفا تکرار کنید

kindly answer (give answer)   لطفا جواب بدهید

kindly ask ('from') him/her (polite form)   لطفا از ایشان بپرسید

kindly pronounce (make pronunciation)   لطفا تلفظ کنید

kindly read   لطفا بخوانید

kindly write   لطفا بنویسید

kindly translate   لطفا ترجمه کنید

kindly open your books   لطفا کتابتان را باز کنید

kindly close your books   لطفا کتابتان را ببندید

kindly repeat again   لطفا دوباره تکرار کنید

kindly repeat aloud   لطفا بلند تکرار کنید

your turn (turn of you)   نوبت شما

excuse me   ببخشید

Notes on pronunciation:

1)   لطفاً   is pronounced like   لطفن.

2) The   و   in   خواهش   and   بخوانید   is silent, thus read as if   بخانید ، خاهش.

3)   کتاب   'book'
    کتابتان 'your book'
    کتاب شما 'your book' (cf. p. 74)

REMEMBER: All assignments should indicate your name, the date,

the number of the lesson, and the page of the textbook.

DRILLS　　　　　　　　　　　　　　　　　　　　　　　　تمرین

A) Read the following and translate:

مِرْسی ـ بِفَرْمائید ـ لُطْفاً تِکْرار کُنید ـ خواهِش میکُنَم گوش کُنید ـ

خِیْلی خوب ـ لُطْفاً دوباره تِکْرار کنید ـ لطفا از ایشان بِپُرسِید ـ

لطفا جَواب بِدَهید ـ خواهِش میکُنَم بُلَنْد تِکْرار کنید ـ

B) In the following, the expressions are given in the wrong word order. Correct and read the expressions:

خوب خیلی ـ جَواب بدهید لُطْفاً ـ ایشان اَز لُطْفاً بِپُرسِید ـ فَرمائید بِه ـ

لطفا پُرْسِید بِه ـ کُنید لطفا گوش ـ خواهِش میکنم کُنید بُلَنْد تِکْرار ـ

لطفا کنید تکرار دوباره ـ

DIALOGUE　　　　　　　　　　　　　　　　　　　　　　گُفتگو

English	Persian
Hello.	سَلام .
Hello to you.	سَلام عَلَیْکُم .
Good morning.	صُبح بِخَیْر .
How are you?	حالِ شُما چِطُور اَسْت ؟
I am fine, thank you.	خوبَم ، مِرْسی .
How about you?	شُما چِطُور ؟
I am fine, too ('not bad').	مَن هَم بَد نیسْتَم .
With (your) permission.	با اِجازه .
Bye, now.	فِعْلاً خُدا حافِظ .
Bye.	خُدا حافِظ (شُما) .

زِبُوْنه مِن ____ نِیسْت

2) <u>PERSONAL PRONOUNS</u>

I	مَن	we	ما
you	تو	you	شُما
he, she	او	they	آنْها

Note: There are polite forms for 'you' (singular) and 'he,' 'she':

	polite	familiar
you	شُما	تو
he, she	ایشان	او

3) <u>ADDRESSING AND NAMES</u>

lady, Mrs.   خانُم   sir, Mr.   آقا

Mrs. Miller   خانُمِ میلِر   Mr. Miller   آقایِ میلِر

The family name is connected to Mr. and Mrs. by the connective
/-e-/. (Stress on first syllable when addressing someone, see p.365.)

Note   آقایِ میلِر : the   ی   is a glide inserted between

two vowels: /āqā-y-e miler/.

چیسْت ؟	اِسْمِ ایشان	آقایِ میلِر
حَسَن اَسْت .	اِسْمِ ایشان	

Mr. Miller, what is his/her name?

His name is Hassan.

چیست ؟	اِسْمِ شُما	آقا
میلِر است .	اِسْمِ مَن	

Sir, what is your name?

My name is Miller.

Note: چیست   is a contraction of   چی است ، اِسْمِ   'name of.'

> Note: From here on as soon as you have understood the point,
> go on to the next drill. Do not spend time getting bored!

DRILLS اِسْمِشان اِسْمِم تَمْرین
اِسْمِتان اِسْمِت
اِسْمِشان اِسْمِش

A) Answer the following questions:

اِسْمِم — اِسْمِتْ یا مَن — هَسْتَم

١) اسمِ شما چیست ؟

٢) اسمِ آقا چیست ؟

٣) اسمِ خانُم چیست ؟

٤) اسمِ ایشان چیست ؟

٥) اسمِ من چیست ؟

B) Ask for the name of other students using the address
Mr. and Mrs. X:

١) آقا اسمِ شما چیست ؟

٢) خانم اسمِ شما چیست ؟

٣) آقای میلر اسمِ ایشان چیست ؟

٤) خانُم میلر اسمِ ایشان چیست ؟

C) Ask as many students as possible all the questions of Drill A
and B:

D) 'First name' in Persian is اِسمِ کوچک 'little name'
(note the short vowel under مِ which connects the two
words). Ask other students their first name. And answer
the same questions put to you by other students according
to the pattern:

Q) آقایِ میلر، اسمِ کوچکِ شُما چیست ؟

A) اسمِ کوچکِ مَن جان است .

E) 'Who' in Persian is کی . Ask questions and answer
according to the pattern:

Q) اسمِ کی آقای میلر است ؟

A) اسمِ من / ایشان میلر اَست .

Q) اسمِ کوچکِ کی جان است ؟

A) اسمِ کوچکِ من / ایشان جان است .

F) Translate the following into Persian:

1) What is your name, sir/lady?

2) What is her first name?

3) My name is Ali (عَلی).

4) Whose name (the name of who) is Hassan (حَسَن)?

5) Please listen again.

6) Please answer aloud.

7) Please, kindly, would you please.

4) <u>'TO BE'</u>

In English there are two sets of 'to be': 'I am, you are,'
etc., and 'I'm, you're,' etc. There are also two sets in
Persian, but there is only one negative set:

I am	هستَم	I'm	ـَ م
you are	هستی	you're	ـ ی
he/she is	هست	he's/she's	ـ اَست *
we are	هستیم	we're	ـ یم
you are (plural)	هستید	you're (plural)	ـ ید
you are (polite)	هستید	you're (polite)	ـ ید
they are	هستند	they're	ـ نُد
he/she is (polite)	هستند	he's/she's (polite)	ـ نُد

I (a)m not	نیستَم
you (a)re not	نیستی
he/she (i)s not	نیست
we (a)re not	نیستیم
you (a)re not (plural)	نیستید
you (a)re not (polite)	نیستید
they (a)re not	نیستند
he/she (i)s not (polite)	نیستند

*Note: اَست is generally written separately while the other
persons are directly added to the preceding word, for these forms
after words ending in vowels see 3Aa, page 343.

5) COUNTRIES, NATIONALITIES, LANGUAGES

English			
America, American	اِنْگلیسی	آمریکائی	آمریکا
Iran, Iranian	فارسی	ایرانی	ایران
England, English	انگلیسی	انگلیسی	انگلیس / اِنْگلِسْتان
Germany, German	آلمانی	آلمانی	آلمان
Russia/Soviet Union, Russian	دوسی	دوسی/روس	روسِه
Japan, Japanese	ژاپُنی	ژاپُنی	ژاپن
China, Chinese	چینی	چینی	چین
Spain, Spaniard, Spanish	اسپانیائی / اسپانیولی	اسپانیائی	اِسْپانیا
France, Frenchman, French	فَرانْسَوی	فَرانْسَوی	فَرانْسَه
Turkey, Turk, Turkish	تُرکی	تُرک	تُرکیِه
Egypt/Egyptian/Arab/Arabic	عَرَبی	مِصْری/عَرَب	مِصْر
Pakistan/Pakistani/Hindu	اُردو	پاکستانی	پاکِسْتان
India/Indian/Hindi	هِنْدی	هِنْدی	هِنْد (-وستان)
Afghanistan/Afghan/Pashto	پُشْتو/فارسی	آفْغان (نی)	اَفْغانِسْتان

Nationality and language are indicated by a stressed ending ی .
After vowels, a glottal stop is inserted, written ئـ , thus
ئی as in اسپانیائی ، آمریکائی . The boxed-in
names differ from the general pattern.

a) <u>Language</u>

است ؟	انگلیسی	آیا زُبانِ شما	
است .	انگلیسی زبانِ من	بُله	
نیست .	انگلیسی زبانِ من	نه	

Is your language English?

Yes, my language is English.

No, my language is not English.

Note: زبانِ means 'tongue of', ⸻ آیا   'whether' functions as

a question mark when one expects a 'yes' or 'no' answer.

<u>DRILLS</u>   تمرین

A) Following the pattern of a) 'language' above, substitute other

languages for   انگلیسی ، .

B) Substitute other persons for   شما   and   من .

C) Substitute both the language and persons at the same time.

b) <u>Nationality</u>

هستید ؟	آمریکائی	آیا شما	
هستم .	آمریکائی	بله ، من	
نیستم .	آمریکائی	نه ، من	

Are you American?

Yes, I am American.

No, I am not American.

DRILLS   تمرین

   A) Following the pattern of b) 'nationality,' substitute other

       nationalities for   آمریکائی .

   B) Substitute other persons for   شما   and   من .

   C) Substitute both the nationality and persons at the same time.

c) <u>From a given country</u>

آیا شما	اَهلِ آمریکا	هستید ؟
بله ، من	اَهلِ آمریکا	هستم .
نه ، من	اَهلِ آمریکا	نیستم .

Are you from America?
Are you American?

Yes, I am from America.
Yes, I am American.

No, I am not from America.
No, I am not American.

Note: x   اَهلِ   means 'inhabitant-of-x.'

DRILLS   تمرین

   A) Following the pattern c) 'from a given country,' substitute

       other countries for   آمریکا .

   B) Substitute other persons for   شما   and   من .

   C) Substitute both the country and persons at the same time.

d) **From which country, from where**

هستید؟	اهلِ کُجا	شما	Where are you from?
هستم .	اهلِ آمریکا / آمریکائی	من	I am from America /American.

هستید؟	اهلِ کجایِ آمریکا	شما	Where are you from in America?
هستم .	اهلِ نیویورک	من	I am from New York.

Note: کجا 'where' ,

اهلِ کجایِ آمریکا   'inhabitant of where "of" America'

DRILLS   تمرین

A) Using   اهلِ کجا or ـــــ اهلِ کجایِ   ask questions.

B) Ask for knowledge of language according to the pattern:

آقای ... آیا شما فارسی بَلَدید؟	Mr., do you know Persian?
بله ، من فارسی بَلَدَم .	Yes, I know Persian.
نَه خِیر ،من فارسی بَلَد نیستم .	No, I don't know Persian.

Note: بَلَد functions as an adjective to which 'to be' is added,

and means 'know' :

بلدم/نیستم	I know/ not
بلدی/نیستی	you know / not
بلد است / نیست	he/she knows/ not

<u>Note</u>:

Instead of the full forms هستیم ، هستی etc., the short forms/personal endings may be used. Note that after vowels a glottal stop is inserted using the letter (alef). Thus, the patterns shown above will read as follows:

آیا ایشان آمریکائی اُنْد ؟				
بله من آمریکائی اَم .				

آیا شما اهلِ آمریکا اید ؟				
بله من اهلِ آمریکا اَم .				

Note that اید / ایم / ای should not be used after words ending in ی , in order to avoid double /i-i/, use هست instead; e.g.:

آمریکائی اَم	آمریکائی هستیم
آمریکائی هستی	آمریکائی هستید
آمریکائی اَست	آمریکائی اُنْد

6) <u>BEING SOMEONE OR SOMETHING</u>

Compare the following:

a) <u>Adjective</u>

است .	خوشحال	او
هستند .	خوشحال	آنها

He is happy.

They are happy.

b) <u>Nationality</u>

است .	ایرانی	او
هستند .	ایرانی	آنها

He is an Iranian.

They are Iranian.

c) <u>Occupation</u>

است .	دانشجو	او
هستند .	دانشجو	آنها

He is a student.

They are students.

You note that, as in English, ایرانی and خوشحال are
singular whether the subject is in the singular (he) or in the
plural (they). However, if an occupation is stated, English
requires the plural: 'a student' vs. 'students.' When you look
at the Persian you notice there is no change at all: whether
the subject is singular (او) or plural (آنها), the
statement of occupation is the singular: (دانشجو); i.e.,
unlike English, in Persian an occupation behaves like a predica-
tive adjective, as it describes a property common to one or more
persons.

7) <u>ASKING QUESTIONS</u>

است ؟	چِطُور	او	How is he?
است .	خوشحال	او	He is happy.
است ؟	اهل کجا	او	Where is he from?
است .	ایرانی	او	He is Iranian.
است ؟	کی چکاره	او	Who is he? What does he do?
است .	دانِشجو	او	He is a student.

Note: چِطُور 'how,' کی 'who,' چکاره 'of what work/what occupation' — 'what' (for 'to be' after /e/ in چکاره see p. 343).

8) و /va/ 'AND'

The 'and' in Persian is و /va/. It is usually pronounced /o/ when the two items are closer connected., e.g.:

عَلی	و	حَسَن	/va/ or /o/
خانِمِ میلر mrs	و	آقا mr.	/va/ or /o/
شُما	و	مَن	/va/ or /o/

من و علی ایرانی هستیم .   I and Ali are Iranian.

آقا و خانِمِ میلر فارسی بلدند.   Mr. and Mrs. Miller know Persian.

لُغَت

VOCABULARY

<u>adjective</u>   صِفَت

happy   خوشحال

at ease, comfortable   راحَت

uneasy, unhappy (note: نا 'un-')   ناراحَت

content   راضی

discontent   ناراضی

wealthy   پولدار

poor   (cf. fakir)   فقیر

ready, present   حاضِر

alone   تَنها

convinced, sure   مُطمَئِن

successful   مُوَفَق

quiet   ساکِت

polite   مُؤَدَب

agreed   مُوافِق

<u>occupation</u>   شُغْل

professor, master   اُستاد

teacher   مُعَلِم

student (university)   دانِشْجو

librarian (book-keeper)   کِتابْدار

secretary   مُنشی

employee   کارمَند

doctor   دُکتُر

waiter (French: garçon)   گارسون

engineer   مُهَندِس

lawyer	وکیل
writer	نویسَنْدِه
singer	خوانَنْدِه
mechanic	مِکانیک

DRILLS تمرین

A) In the following pattern, substitute خوشحال with other adjectives, e.g.:

او راحت است .

B) Change persons in Drill A, e.g.:

ما راحت هستیم .

C) In the following pattern substitute دانشجو by other occupations, e.g.:

حسن استاد است .

D) Use two nouns or names in the patterns of Drills A and C, e.g.:

حسن وعلی خوشحال اند .

من و شما دانشجو هستیم .

E) Answer the following questions:

۱) آیا شما فرانسوی هستید ؟

۲) اسمِ شما چیست ؟

۳) شما کجائی هستید ؟

۴) آیا زبانِ شما انگلیسی است ؟

F) Fill in the blanks as you see fit:

۱) او ـــــ است . ایرانی

۲) من ـــــ هستم . راضی

۳) آیا شما ـــــ هستید ؟ راضی

۴) حسن ـــــ است .

۵) ایشان ـــــ هستند .

۶) ـــــ چکاره است ؟

۷) من خوشحال هستم

۸) او کجا است ؟

۹) ـــــ او چیست ؟

۱۰) ـــــ من انگلیسی است .

G) Read and translate into English:

۱) آقای میلر استاد است . prof.

۲) حسن و علی دانشجو هستند . students

۳) مَرْیَم خیلی مؤدب است .

۴) آیا حسن موفق است ؟

۵) آیا گارسون تنها ست ؟

۶) آیا نویسنده و خواننده موفق هستند ؟

۷) آیا آنها راحت هستند ؟

۸) کتابدار پولدار نیست .

۹) وکیل موافق نیست .

H) Translate into Persian:

1. She is happy. او خشحال (است)

2. They are employees. آنها کرمند ه

3. Hassan and Ali are very quiet.

4. How is he?

5. What do John and Mary do?

6. What is your first name?

7. Where are Bizhan and Manizhe from?

8. Whose language (the language of who) is German?

9. Please ask the secretary.

10. The waiter is from Spain.

I) Use کجا ، 'who' کی ، چکاره ، اهل کجا ، چطور

to ask ten questions; then answer.

خانهٔ روستایی
و آلاچیق ترکمنی

LESSON FOUR

درس چهار

NUMBERS AND COUNTING

عـــدد و شـــمارش

1) Basic notes on numbers, 2) counting things; vocabulary; drills,

3) prices; vocabulary; drills, 4) time; drills; more drills;

dialogue; reading

_____

1) BASIC NOTES ON NUMBERS

a) Number symbols

۱۰	۹	۸	۷	۶	۵	۴	۳	۲	۱	۰
۲۰	۱۹	۱۸	۱۷	۱۶	۱۵	۱۴	۱۳	۱۲	۱۱	

Variants

٣= ٣   ٤= ٤   ٥= ٥   ٦= ٦

b) The names of the numbers are as follows:

yek	1	یک	11	یازده	10	ده	100	صد
Do	2	دو	12	دوازده	20	بیست	200	دویست
Seh	3	سه	13	سیزده	30	سی	300	سیصد
chahar	4	چهار	14	چهارده	40	چهل	400	چهارصد
panj	5	پنج	15	پانزده	50	پنجاه	500	پانصد
shesh	6	شش	16	شانزده	60	شصت	600	ششصد
haft	7	هفت	17	هفده	70	هفتاد	700	هفتصد
hasht	8	هشت	18	هجده	80	هشتاد	800	هشتصد
No	9	نه	19	نوزده	90	نود	900	نهصد
Da	10	ده	20	بیست	100	صد	1000	هزار

55

| 10,000 | ده هزار | 1,000,000 | یک میلیون |
| 100,000 | صد هزار | 1,000,000,000 | یک بیلیون |

c) <u>Combinations of numbers</u> are extremely regular, beginning with 20 = ۲۰ . The sequence is as in English:

21	بیست و یک	31	سی و یک
22	بیست و دو	32	سی و دو
23	بیست و سه	33	سی و سه
24	بیست و چهار	34	سی و چهار
25	بیست و پنج	35	سی و پنج
26	بیست و شش	36	سی و شش
27	بیست و هفت	37	سی و هفت
28	بیست و هشت	38	سی و هشت
29	بیست و نه	39	سی و نه

Hundreds and thousands, etc. are conjoined by

هزار و نُهصُد و بیست و نُه   ۱۹۲۹ = 1929.   'and': /o/ و

d) <u>Applications</u>

<u>Measures</u>

You will find the following measurements used:

کیلو   مِتر   لیتر

کِرُم   سانْت / سانْتی مِتر

۱ مَن = ۳ کیلو ، ۱ سیر = ۷۵ گرم ، ۱ کیلو = ۱۰۰۰ گرم

Prices قیمَت

The official unit of Iran is the ریال rial.

$1.00 is approximately 70 rials. Thus, the coins and bills

read:

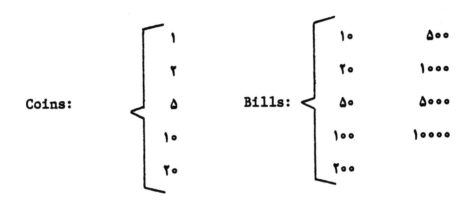

Coins: {
١
٢
۵
١٠
٢٠
}

Bills: {
١٠
٢٠
۵٠
١٠٠
٢٠٠
}

۵٠٠
١٠٠٠
۵٠٠٠
١٠٠٠٠

Unofficially, one ریال is also called قِران.

qeran or زار (he)zār; another unofficial unit

is تومان = 10 rials.

Telephone numbers شُماره‌یِ تِلِفُن

Telephone numbers are read in pairs (not by single

digits as in America). Thus:

637499   is   63-74-99

Dates تاریخ

Dates in Persian read leftward, day first, e.g.:

١٩٧٧ / ٣ / ۵   5th March, 1977

yr. mo. day

2) <u>COUNTING</u>   دوره،
   شمردن

Numbers precede their noun as in English. However, the noun

remains singular, as plural is already implied by the

preceding number. The question word is   چَند   'how many.'

one lesson   یک درس   one book   یک کتاب

several lessons   چند درس   ten books   ده کتاب

When one wants to emphasize individual tangible items, a single item

is   یک دانه ; all other numbers are followed by تا .

Without nouns, these <u>must</u> be used, e.g.:

کتاب	(تا)	چند	how many (items of) books
کتاب	(تا)	ده	ten (<u>items</u> of) books
کتاب	(تا)	چند	several (items of) books
کتاب	(دانه)	یک	one (<u>single</u>) book
	دانه	یک	one (item)
	تا	ده	ten (items)
	تا	چند	several; how many (items)

For counting people, the itemizing count word is   نَفَر .

'person' or also تا , e.g.:

ایرانی	نفر	یک	one Iranian (<u>person</u>)
ایرانی	نفر/ تا	ده	ten Iranians (<u>persons</u>)
	نفر	ده	ten (persons)
	نفر	چند	how many (persons)

VOCABULARY لغت

(sheet of) paper	کاغذ (وَرَقِ)
briefcase, purse	کیف
pencil	مِداد
notebook, office/small notebook	دَفتَر /دَفتَرچِه
pen	خودکار
lesson	دَرس
university	دانِشگاه
school	مَدرِسِه
room	اُطاق
chair	صَندَلی
table	میز
window	پَنجِرِه
door	دَر
wall	دیوار
lamp	چِراغ
blackboard	تَختِه سیاه

'have' (Note that the endings are like 'to be' except for 3rd person
singular which is /ad/ not /ast/:

I have	دارم	we have	داریم
you have	داری	you have	دارید
he/she has	دارد	they have	دارند

I have not	ندارم	we have not	نداریم
you have not	نداری	you have not	ندارید
he/she has not	ندارد	they have not	ندارند

DRILLS   تمرین

A) Practice 'to have' with the vocabulary given above:

چند تا کتاب دارید؟

یک دانه کتاب دارم .

B) Practice this pattern by adding different subjects, e.g.:

		Subject
دارد؟	چند (تا) کتاب	حسن
دارم ؟	چند (تا) مداد	من
دارند؟	چند (تا) کلاس	علی و جواد

Then answer.

C) Practice this pattern with the nouns referring to furniture,
etc., using the subject   اطاق حسن   (the room of
Hassan), e.g.:

		Subject
دارد ؟	چند تا پنجره	اطاق حسن

Then answer.

D) Ask each other for your age (which you need not tell truly,
of course), using the pattern: (سال = year ; never use تا):

Q) شما چند سال دارید ؟

A) من (بیست و دو) سال دارم .

hejdah

3) <u>Prices</u> قِیمَت

There are two patterns, one using چَند اَست , the other,

چِقَدر میشَوَد :

چَند اَست ؟	سیب	How much are the apples?
چِقَدر میشَوَد؟	سیب	How much will the apples cost?

meshaved / che/dad

چقدر است is the standard way of asking for the price

per unit. چقدر میشود is more general and is more or less

equivalent to 'how much will it be/cost me (altogether).'

Note the use of these two expressions in the following dialog:

چه فَرمایِشی داریِد ، خانِم / آقا ؟   What can I do for your, Madam/Sir?

سیب میخواهم .   I want/ need apples.

بله خانِم /آقا ، سیب خیلی خوب داریم .   Yes, Madam/Sir, we have very good apples.

سیب   چَند اَست ؟   How much are the apples ?

فَقَط پَنج تومان ، خانِم /آقا .   Only 5 Tomans, Madam/Sir.

لطفا چهار کیلو بِدَهید .   Please, give me 4 kilos.

چُشم ، خانِم ، آقا .   Certainly, Madam/Sir .

چِقَدر میشود ، آقا ؟   How much will that be, Sir?

بَرای شما بیست تومان .   For you 2o Tomans.

خیلی زیاد است ، آقا .   That is too much, Sir.

خیلی خوب ، ۱۷ تومان بَرای شما .   Very well, 17 Tomans for you.

VOCABULARY

لغت

rice	بِرِنْج
pea	نُخود
bean	لوبیا
onion	پیاز
potato	سیبِ زَمینی
yoghurt	ماسْت
butter	کَرِه
cheese	پَنیر
oil	رُوْغَن
tea	چای
coffee	قَهْوِه
apple	سیب
peach	هُلو
pear	گُلابی
sweet orange	پُرْتُقال
watermelon	هِنْدِوانِه
cantelope	طالِبی
melon	خَرْبُزِه
grape	اَنْگور
tangerine	نارَنْگی
sour orange	نارِنْج
sweet cherry	گیلاس
tree	درخت

Note: You are not supposed to learn by heart the words in this or the following lists, each dealing with a particular subject matter.

Just try to use as many of them in the drills of this lesson, and wherever fitting in the following lessons.

As a suggestion, you may start your own notebook, listing the words by subject matter, adding to them as you go along, and also add the new words in the dialogues, readings, etc.

<u>DRILLS</u>   تمرین

A) Imagine yourself in a grocery store either as a seller
or a buyer and ask for prices.

Use the dialog on p. 61 as the pattern for this drill.

4) <u>TIME</u>   وَقت

   a) <u>Counting hours</u>

کار میکُنید؟	چَند ساعَت	روزی	How many hours do you work per day?
کار میکنم.	یک ساعت	روزی	I work (for) one hour per day.
کار میکنم.	ده ساعت	روزی	I work (for) ten hours per day.

Note: کار 'work,' میکُنم 'I do,' میکُنید 'you do.'

Negative: نه   thus: نمیکُند 'he does not do', etc.

Vocabulary:		unstressed ی		stressed ها	
today	اِمروز	per day	روزی	in the mornings	صُبح ها
tomorrow	فَردا	per week	هَفته ای	in the afternoons	بَعدْازظُهرها
every day	هَر روز	per month	ماهی	in the nights	شَبها

<u>DRILLS</u>   تمرین

A) Ask for each other's working hours, using the pattern
and vocabulary above.

b) <u>Telling time 'o'clock'</u>

الان	ساعَتْ چَنْد	است ؟
الان	ساعَتِ یک	است .

What time is it now?

Now it is one o'clock.

الان 'this moment, now'

ساعَتِ چند	کارمیکنید؟
ساعَتِ سه	کارمیکنم .

What time do you work?

I work at three o'clock.

3:05	سه و پنج دقیقه	2:55	پنج دَقیقِه بِه سه
3:15	سه و رُبْع	2:45	یک رُبْع بِه سه
3:30	سه و نیم	about 3:00	تَقْریباً ساعَتِ سه

Note 1:

minute	دَقیقِه	half	نیم
second	ثانیه	quarter	رُبْع

Note 2:

six o'clock <u>in the morning</u>   ساعتِ ششِ صُبح

six o'clock <u>in the evening</u>   ساعتِ ششِ شب

<u>DRILLS</u>   تمرین

A) Practice asking and telling time.

B) Practice asking and answering time of work. Use also

    fractions of hours as well as 'morning' and 'evening' hours.

MORE DRILLS   تمرین

A) Read the following and translate:

The room has 2 windows

۱) اُطاق دوتا پَنجره دارد .

۲) کِلاس یک دانه تَخته سیاه دارد . _the class has one black board_
(black board)

۳) چَند تا دانشجو ایرانی هستند ؟ _how many / How many students are iranian_

۴) فَرهاد و شیرین چند تا کتاب دارند ؟ _How many sons do farhad w sharen have_ _girls nord_

۵) اطاقِ حسن چهار تا صَندلی دارد . _Husan's room has 4 chairs_

۶) آنها چند سال دارند؟ _How old are they_

۷) اَنگور چند است ؟ _How much is the grape_ _ask price_ _grape_

۸) دوکیلو برنج چقدر میشود؟ _How much is 2 kilos of rice_

۹) حالِ شما چطور است ؟ شما چطور ؟ _How are you? And you?_

۱۰) شب‌ها چند ساعت کار میکنید؟ _How many hours do you work @ night_ _night_

۱۱) من یک دَفتَر دارم . _I have one office / note book_

B) Fill in the blanks appropriately:

۱) چند ــــــ مُعلم آمریکائی هستند ؟ _How many American teachers_

this place, here   ۲) ده ـــــ صَندلی اینجا است . _There are 10 chairs here_

۳) یک ـــــ مِداد دارم .

۴) شما ـــــ سال دارید ؟

۵) پُرتقال ـــــ است ؟ _orange_

۶) اَلآن ـــــ چند است ؟

C) The following sentences are scrambled. Unscramble them:

۱) حَسَن ــ عَلی ــ و ــ اند ــ خوشحال .

۲) تَنها ــ گارسون ــ میکند ــ کار .

۳) دانشجو ــ چند ــ ایرانی ــ نفر ــ هستند ؟

۴) دانه ــ میز ــ اینجا ــ است ــ یک

۵) دارد ــ پُنْجِره ــ اطاقِ حسن ــ تا ــ چند ؟

۶) سال ــ حسن ــ دارند ــ علی ــ و ــ چند ؟

۷) چِقَدر ــ میشود ــ چای ــ کیلو ــ یک ؟

۸) کار میکنم ــ ساعت ــ دو ــ بَعْد اَز ظُهْر ها .

۹) ساعت ــ است ــ الان ــ چند ؟

۱۰) هشت ــ ساعت ــ است ــ شب ــ الان .

D) Translate the following into Persian:

1) What time is it? a) 2:40, b) 8 P.M.

2) How many hours do you work per week?

3) How are you?

4) How many have you?

5) How much are the cherries?

6) I am 24 years old.

7) George's room has two windows.

8) I have two.

DIALOGUE

	گفتگو
I stay, remain	شما چند روز در ایران میمانید ؟ (A
	دو هَفته میمانم . (B
	چقدر پول دارید ؟ (A
approximately	تَقریباً ۵۰۰۰ فرانک فرانسوی . (B
suitcase	چند تا چُمدان دارید ؟ (A
from - to, until	دوتا ، از اینجا تا هُتِلِ هیلتون چقدر میشود ؟ (B
	بیست تومان . (A

هُتَل

READING

خواندنی

ask — ژان و شارل به هُتِل میرَوَند . مُدیر هتل از ایشان میپُرسد چند تا اُطاق لازم دارند . جواب میدَهند که یک اُطاقِ دو نَفره لازم دارند . بَعْد میپُرسند قیمَت چند است . مُدیرِ هتل به آنها میگوید شبی ۱۲۰ تومان است .

I go to	به ... میرَوَم	double (room)	دو نَفره
manager	مُدیر	after, afterwards	بَعد
I need	لازم دارم	price	قیمَت
that	که	I say to	به ... میگویَم
		per night	شبی

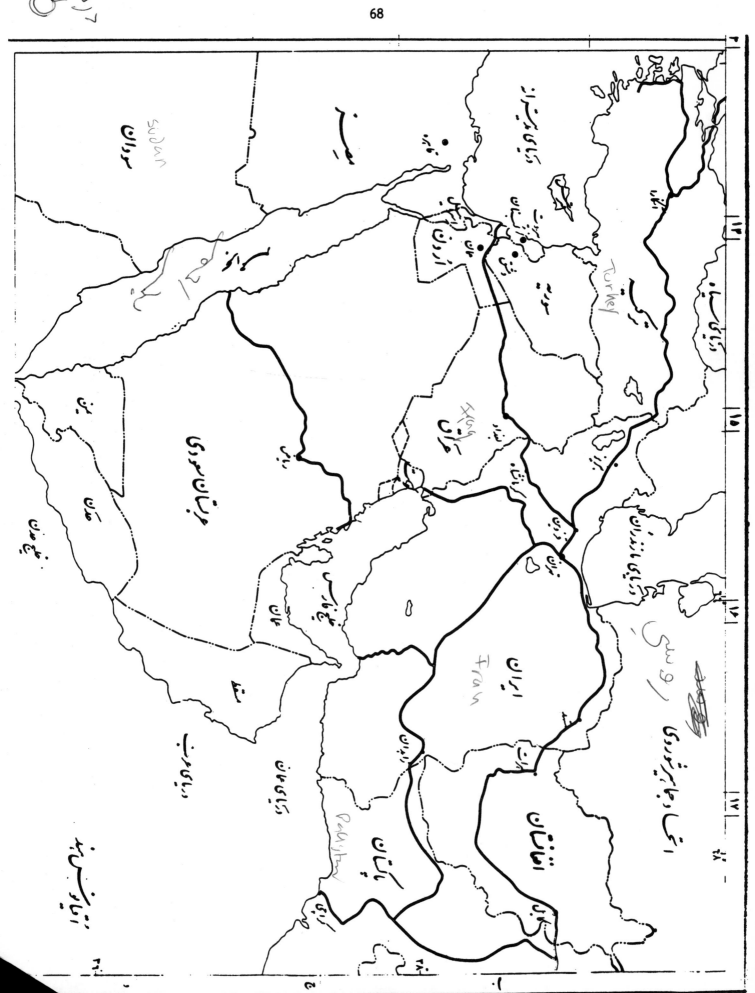

L E S S O N   F I V E

درسِ پنـــــــج

W O R D   O R D E R ,   P R O N O U N S

کُرتیبِ جُـــــمْلِه و ضَمایِــر

1) A note on Persian word order; drills; dialogue 1; reading 1;

2) personal suffixes; vocabulary; drills, 3) mine, yours, etc.,

4) demonstratives, vocabulary; drills; dialogue 2; reading 2

---

1) ## A NOTE ON PERSIAN WORD ORDER

a) The most basic rule of Persian word order is: the verb

comes last; the basic word order is:

SUBJECT	PREDICATE NOUN	VERB

b) The question word   آیا   "whether" (expecting 'yes' or 'no' as

an answer) is placed before the entire sentence; e.g.:

Are you American?   آیا شما آمریکائی هستید؟

The same is true for the equivalent of English 'do'

questions (<u>Does</u> Hassan work?). In Persian, yes-no

questions are introduced by   آیا:

Hassan works? = Does he...   آیا حسن کار میکند ؟

69

c) All <u>other question</u> words are usually <u>not</u> placed in the beginning as in English, but <u>exactly where the answer word will occur</u> in the sentence, e.g.:

Q - A

است ؟	<u>چی</u>	اسم ِ ایشان
است .	حسن	اسم ِ ایشان

What is his name?

His name is Hassan.

Q - A

هستید؟	اهل ِ <u>کجا</u>	شما
اهل ِ آمریکا هستم .		من

Where are you from?

I am from America.

Q - A

فارسی است ؟	زبان ِ <u>کی</u>
فارسی است .	زبان ِ حسن

Whose language is Persian?

Hassan's language is Persian.

Q - A

اهل ِ ایران است ؟	<u>کی</u>
اهل ِ ایران است .	حسن

Who is from Iran?

Hassan is from Iran.

Q - A

کتاب دارد؟	<u>چندتا</u>	حسن
کتاب دارد .	سه تا	حسن

How many books does Hassan have?

Hassan has three books.

DRILLS *(will be on Exam)* تمرین

The word order in the following sentences is scrambled.

Unscramble them:

Is his name ——

۱) آیا ـ حسن ـ ایشان ـ است ـ اسم ؟

۲) هستند ـ جان ـ چه کاره ـ مری ـ و ؟

۳) آلمانی ـ زبانِ ـ است ـ کی ؟

۴) است ـ او ـ چطور ؟

۵) مؤدب ـ مریم ـ است ـ خیلی .

۶) میلر ـ استاد ـ آقای ـ است .

۷) کجا ـ هستید ـ اهلِ ـ شما ؟

۸) نیستم ـ من ـ آمریکا ـ اهلِ .

۹) کی ـ جان ـ اسم ـ است ـ کوچک ؟

۱۰) جواب ـ دهید ـ به ـ خواهش ـ میکنم ـ بلند .

۱۱) است ـ کی ـ منشی ؟

۱۲) علی ـ شما ـ و ـ هستید ـ چکاره ؟

گفتگــو ۱

DIALOGUE 1

you know   A) فارسی بَلَدید ؟

a little   B) یکْ کَمی

that's fine ('plenty') بسیار   A) بِسیارْ خوب

A) شما آلمانی هستید؟

B) نه خیر ، من فرانسوی هستم .

پاسپورتِ شما   A) پاسْپورتِتان ، خواهش میکنم .

B) بفرمائید .

A) اسمِ شما چیست ؟

B) دوگُل.

اسمِ کوچکِ شما   A) اسمِ کوچکتان ؟

B) شارل .

خواندنــــــی ۱

READING 1

also   زبانِ آقایِ میلر انگلیسی است . او فارسی هَم یک‌کمی

بلد است . اسمِ کوچکِ او تام است . تام و دوسْتَش در (دوستِ او)

live   ایران زندگی میکنند. آنها مهندس هستند.

2) PERSONAL SUFFIXES

Sequences like اسم من mean 'mý name', with stress,
(as opposed to somebody else's). Thus, in Persian as in
English, you can say 'mý name is' or 'my náme is'. While
in English the difference is simply indicated by stress
either on 'my' or 'name,' in Persian the unstressed version
is expressed by 'personal suffixes', which are directly
added to the noun, e.g.:

اسم من	my name	اسمَم	my name
اسم تو	your name	اسمَت	your name
اسم او	his/her name	اسمَش	his/her name
اسم ما	our name	اسمِان	our name
اسم شما	your (plural) name	اسمِتان	your (plural) name
اسم شما	your (polite) name	اسمتان	your (polite) name
اسم آنها (ایشان)	their name	اسمِشان	their name
اسم ایشان	his/her (polite) name	اسمِشان	his/her (polite) name

Q - A

چیست ؟	اسمِ شما
چیست ؟	اسمِتان
جواد است .	اسمِ من
جواد است .	اسمَم

What is your name?

What is your name ?

My name is Javad.

My name is Javad.

The personal suffixes are always last, also when they occur
after two nouns:

(پِدَر و ماَدَر)َم   <u>my</u> father and mother

(بَرادَر و خواهَر)َم   <u>my</u> brother and sister

(و in خواهَر is silent)

<u>Orthographic note</u>: After words ending in a final /-e/ ه ,
these endings are written as follows (see p. 343):

خانه اَم / خانه اِمان   my/our house

خانه اَت / خانه اِتان   your/your house

خانه اَش / خانه اِشان   his/her/their house

VOCABULARY   لغت

I live	زِندِگی میکُنم	friend	دوسْت
you live	زندگی میکنی	co-worker	هَمْکار
he/she lives	زندگی میکند	classmate	هَمْکِلاس
we live	زندگی میکنیم	roommate	هَمْ اُطاق
you live	زندگی میکنید	girlfriend	دوستِ دُخْتَر
they live	زندگی میکنند	boyfriend	دوستِ پِسَر
		house	خانِه
negation:		landlord	صاحِبْخانِه
I don't live	زِندِگی نِمیکُنم	car	ماشین
you don't live	زندگی نمیکنی	bus	اُتوبوس
he/she doesn't live	زندگی نمیکند	bicycle	دوچَرْخِه
we don't live	زندگی نمیکنیم	father	پِدَر
you don't live	زندگی نمیکنید	mother	مادَر
they don't live	زندگی نمیکنند	grandfather	پِدَر بُزُرگ
		grandmother	مادَر بُزُرگ
		child	بَچِه
	اینجا	boy/son	پِسَر
		girl/daughter	دُخْتَر
		brother	بَرادَر
		sister (silent و)	خواهَر
		woman/wife	زَن
		husband	شَوهَر
		man	مَرد

م - my
ت - you
ش - he/she
مان - our
تان - you
شان - they

DRILLS   تمرین

A) Ask each other's names using the personal suffixes.

B) Read the following and translate:

My friend lives here ———— ۱) دوستم اینجا زندگی میکند .

How how is your child ———— ۲) بچه‌ات چند سال دارد ؟
has years how your child

His friend has 2 cars ———— ۳) دوستش دوتا ماشین دارد .
has

Where is your bike? ———— ۴) دوچرخه‌ات انا نکجاست ؟

My sister doesn't have a husband ———— ۵) خواهرم شوهر ندارد .

My classmate doesn't have an apartment ———— ۶) هم‌کلاسم آپارتمان ندارد .

Their car doesn't work ———— ۷) ماشینشان کار نمیکند .

My grandpa and grandma live here ———— ۸) پدر و مادر بزرگم اینجا زندگی میکنند .

My teacher is very happy today ———— ۹) معلمم امروز خیلی خوشحال است .

what time does his son and daughter work? ———— ۱۰) پسر و دخترش ساعت چند کار میکنند ؟

our lawyer doesn't agree ———— ۱۱) وکیلمان موافق نیست .
doesnt agree   our lawyer

Is your doctor sure? ———— ۱۲) آیا دکترتان مطمئن است ؟
is sure your doctor

C) Translate into Persian:

1) My girlfriend is my roommate.

2) His brother and sister are students.

3) My (our) father and mother live here.

4) Our son and their daughter are friends (with each other) (باهم).

5) His car does not work.

mashinash kár nemikonand.

3) 'MINE, YOURS,' ETC.

Persian does not have a separate set of independent possessive pronouns equivalent to English 'mine, yours, his/hers,' etc. Instead they use the word مال 'property,' thus:

Q - A

است ؟	کی مال	کتاب ِ	The book is whose?
است .	مال من	کتاب	The book is mine.
	مال تو		yours.
	مال او		his/hers.
	مال ما		ours.
	مال شما		yours.
	مال آنها		theirs.

Note: Since 'mine, yours,' etc. is always stressed, always use the independent pronoun after مال, never the personal suffixes.

4) DEMONSTRATIVES

Compare the patterns:

کتاب	—	the book
کتاب	این	this book
کتاب	آن	that book

Note: There is no article in Persian. Thus, whenever English has 'the,' as in 'the book' (which I am talking about, etc.), Persian has simply کتاب .

a) <u>Demonstrative with noun:</u>

Q - A

است ؟ خوب	کُدامُ کتاب	Which book is good?
است . خوب	این کتاب	This book is good.
است . خوب	آن کتاب	That book is good.

b) <u>Demonstrative without noun:</u>

Q - A

است ؟	چی		What is it?
است .	کتاب		It's a book.
است ؟	چی	این	What is this?
است .	کتاب	این	This is a book.
است ؟	چی	آن	What is that?
است	کتاب	آن	That's a book.

Note: Persian has no equivalent word for English 'it.'
'It' is simply understood from the context. But این

or آن are also often used instead.

c) <u>Demonstrative with numbers</u>

Q - A

مالِ کی است ؟	دوتا کتاب	Whose are the two books?
مالِ حسن است .	دوتا کتاب	The two books are Hassan's.
مالِ کی است ؟	این دوتا کتاب	Whose are these two books?
مالِ جواد است .	این دوتا کتاب	These two books are Javad's.
مالِ کی است ؟	آن دوتا کتاب	Whose are those two books?
مالِ ژاله است .	آن دوتا کتاب	Those two books are Zhale's.

d) <u>Focusing demonstrative:</u>

'just this/that' is expressed by هَمین and هَمان (stress

on هَـ):

کتاب	هَمین
کتاَب	هَمان

just this book, exactly
this book, this very book,
the same book

just that book, exactly
that book, that very book,
the same book

VOCABULARY لــغت

expensive	گِران	yellow	زَرد
cheap	اَرزان	orange	نارِنْجی
big	بُزُرْگ	pink	صورَتی
small	کوچِک	purple	بَنَفْش
bad	بَد	white	سِفید
high, tall	بُلَند	green	سَبز
short	کوتاه	red	قِرْمِز
tall (person)	قَدْبُلَند	brown	قَهْوه ای
short (person)	قَدْکوتاه	black	سیاه
beautiful	قَشَنْگ	blue	آبی

DRILLS   تمرین

A) Look around the room and ask for the names of colors according to
the pattern:

است	رَنگی	چه	این
است	رنگی	چه	آن

رنگ 'color'; ی is not stressed.

B) Translate the following into Persian:

1) This car is expensive.

2) That orange is not orange.

3) This class is not big.

4) Which room is quiet?

5) This (same) singer is very good.

C) Practice each of the sentences above using different adjectives.

D) Translate the following into English:

mine

Mine is here → ۱) مالِ من اینجاست.

My friend lives here → ۲) دوستِ من اینجا زندگی میکند.

those are these 2 kilos of potatoes ۳) این دو کیلو سیبْ زَمینی مالِ کی است؟

That pen is blue ۴) آن خودْکار آبی است.

my girlfriend works in
(cf. p. 63) to morning ۵) دوستِ دخترم صُبحها کار میکند.

Its is mine ۶) مالِ من است.

His answer is good → ۷) این جوابَش خوب است.

Which class is very good? ۸) کدام کلاس خیلی خوب است؟

This employee doesn't have ۹) این کارْمَند کار ندارد.
enough work to do.

E) Make up sentences with the following words:

۱) مال ـ مداد ـ این ـ نیست ـ من .   *This is not my pencil*

۲) پدرتان ـ است ـ کاره ـ چه ؟   *what is the occupation of your father*

۳) دانشجو ـ خیلی ـ نیست ـ راضی .   *student is not very satisfied*

۴) آن ـ مال ـ پدر ـ است ـ خانه ـ و ـ مادرم .

۵) زبان صاحبخانه ـ آیا ـ فارسی ـ اِتان ـ نیست ؟

F) Fill in the blanks appropriately:

۱) اسم دوست من پرویز است .

۲) آن خانه مال پدرم است .

۳) این مداد مال او نیست .

۴) آن دفتر چه مال حسن است .

۵) ماشین خوب است ؟

۶) امروز هوا خیلی خوب است .

۷) شما ساعت چند کلاس دارید؟

۸) جواد سؤال دارد .

۹) امروز سه ساعت کار میکنم .

۱۰) ـــ نفر آمریکائی در این کلاس هستند .

۱۱) پدر چکاره است ؟

DIALOGUE 2   گفتگو ۲

(A   این دوتا گُلِدان مال کیست ؟

sirs (/ān/is polite plural)   آقایان ، مال شماست ؟
   note the glide in /āqā-y-ān/
     cf. p. 40 # 3
     for /-ān/ see p. 131

(B   نه خیر .

(A   آقا ، شما ؟

one of them (for inanimate plural   (B   یکی اَش مال من است .
   the singular may be
   used, here   ش)

(A   کدام ؟

(B   همین است .

how about   (A   آن یکی چطور؟

know   (B   نمیدانم .

READING 2   خواندنی ۲

اسمِ دوستم پرویز است . او در یک خانهٴ بزرگ زندگی میکند .
خانه مال او نیست . مالِ صاحبخانه است . پرویز خودش یک
آپارتمانِ کوچک دارد . آپارتمانِ او فَقَط یک اطاق دارد . او
صبح ها ساعتِ هشتِ سرِ کار میرود و شبها ساعتِ هفت و رُبع
به خانه اش بَرْمیگَردَد .

house owner	صاحبخانه	
himself	خودش	to, at work سَرِکار
only	فقط	I return to بَرْمیگَردم ... به

'crab' خرچنگ

چنگ

خر

LESSON SIX

درس شـــــش

CONNECTIVE /-e-/ AND PLURAL

اضافـــه و جمـــع

1) Noun-noun, 2) noun-adjective, 3) combinations, 4) further

notes on اضافه , 5) plural; vocabulary; drills

---

1) ## NOUN-NOUN

Two nouns are connected by /-e-/ which is very often the

equivalent of 'of'.

Note on orthography: after ا and و a glide ی is inserted

(see p. 344); e.g.:

after consonant:	کتابِ من	my book
after ا :	آقای میلر	Mr. Miller
after و :	دانشجوی کلاس	the student of class

As indicated, the connective /-e-/, which is a short vowel,

is represented by the short vowel sign ِ .

However, like all short vowels it is usually not written,
although the connective ی stays:

کتاب من

آقای میلر

دانشجوی کلاس

While this omission may fool one occasionally (even Persian

professors and professors of Persian) the context is usually

clear enough to recognize that nouns are connected.

Note: With names (and a few other words) English has two

ways of connection; in Persian there is only one way:

کتاب حسن   the book of Hassan
Hassan's book

2) <u>NOUN-ADJECTIVE</u>

In Persian the adjective: a) <u>follows</u> the noun (exactly opposite

most English adjectives); and b) is connected to the preceding

headnoun by /-e-/, e.g.:

<div dir="rtl">اسم کوچک</div>	first name
<div dir="rtl">کتاب خوب</div>	good book
<div dir="rtl">قالی گران</div>	expensive carpet
<div dir="rtl">پول آمریکائی</div>	American money

3) COMBINATIONS

Nouns and adjectives can be combined as follows:

(the Persian class) of Homa   (کلاس فارسیِ) هما

(the book) (of the Persian class)   (کتابِ) (کلاس فارسی)

(the large car) (of the
Iranian teacher)   (ماشینِ بزرگِ) (معلمِ ایرانی)

Coordinated nouns and adjectives follow the same rules.

Pronouns and pronominal suffixes are final, e.g.:

(the parents) (of my teacher)   (پدر و مادرِ) (معلمِ) من

       (پدر و مادرِ) (معلم)َم

(my) (good and expensive) (book)   (کتابِ (خوب و گران)ِ من

       (کتابِ (خوب و گران)َم

خطِ سیاق ۵۱۵/۱/۷

4) __FURTHER NOTES ON__ اضافه

Possession is only one of a number of اضافه phrases; some
of those were mentioned earlier. Among the more frequent
phrases there are:

a) __name__ آقای میلر Mr. Miller

حسنِ بَهْرامی Hassan Bahrami

b) __time__ ساعتِ سه three o'clock

ساعتِ ششِ صبح three o'clock in
the morning

c) __where from__ اهلِ آمریکا from America

d) __generic noun and name__ روزِ جُمعه (the day of) Friday

شَهْرِ تهران the city of Tehran

خیابانِ دَرّیا Darya street

دوستِ دختر girlfriend

5) <u>PLURAL</u> جَمْع

The general plural marker is <u>stressed</u> ها (always written
separately after final /-e/ ; elsewhere it may or may
not be connected), e.g.:

خانه ــ خانه ها   house - houses

کتاب ــ کتاب ها ، کتابها   book - books

قالی ــ قالی ها ، قالیها   carpet - carpets

The glide ی is inserted between ها and the connective
/-e-/; e.g.:

کتابهای خوب   good books

کتابهای فارسی   Persian books

کتابهای حسن   Hassan's books

روزهای جمعه   Fridays

Personal suffixes are connected to ها by inserting ـ ,
e.g.:

کتابهایَم   my books

کتابهایَت   your books

کتابهایَش   his/her books

کتابهایمان   our books

کتابهایتان   your books

کتابهایشان   their books

88

VOCABULARY لغت

sell	میفُروشَم	stop, station	ایستگاه
go	به ... میرَوَم	side	طَرَف
come	از ... میآیم	traffic	تِرافیک
empty (place)	خَلوَت	ticket	بِلیط
crowded (place)	شُلوغ	street	خیابان
empty	خالی	square	مَیدان
full	پُر	driver	رانَنده
direct	مُستَقیم	heavy	سَنگین

DRILLS تمرین

A) Read the following and translate:

۱) امروز ترافیکِ تهران خیلی سنگین است .

۲) ایستگاهِ اتوبوس آن طرفِ خیابان است .

۳) روزِ جمعه پدر و مادرم به شیراز میروند .

۴) این اتوبوسِ قرمز مستقیماً به مَیدانِ وَنَک میرود .

۵) معلمِ آلمانیِ کلاسِ فارسیِ دانشگاهِ ما صبح ها ساعتِ هشت به کلاس میآید .

B) Translate into Persian:

a) Today is Friday.

b) The city of New York is large.

c) Our taxi driver lives on Sa'di street.

d) Where do they sell Russian tea?

e) Mrs. Miller lives in (دَر) the house of the brother of her husband.

C) Multiple substitution:

۱	۲	۳	۴	۵	
ماشینِ	دوستِ	آمریکائیِ	من	بزرگ	است .

a) Substitute ماشین by: دوچرخه ــ کلاس ــ کیف (bag)

اطاق ــ خانه ــ دانشگاه

b) Do the same, but use the plural.

c) Substitute دوست by: family members, occupations

and other persons (like هم اطاق).

d) Do the same, but use the plural.

e) Substitute من by other persons, such as personal

suffixes, pronouns, names, occupations, etc.

f) Do the same, but use the plural.

g) Substitute آمریکائی by other nationalities.

h) Substitute بزرگ by other adjectives (including

colors) and find the appropriate nouns for it.

تِهران

کِیومَرث و ثُرَیّا دَر تِهران زِندِگی می کُنند .

تِهران پایتَختِ ایران اِست .

capital

تِهران شهرِ بُزُرگی اِست .

دَر تِهران اُتوبوس هایِ دو طَبقه هَم هست .

تِهران باغِ وَحش دارد . کِیومَرث و ثُرَیّا

zoo

بِه تَماشایِ باغِ وحش می رَوند .

watch, observation

ث ث

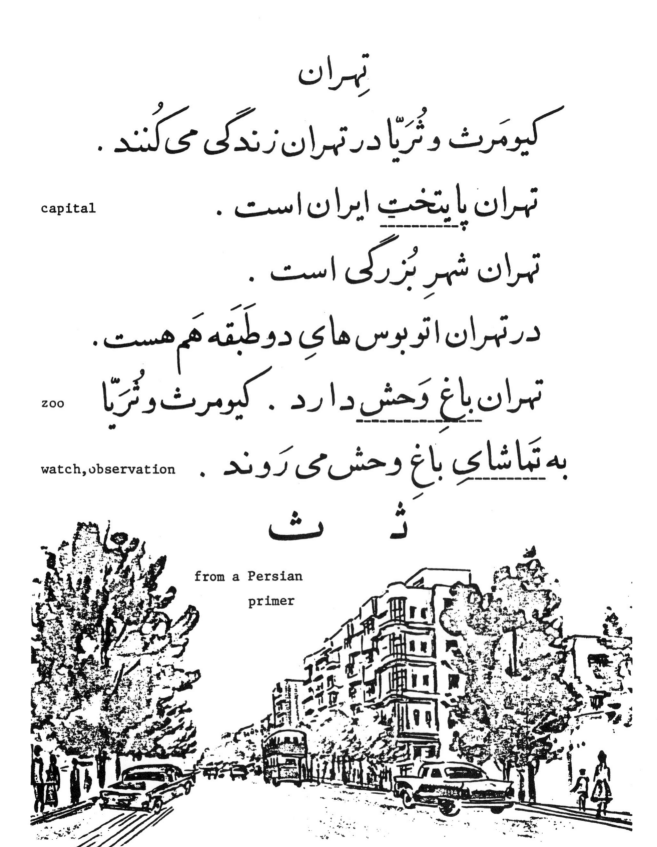

from a Persian
primer

درس هــفت

NOTES ON THE VERB

فِعْـل

1) Present and past, 2) personal endings, 3) the present prefix,
4) main uses of the past, 5) verbs with prepositions, 6) noun-verb
constructions; vocabulary; drills; reading

---

1) <u>PRESENT AND PAST</u>

Foreigners learning English have a hard time learning verbs;
quite a number of English verbs have three different stems,
one for the present, one for the past, and one participle,
e.g. swim, swam, swum; while other verbs have just one stem,
e.g. put, put, put. Fortunately, many verbs are regular
('weak'), they add /-ed/, e.g.: work, worked, worked. Persian
is much easier. First, the majority of the verbs are regular;
their past stem ends in / ـد /.

Second, Persian verbs have just two stems, the present stem
and the past stem. Thus, one only has to learn two stem forms,
e.g.:

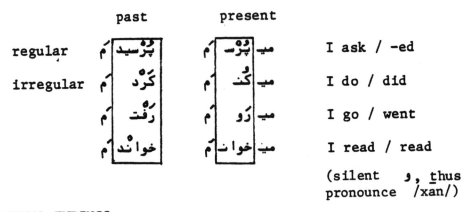

	past	present	
regular	پُرسیدَم	میپُرسَم	I ask / -ed
irregular	کَردَم	میکُنَم	I do / did
	رَفتَم	میرَوَم	I go / went
	خواندَم	میخوانَم	I read / read

(silent و , thus
pronounce /xan/)

2) PERSONAL ENDINGS

The personal endings are identical with the verb 'to be',
except for the 3rd person singular: the ending in the present
is دَ (and not اَست); in the past it is zero, i.e.
no ending; e.g.:

to arrive

present	past
میرَسَم	رَسیدَم
میرَسی	رَسیدی
میرَسَ دَ	رَسید □
میرَسیم	رَسیدیم
میرَسید	رَسیدید
میرَسَند	رَسیدَند

3) <u>THE PRESENT PREFIX</u>

The basic pattern is مـی ‑ کُنـ ‑ م .

کُنـ ‑ is the present of 'do, make'; م is the personal
ending 'I'; می indicates <u>incomplete</u> action, i.e. an action
that is going on at the moment or that always goes on or
that will go on. Thus, depending on the context می کنم may
mean:

'I am doing (now)'

or   'I do (always)'

or   'I do (tomorrow)/I'll do'

The negative is نـه ‑ می , thus: نِمیکنـم 'I don't do.'
(The prefix بـ which is found in the expressions of pp. 37-38 will be
discussed in lesson 18, p. 231.)

Note: The verbs 'have' and 'be' do not take the prefix

مـی :

past	pres.		past	pres.
داشتم	دارم		بودم	ام
داشتی	داری		بودی	ای
داشت	دارد		بود	است
داشتیم	داریم		بودیم	ایم
داشتید	دارید		بودید	اید
داشتند	دارند		بودند	اند
نداشتم	ندارم		نبودم	نیستم
نداشتی	نداری		نبودی	نیستی
نداشت	ندارد		نبود	نیست

4) <u>MAIN USES OF THE PAST FORMS OF VERBS</u>

The past form of verbs is used:

1) To narrate an event in the past, e.g.:

به آنجا رَفْتم .	I went there.
ساعت سه آمَد .	He came at three.
به مُنْشی گُفتم .	I told the secretary.
به پَرْوین تِلِفُن کردم .	I telephoned Parvin.

2) To refer to an event that <u>just happened</u>, where English

often uses the perfect with have -; e.g.:

رِسیدیم	We have just arrived, here we are.
فَهْمیدیم	I understand (have just understood).
آمَد	He has just come, is here.

5) <u>VERBS WITH PREPOSITIONS</u>

Many verbs in English are followed by prepositions, e.g.

'to count <u>on</u>', 'to take <u>from</u>', 'to ask <u>of</u>', 'to go <u>to</u>'.

The same is true in Persian. e.g.:

به او کتاب میدَهم / دادم .	I give/gave him a book/<u>to</u> him.
به تهران میرِسم / رِسیدم .	I will arrive/arrived <u>at</u> Tehran.
به حسن تِلِفُن میکنم / کَردم .	I call/called Hassan. (note به)
از حسن میگیرم / گِرِفتم .	I take/took it <u>from</u> Hassan.
از حسن میپُرسم / پُرسیدم .	I ask/asked (<u>of</u>) Hassan. (note اَز)
از شما تَشَکُر میکنم / کردم .	I thank/thanked you. (note اَز)

Evidently, the Persian prepositions do not necessarily agree

with English prepositions, such as به ... تِلِفُن میکنم 'I call',

از ... تَشَکُر میکنم 'I thank'.

6) <u>NOUN-VERB CONSTRUCTIONS</u>

In English, an action is either expressed by a single verb or
by a combination of noun-verb, e.g.: 'I teach' vs. 'I give a
lesson'; 'I study' vs. 'I learn a lesson.' In Persian many
actions can <u>only</u> be expressed by noun-verbs. Take, for
example, the notions of 'study' and 'teach'; there are no
simple verbs for these; instead, the verbs خوان 'read' and
ده 'give' are used in combination with nouns, e.g.:

a. <u>'read' ———— 'study'</u>:

میخوانم.	I read
کتاب میخوانم.	I read a book, I read
درس میخوانم.	I read a lesson, I study (a lesson)
فارسی میخوانم.	I study Persian (<u>never</u>:

(فارسی درس میخوانم)

b. <u>'give' ———— 'teach</u>

میدهم.	I give
درس میدهم.	I give a lesson, I teach (a lesson)
فارسی درس میدهم.	I teach Persian

c. <u>The helpful dummy</u> میکنم / کردم 'do':

One of the most frequent verbs used in these noun-verb
constructions is کردم / میکنم I do/did,' e.g.:

میکنم.	کار	I do work ——► I work
میکنم.	ترجمه	I do translation ——► I translate
میکنم.	بازی	I do playing ——► I play (a game)

VOCABULARY

لُغت

ask	از ... سُوال میکنم / کردم
listen	به ... گوش
repeat	تِکرار
request	از ... خواهش
pronounce	تلفُّظ
talk with	با ... صُحبت
practice	تمْرین
watch	تماشا

answer	به ... جَواب میدَهم / دادم
have an examination	اِمْتِحان

like, love	دوست دارم / داشتم
need	لازم

come	میآیم / آمَدم
go, leave	میرَوم / رَفْتم
sit (down)	مینْشینم / نِشَسْتم
sleep, lie (down)	میخوابم / خوابیدم
return	بَرْ میگَرْدم / بَرْگَشْتم
arrive, reach	میرسم / رسیدم
write	مینویسم / نِوِشْتم
ask	از ... میپُرسم / پُرسیدم
buy	میخَرم / خَریدم

Collect all the verbs up to here and enter them in your notebook

    a) verbs with کردن,   b) with دادن ,   c) with داشتن ,

    d) others.

DRILLS   تمرین

A) Practice each of the following sentences by substituting
   systematically 2nd, 3rd singular and 1st, 2nd,
   3rd plural. Practice until you can pronounce the six
   forms of each sentence in about a minute's time:

   ۱- من امروز به دانشگاه میروم .

   ۲- من هر روز فارسی تمرین میکنم .

   ۳- من به سوال معلم جواب میدهم .

B) Practice the following sentences in the same fashion as in
   Drill A, but in the past tense.

   من از ایران به آمریکا برگشتم .

   last night   من دیشب تلویزیون تماشا کردم .

   من به سوال معلم جواب دادم .

C) Fill in the blanks as indicated:

   (to listen)   ۱) دیشب دو ساعت به رادیو ——— .

   (crowded)   ۲) این کتابخانه شب ها خیلی ——— است .

   (our, like)   ۳) برادر کوچک ——— خیلی موسیقی ——— دارد .

   (yesterday)   ۴) ——— امتحان زبان فارسی خیلی خوب بود .

   (just   ۵) آیا حسن و علی اینجا هستند ؟ بله الان ——— .
   arrived)

98

D) Translate into Persian:

1) Did you go to your friend's house last night?

2) I talked to him in the library.

3) Ali bought a Persian dictionary yesterday.   (لغت نا مه)

4) My friend and I talked to our teacher in his office. (دفتر)

5) Did you play with your friend tonight?

6) Here we are (have arrived).

E) Read the following and translate:

۱) خواهرم به شُوهَرش نامه نوشت .

۲) علی هَمیشه۱ در کلاس فارسی به تلفظ معلمش خوب گوش میکند .   always

۳) پدر و مادرم از من پرسیدند .

۴) دیروز جان و مری امتحان فارسی دادند و از امتحان خیلی راضی هستند .

۵) برادرِ کوچکم شبها ساعتِ نه میخوابد .

۶) دوستِ دخترم آلمانی است و او سیب زمینی خیلی دوست دارد .

۷) کتابْدار دپارتمانِ ما فارسی بلد نیست .

۸) دیشب سه ساعت در کتابخانه نشستیم و درس خواندیم .

۹) پدر بزرگ و مادر بزرگم یک خانهٔ ساکِتْ لازِم داشتند .

۱۰) دیشب رستورانِ دانشگاه خیلی شلوغ بود و ما به خانه برگشتیم .

READING خواندنی

دیروز ساعتِ چهار بعد از ظُهر به دوستم پرویز تلفن کردم . پرویز

منزل نبود . او ساعت پنج ونیم به منزلش آمد و به من تلفن کرد و

گفت : اِمتِحانِ مِشکِلی بود ولی خوب امتحان دادم . او خیلی خوشحال بود .

به او گفتم : امشب با هم به سینما برویم . پرویز ماشین نداشت .

من با ماشین به منزل آنها رفتم . ساعت هفت بود . اول با هم به

یک رستوران رفتیم . رستوران کوچک بود ولی خیلی قشنگ بود . جواد ،

دوستِ پرویز ، آنجا بود . او در آن رستوران کار میکرد . چند تا از

دوستهای من هم آنجا بودند . ساعت هشت ونیم از رستوران بیرون آمدیم .

جلویِ سینما خیلی شلوغ بود . دو تا بلیط گِرِفتیم و به سینما رفتیم .

فیلم زیاد جالبی نبود .

_____

(* For unstressed ی 'a' etc. see p.115)

_____

home	<div dir="rtl">مَنْزِل</div>
difficult	<div dir="rtl">مُشْکِل</div>
tonight	<div dir="rtl">اِمْشَب</div>
together	<div dir="rtl">با هَم</div>
let's go (note بـ)	<div dir="rtl">بِرَویم</div>
first	<div dir="rtl">اَوَل</div>
beautiful	<div dir="rtl">قَشَنْگ</div>
out(side)	<div dir="rtl">بیرون</div>
in front of, before	<div dir="rtl">جلوی</div>
crowded	<div dir="rtl">شلوغ</div>
ticket	<div dir="rtl">بلیط</div>
(too) much	<div dir="rtl">زیاد</div>
interesting	<div dir="rtl">جالب</div>

LESSON EIGHT

درس هشـت

را

را ; voçabulary; drills; reading

A.

من	کی	را	می بینم ؟
من	کتاب	را	می بینم .
من	حسن	را	می بینم .
من	شما	را	می بینم .
من	پدرتان	را	می بینم .
من	این کتاب	را	می بینم .
من	چه چیزی	را	می بینم ؟

B.

من	چه		میخوانم ؟
من	کتاب		میخوانم .

A. Whom do I see?

I see the book, Hassan, you, your father, this book.

What (particular thing) do I see?

B. What do I read?

I read a book.

101

What have the direct objects with را of A in common as opposed to B? TRY TO ANSWER BEFORE READING ON.

The direct objects of A are <u>specific persons or specific items referred to</u>, while the direct object in B is unspecific, i.e. <u>there is no specific book or books referred to</u>. 'Book' is used here in the 'generic' sense.

RULE: را is obligatory with specific direct objects.

را is a marker of reference. It is most frequently found with specific direct objects.

A direct object is that part of a sentence which identifies the immediate objective of a verb, as opposed to an indirect object, e.g.:

من کتاب را به او میدهم .   I give <u>the book</u> to him.

Here, کتاب را 'the book' is the immediate objective of 'give' and thus the 'direct object' of the sentence while به او 'to him' identifies the indirect object here.

In this example, کتاب را refers to a specific book: 'the
book,' i.e. a book the speaker and the hearer know about
so that the speaker can refer to it as کتاب را 'the book.'

Whenever such a specific direct object is referred to by the
speaker, را is obligatory.

A direct object is not always a specific item referred to,
e.g.:

I gave him a book. به او کتاب دادم .

Here, too, کتاب 'a book,' is the immediate objective of
میدهم 'I give' and is thus the direct object of the sentence
(and به او 'him' is the indirect object). However, it is
not a specific book which the speaker refers to, although
he probably knows which book he gave. کتاب 'a book'
here simply tells the hearer that 'a book' was given.
That is, the speaker leaves the book he gave unspecified,
he does not refer to it 'specifically.' The issue is 'book
giving,' not which book.

Whenever no specific direct object is referred to, there
is also no marker of specific reference, i.e. no را .

Persian has no equivalent of English 'the'. As a rule of thumb, whenever the equivalent of a Persian direct object in English would have 'the', را should be used; e.g.:

دَر را باز کن .

بلیط ها را خریدی ؟

چرا حَیْوانها را میگُشند؟

چند تا از لُغَت ها را نمیدانم .

Open <u>the door</u>!

Did you buy <u>the tickets</u>?

Why do they kill <u>the animals</u>?

I do not know <u>some of the words</u>.

'Shopping list' for را

In addition to items which in English would have 'the', there are a number of words which implicitly refer to <u>individual</u> items and persons, or groups of items and persons as a <u>unit-whole</u>. These are thus specific by definition, so to speak, and require as direct objects:

a) <u>Proper names</u> refer to specific individuals:

حسن را قَبول کردند .

They accepted Hassan.

b) <u>Personal pronouns</u> refer to individuals and thus specific persons:

آنها را رَد کردند .

They flunked them.

c) <u>Personal suffixes</u> refer to individuals and thus specific

persons:

كتابم را گُم كردم .   I lost <u>my</u> book.

اسمتان را بنويسيد .   Write <u>your</u> names!

d) اين 'this' and آن 'that' (similar to 'the') by defini-

tion refer to 'this' or 'that' individual and thus

specific persons or items:

اين غذا را خيلى دوست دارم .   I like <u>this</u> food very much.

e) Such <u>question words</u> as كى 'who,' كُدام 'which,'

چندُم 'number what' ask for specific items or person:

كُدام صفحه را ميخواستيد ؟   <u>Which</u> record album did
you want?

f) Words like هر '<u>each</u>...' refer to individuals and

'all, every<u>one</u>' refer to a group as a unit-whole and

thus specific items or groups:

همه را بوسيد .   He kissed every<u>one</u>/all.

g) Words like يكى 'some<u>one</u>,' ديگرى 'another <u>one</u>,' هَمديگَر

'<u>each</u> other,' كَسى 'some<u>one</u>, single person,' خود 'self,

<u>own</u>' refer to individuals and thus specific persons

or items   (see p. 118):

كسى را نديدم .   I didn't see any<u>one</u>.

Thus, in all these cases use را . This means that one will initially go down this 'shopping list' each time one comes across a direct object, but one will learn to do it faster soon. Thus, the questions to ask are:

1) Direct object?

2) Yes? (Now one goes down the shopping list.)

3) Yes!: Use را .

No!: Don't use را .

So, when **not** to use را ? Whenever no specific person or item, etc. is implied, i.e. when they are used in the <u>generic sense</u>. In English these differ as to whether they are count nouns or mass nouns, they also can be singular or plural. In Persian, however, there is no difference whatsoever.

I have money.	من پول دارم .
<u>a</u> brother.	برادر
<u>a</u> book.	کتاب
book<u>s</u>.	کتاب

Verbs with and without Direct Objects

The difference between verbs with and verbs without direct

objects (D.O.) may be illustrated by the following pairs:

II	I	II	I
with D.O.	no D.O.		
داشتن (دارم)	بودن	have	- be
آوُردن (می‌آورم)	آمَدن (می‌آیم)	bring	- come
بُردن (می‌برم)	رَفتن (می‌روم)	take, carry	- go, leave
رِساندن (می‌رسانم)	رِسیدن (می‌رسم)	take to	- arrive
خواباندن (می‌خوابانم)	خوابیدن (می‌خوابم)	put to sleep	- sleep
پیْدا کردن	پیْدا شدن	find	- be found, appear
دیدن (می‌بینم)	پیْدا بودن	see	- be evident
دوست داشتن	از ... خوش آمدن	love, like	- like, delighted by

Note that English and Persian do not always coincide; for

example, the following verbs do not take the direct object

in Persian but instead have prepositions:

به او کُمَک می‌کنم .	I help <u>him</u>.
به او تلفن می‌کنم .	I call <u>him</u> (on the phone).
از او سوال می‌کنم .	I ask <u>him</u>.
از او تَشَکُّر می‌کنم .	I thank <u>him</u>.

را always occurs at the very end of the noun phrase, so that

sometimes one has to wait quite a time until one reaches را ,

e.g.:

the book	(کتاب) را
the big book	(کتاب بزرگ) را
the big book of the teacher	(کتاب بزرگ معلم) را
the big book of the good teacher	(کتاب بزرگ معلم خوب) را
the big book of the good Iranian teacher	(کتاب بزرگ معلم خوب ایرانی)را
the big book of my good Iranian teacher	(کتاب بزرگ معلم خوب ایرانیم)را
the book and the pencil and the small notebook	(کتاب و مداد و دفترچه) را

Note: مَرا   instead of   من را

تُرا   instead of   تو را

Archaeological Museum

موزهٔ ایران باستان به فرمان رضاشاه کبیر سرسلسله
خاندان پهلوی در سال ۱۳۱۶ تأسیس گردید

VOCABULARY

لغت

winter	زِمِسْتان	see	میبینم / دیدم
summer	تابِستان	want	میخواهم / خواسْتم
fall	پائیز	know (thing)	میدانم / دانِسْتم
spring	بُهار	understand	میفَهْمم / فَهْمیدم
air, weather	هَوا	buy	میخَرم / خَریدم
cold	سَرْد	take	میگیرم / گِرِفْتم
warm	گَرْم	put, let	میگُذارم / گُذاشْتم
shoe	کَفْش	know (acquainted)	میشِناسم / شِناخْتم
overcoat	پالْتو	find	پَیْدا میکنم / کردم
shawl	شالْ گَرْدَن	take out, off	دَرْ میآوَرم / آوُرْدم
shirt	پیراهَن	put on, wear	میپوشم / پوشیدم
suit	کُتُ شَلْوار	learn	یاد میگیرم / گِرِفْتم
dress	لِباس	build	میسازم / ساخْتم
field of study	رِشْته	bring	میآوَرم / آوُرْدم
letter	نامه	sing	میخوانم / خواندم
vacation/closed	تَعْطیل	drive	میرانم / راندم
to	به	meet	مُلاقات میکنم / کردم
with	با	invite	دَعْوَت میکنم / کردم
in	دَر	wait for	مُنْتَظِرِ (او) هستم / بودم
before ...	قَبْل از	wait	صَبْر میکنم / کردم
on (top)	رویِ	song	آواز
for	بَرایِ	afternoon	بَعْد از ظُهْر

<u>DRILLS</u>   تمرین

A) Recognition drill:

In the following sentences indicate whether را is needed or not.

Explain the reason for each case. Use the shopping list:

library   ۱) جواد هر روز من ــــ در <u>کتابخانه</u> میبیند .

shirt   ۲) فَردا صبح <u>پیراهن</u> ــــ میخرم .

very   ۳) این هوا ــــ <u>زیاد</u> سرد نیست .

              ۴) پدر دوستم ــــ هر روز <u>ملاقات</u> میکنم .

when?   ۵) برای دانشگاه <u>کِی</u> کتابخانه ــــ میسازند؟

              ۶) زمستانها لباسِگرم و پالتو ــــ میپوشم .

yesterday   ۷) <u>دیروز</u> در هوای سرد نیم ساعت ــــ منتظرِ او بودم .

each   ۸) پرویز <u>هر</u> هفته برادرش ــــ دعوت میکند .

It is important to note that whether a direct object is specific, or
not, ususally requires more context than a single sentence. This is especially the case when none of the criteria of the 'shopping list' (pp.
104-106) applies. In that case, the decision of whether to use را, or not,
depends on your imagination, i.e. how you as the speaker imagine the context of the sentence. - For example, in this drill, sentences 2,5,6 clearly have direct objects; but their context may be imagined as specific, or
not. Thus, sentence 2 :

Tomorrow morning I will buy   فردا صبح پیراهن <u>را</u> میخرم .

<u>the shirt</u> (I told you about)

<u>but</u>: I'll buy <u>a shirt/shirts</u> to-   فردا صبح پیراهن ـــ میخرم .

morrow morning. (I need some.)

B)   Translate and answer the questions:

what field (use p. 138)   ۱) مَریَم چه رشته ای میخواند ؟
   (unstressed ی)

                      ۲) پرویز دیروز چی پیدا کرد؟

party   ۳) آیا او فردا در مِهمانی آواز میخواند؟

                    ۴) کتابِ علی را کجا گذاشت ؟

              ۵) حسن کدام کلاس را خیلی دوست دارد ؟

                  ۶) آیا پدرِ علی کارمند است ؟

                  ۷) این درس را یاد گرفتید ؟

            ۸) جواد بعد از ظهرها چکار میکند ؟

         ۹) امروز صبح در کتابخانه کی را دیدید ؟

chess   ۱۰) آیا حسن بازی شَطرَنج را دوست دارد ؟

state /eyālat/   ۱۱) کدام ایالَت در آمریکا خیلی بزرگ است ؟

closed   ۱۲) دانشگاه هفتهٔ قبل چند روز تعطیل بود ؟

C)   Translate into Persian.

1) Did you see the movie last night? (فیلم).

2) My friend sold his car.

3) Which movie did you see?

4) We invited a Persian teacher to our house.

5) Where did you buy this nice dress?   (قشنگ)

6) Please repeat this again.

7) Do you <u>understand</u> this question? (past form!)

8) They are our Iranian friends. (use singular, cf. p. 49)

9) He likes my sister very much.

10) Please, answer (give an answer).

112

D) Completion and transformation drill

This drill contains two types of blanks:

a) The blanks indicated by ... are to be filled by را

if appropriate.

b) The blanks indicated by ____ are to be filled by

one of the following prepositions:

به ــ با ــ در ــ روی ــ برای

Note: Sentences 1,7,13,14 allow را or not. Explain the difference.

۱) کتاب ... میآورم .

۲) ____ دکتر میروم .

۳) ____ تهران ____ ماشین میروم .

۴) حسن .... ناراحت میکنم .

۵) نامه ... ____ میز میگذارم .

۶) امروز ____ کتابخانه نمیروم .

۷) ماشین .... میخرم .

۸) یک جواب .... میدهم .

۹) اینجا خانه های بزرگ ... میسازند .

۱۰) ____ حسن ... صبر میکنم .

۱۱) منتظر حسن ... هستم .

۱۲) این تمرین ... یاد میگیرم .

۱۳) درس ... میخوانم .

۱۴) دوچرخه ... میرانم .

۱۵) ____ رادیو ... گوش میدهم .

۱۶) یک فیلم ... تماشا میکنم .

۱۷) یک آواز ... میخوانم .

c) **Translate** the sentences in this drill.

d) **Put all** sentences in the past tense.

e) **Wherever** appropriate, change the nouns to the plural.

E) **Make up sentences with the following words:**

۱) کتاب ــ آیا ــ این ــ از ــ کتابخانه ــ را ــ گرفتی

۲) مِداد ــ آن ــ کجا ــ را ــ خَریدی ــ از

۳) بازی ــ بچه ــ را ــ ها ــ دوست دارند ــ خیلی

۴) دیروز ــ حسن ــ فارسی اش ــ کتاب ــ در کلاس ــ گذاشت ــ را

۵) جواد ــ را ــ دوست دارد ــ برادر

Drawing from an edition of Molla Nasroddin stories

READING خواندنی

دیروز در کتابخانه علی را دیدم . علی دوست من است ودر همین
دانشگاه درس میخواند . او کتابی میخواست ولی اسم نویسندهٔ کتاب
را نمیدانست . با هم به طَبَقهٔ دوم رفتیم و یکی از منشی ها را
دیدیم که با من دوست بود . از او خواهش کردیم به ما کمک بکند تا
کتاب را پیدا بکنیم .

he was wanting/looking for a book (unstressed ی)	کتابی میخواست .
he did not know	نمیدانِست
together	باهم
one of the secretaries	یکی از منشی ها
(here) who	که
that she may help us so that we may find	به ما کمک بکند تا پیدا بکنیم (see lesson 18, p. 231)
third floor (groundfloor not counted)	طَبَقه دوم

A proper question سوال رجا

بچه : مامان ، چرا گُرگ ها را میکُشَند ؟
مادر : بَرای اینکه گوسفَند ها را میخورند .
بچه : پَس چرا قَصاب ها را نمیکُشَند ؟

* * *

Child: Mommy, why do they kill the wolves?

Mother: Because they eat the sheep.

Child: Then, why don't they kill the butchers?

L E S S O N   N I N E

درس نــه

ی

1) Unstressed ی ; drills; dialogue 1; story; 2) the stressed suffix ی;
dialogue 2.

_____   _____

1) UNSTRESSED ی

a) General function

The unstressed ی selects an item or a group of items
from among others. It occurs with both singular and plural
noun phrases. The nearest (yet still quite different) English
equivalents are 'some, certain', and 'a' in the sense of
'some, certain,' or the article-less plural in the sense of
'some, certain.' Never assume that   ی is the exact
equivalent of 'a.'

کتاب جالبی نوشته است .   He has written (some, a certain)
                            an interesting book.

کتابهای جالبی نوشته است   He has written some, certain
                            interesting books.

as opposed to:

یک کتاب جالب نوشته است .   He has written an (one) interesting
                            book.

کتابهای جالب نوشته است .   He has written interesting books.

115

Without ی , these sentences are simply descriptive; they tell about his <u>writing</u> interesting books. With ی , a selection is implied and a comparison with other books; and his books are "selectively" identified as '<u>interesting books</u>'.

ماشینِ قِرمِزِ بود ؟   Was it a <u>red</u> car?

ماشین قرمزی بود ؟   Was it a <u>certain/some</u> red car?

Without ی , a simple descriptive question is asked about the color of the car. With ی , the car in question is compared to and selected from among other cars (which were also in the area when the accident occured, etc.).

کار دارم .   I have <u>work</u> to do.

کاری دارم .   I have <u>some work/a certain job</u> to do.

Note that similar to the use of را (see p. 110) the use of ی is determined by a context larger than a single short sentence.

b) <u>ی of first mention</u>

Persons, items, time, etc. at first mention usually take ی :

روزی مُلانَصرالدّین به مَسجِدی رفته بود.   <u>Someday/on a certain day</u> Molla Nasroddin had gone to <u>a/some/a certain</u> mosque.

در زد . چِراغی رَوشَن شُد و مَردی از پنجره به بیرون نِگاه کرد.   He knocked. <u>A/some</u> lamp lit up and <u>a/some</u> man looked out of the window.

c) ــ ی ــ 'what a, any (particular)'

Exclamations, questions, and negation often imply comparative
selection. In such cases, the approximate English equivalents
are 'what a, any (particular).'

<u>Exclamation 'what a !'</u> ــــ ! ی ــ چی ــــ

چه هوای خوبی .   What (a) fine weather/some fine weather!

چه خری هستی .   What an ass you are/some ass you are!

<u>Question 'what a'</u> ــــ ؟ ی ــ چه ــــ

چه رِشته ای میخوانید؟   What (a) field do you study?

چه رَنگی است ؟   What (a) color is it?

d) <u>Question 'any particular'</u> ــــ ؟ ی ــ ــــ

سوال دارید؟   Do you have <u>a question</u>?

سوالی دارید ؟   Do you have <u>any (particular)</u>
question?

e) <u>Negation</u> ــــ نه ــ ی ــ ــــ

سوال ندارم .   I don't have <u>any</u> question.

سوالی ندارم .   I don't have <u>any particular</u> question.

f) ــ ی ــ with measure (cf. p. 63)

هفته ای دوبار   twice a/per week

روزی یک دَفْعه   once a/per day

متری یک تومان   one toman a/per meter

g) <u>ی</u> 'some ---'

کَمی	somewhat, a little
قَدْری	some amount, a little
(یک) جائی	somewhere
(یک) وَقْتی	sometime
(یک) چیزی	something
(یک) کَسی	someone
(یک) دوسه روزی	some 2 or 3 days
(یک) چهار پنج کتابی	some 4 or 5 books

Orthographic note: A glottal stop or ب is inserted
after vowels as follows: خانه ای / دانشجوئی ـ آقائی / آقایی
(cf. p. 344).

<u>Final Note</u>

When an adjective stands alone, as in the following

example, it <u>cannot</u> take ی :

The book is small . کتاب کوچک است

<u>Never:</u>

. کتاب کوچکی است

DRILLS

In the following sentences indicate where ی ‪ِ‬ is appropriate, and what the difference in meaning is when both (ی) and (no ی) are possible:

۱) ماشینِ قرمز ‫ـــــ‬ داری .

۲) پرویز اطاقِ کوچک ‫ـــــ‬ دارد .

buy ۳) چه ماشین ‫ـــــ‬ خریدی ؟

quiet ۴) دوستِ برادرم اطاقِ ساکت ‫ـــــ‬ دارد .

crowded ۵) خانهٔ ما در خیابانِ شلوغ ‫ـــــ‬ است .

field ۶) این دانشگاه رشتهٔ مُهَنْدِسیِ خوب ‫ـــــ‬ دارد .

purse ۷) این کیفِ قشنگ ‫ـــــ‬ را از کجا خریدید ؟

۸) چه تلفظِ خوب ‫ـــــ‬ دارید !

۹) جا ‫ـــــ‬ نرفتم .

۱۰) اطاقِ بزرگ ‫ـــــ‬ لازم دارم .

DIALOGUE 1 (Review)   گفتگو ۱

late   A) خیلی دیر آمدی .

I know   B) بله ، میدانم . اتوبوس خیلی شلوغ بود .

(note glide in /na-y-āmadi/)   A) چرا با دوچرخه‌ات نیامدی ؟

days   B) این روزها دوچرخه ندارم .

before, last/('gave it';cf.p.78)   هفتهٔ قَبْل به دوستم دادم .

then   A) پس‌صبحها با چی به دانشگاه میروی ؟

on foot   B) با ماشین پدرم ، ولی امروز صبح پیاده

cold   آمدم . خیلی سرد بود .

far   A) خانهٔ شما از اینجا خیلی دور است ؟

                        B) خیلی دور نیست .

STORY   قصّه

یکی بود ، یکی نبود . غَیْر از خُدا هیچکس نبود .

پادشاهی بود ، پسری داشت .

روزی از روزها رفته بود در جنگلی شکار کند .

در آن جنگل درختهای عَجیبی بود .

هَرْ یکی به اندازهٔ یک کبریت .

ناگهان با پیرزنِ جادوگری روبرو شد .

جادوگر گفت : سوالی دارم از تو .

جواب بِدَهی تو را رَها میکنم ، نَدَهی تو را میخورم .

پسر پادشاه گفت : چه میخواهی از من ؟

جادوگر حرفش را قطع کرد و گفت :

چه حرفهائی ، چه حرفهایِ بیخودی میزنی .

گوش کن : سه تا زن بود ، یک مرد

زنِ اول پیر بود، زنِ دوم جوان بود .

زنِ سوم نه پیر بود و نه جوان بود .

Note the <u>subjunctives</u>: (see lesson 18, p. 231)

رفته بود شکار <u>کند</u> .	he had gone to hunt
نمیتوانی مرا <u>بترسانی</u>	you cannot frighten me
جواب <u>بدهی</u>	should you give an answer
<u>ندهی</u>	should you not give (an answer)

sorcerer, witch	جا دوگر	except for	غَیْر از
come to face with, meet	روبِرومیشَوَم / شُدَم	nobody	هیچکَس
release	رَها میکنم	king	پادِشاه
eat	میخورم / خوردم	had gone	رَفته بود
I can	میتَوانم / تَوانِستم	woods	جَنگَل
I frighten	میتَرْسانم / تَرْساندم	hunt	شِکار میکنم
word, speech	حَرْف	strange	عَجیب
cut (off)	قَطْع میکنم	size, measure	اَنْدازه
meaningless, useless	بیخود	match	کِبْریت
speak	حَرْف میزَنم / زَدم	suddenly	ناگِهان
young	جَوان	old woman	پیرِ زَن

In the story above underline all occurrences of unstressed ی

and explain which kind of unstressed ی it is.

در دورهٔ اشکانی صنعتگران چیره‌دست ایرانی
ظرفهای بسیار ظریف وزیبا ازفلزات قیمتی می‌—
ساختند. از این ظرفها نمونه‌هایی درموزهٔ ایران
باستان و موزه‌های کشورهای دیگر وجود دارد .

2) <u>THE STRESSED SUFFIX ی</u>

Stressed ی is the most productive suffix in Persian to
derive words from others, e.g.:

<u>origin</u>

کجا ــ کجائی	where - wherefrom
ایران ــ ایرانی	Iran - Iranian
شیراز ــ شیرازی	Shiraz - from Shiraz

<u>location/store</u>

قالی فُروش ــ قالی فُروشی	carpet seller - carpet store
نانُوا ــ نانُوائی	baker - bakery
بُقال ــ بُقالی	grocer - grocery

<u>habit</u>

تِرْیاک ــ تِرْیاکی	opium - opium addict

<u>abstract nouns</u>

جادوگر ــ جادوگری	witch - sorcery
خوشحال ــ خوشحالی	happy - happiness
سَبْز ــ سَبْزی	green - vegetables
شیرین ــ شیرینی	sweet - sweets

colors

آبی ــ آب	water - blue
خاکی ــ خاک	dirt - khaki
نارِنْجی ــ نارِنْج	orange - orange
قهوه ای ــ قهوه	coffee - brown

adjectives

کتابی ــ کتاب	book - literary
امروزی ــ امروز	today - of today
رَسْمی ــ رَسْم	custom - official (adjective)
دونَفَری ــ دو نَفَر	two persons - double (room)

the one

قَبْلی ــ قَبْل	before - the one before
پَهْلوئی ــ پَهْلو	side - the one beside
دُوُّمی ــ دُوُّم	second - the second one

gerund

دیدَنی ــ دیدَن	seeing - worth seeing
خوردَنی ــ خوردَن	eating - edible

verbal use (rare)

رفتنی هستم ــ رفتن	going - I am to go/going
ماندَنی هستم ــ ماندَن	staying - I am to stay/staying

adverbial phrases 'by, in it'

کیلوئی	by the kilo
(در) این نَزْدیکیها	in this vicinity (ها = plural)
ده فَرْسَنْگیِ قم	at 10 farsang from Qom (f. = 6.24 km.)
دونَفَری	(as a group of) two persons
به زودی	quickly, with quickness
کتاب به این دِرازی	a book that long
به سِفیدیِ برف	of the whiteness of snow/as white as snow
چطُوری	how, by what means

Note: /-e/ – /eg-/

بَچِگی — بَچِه	child – childhood
خَسْتِگی — خَسْتِه	tired – fatigue

Final Note:

Do not mistake stressed ی for unstressed ی ; e.g.:

unstressed

کیلوئی سه تومان	3 toman per kilo
هفته ای دودَفْعه	twice a week

stressed

فَقَط کیلوئی میفُروشیم	we only sell it by the kilo
مَجَلهءِ هَفْتِگی	weekly magazine

DIALOGUE 2   گفتگو ۲

This dialogue uses a good amount of linguistic تَعارُف'polite behavior'
for which Iranians are famous.

(A   به به ، چشم ما روشن ، کی تشریف آوردید ؟

(B   والله ، تقریباً یک هفته است .

(A   جدی ؟ من تا امروز خبر نداشتم . امروز صبح آقای جوادی به من گفت .

(B   دُرست است ، دیشب هم با هم بودیم و خیلی هم ما را خجالت دادند .

(A   بعد از همهٔ این حرفها ، خیلی دلم برای شما تنگ شده .

(B   خواهش میکنم ، لطف دارید .

(A   خوب کِیْ خدمت برسیم ؟

(B   اختیار دارید ، خدمت از ماست .

(A   فردا شب ساعت نه چطور است ؟

(B   بسیار خوب .

ـــــــ(ادامه دارد)ـــــــــ

Note the use of ما ـ یم for 'I' (alternating with من ـ م), of شما ـ ید
for 'you(singular)' and of ایشان ـند for 'he(she)' (alternating
with the 3rd person singular.

comes, arrives (2nd or 3rd person: 'bring honor')	تَشْریف میآوَرند / آوُردند
well, well	بَه بَه
how nice to see you (new arrival: 'our eyes are bright')	چُشْمِ ما رَوْشَن
well ('God')	وَاللّٰه
about approximately	تَقْریبًا
seriously; is that right (stressed ی)	جِدی
know about ('have news')	خَبَر دارم / داشتم
right, correct	درست
together	با هَم
too nice of you/him ('gave me shame')	ما را خِجالَت دادید / دادند
all of	هَمهٔ
I miss you ('my heart got tight for...')	دِلَم بَرای ... تَنْگ شُده
very kind of you ('you have kindness')	لُطف دارید / داشتید
I come to see you (only 1st person: 'arrive for your service')	خِدمَت میرسم / رسیدم
please, I beg you, your pardon ('you have the liberty')	اِختیار دارید
It is our obligation to see you ('the service is of us')	خِدمَت از ماسْت
continuation	اِدامه

DIALOGUE (continued) گفتگو (ادامه)

B) ماشین قشنگی دارید .

A) اختیار دارید ، چشمهای شما قشنگ میبیند .

B) خواهش میکنم .

A) خوب ، کجا برویم ؟

B) هرجا میل شماست .

A) چطور است به یک رستوران ایرانی برویم ؟

B) بسیار عالی است .

A) مثل اینکه به موقع رسیدیم .

B) چطور مگر ؟

A) چون اینجا برنامه ها از ساعت ده شروع میشود .

B) جدی ! الان پنج دقیقه داریم به ده .

A) خدا کند یک جائی برای پارک پیدا کنیم .

B) مثل اینکه جلوی آن کامیونها یک جای پارک است .

──── (پایان) ────

thank you (for your judgement: 'your eyes see nicely')	چِشْمِ شما قَشَنْگ میبیند
inclination, wish	مَیْل
great, excellent	عالی
it seems	مِثْلِ اینکه
in time	به مَوْقِع
how is that	چطور مَگَر
because	چون
program	بَرْنامه
begins	شروع میشود/شد
I hope ('may God make')	خُدا کُند
before, in front	جِلو
truck	کامِیون
end	پایان

Note the subjunctives (see lesson 18, p. 231):

shall we arrive	برسیم
shall we/let us go	برویم
may be some place	جائی ... باشد

M O R E   O N   P L U R A L   A N D   S I N G U L A R

مُفرَد و جَمع (ادامه)

1) Other uses of ها , 2) plural in ـ ان , 3) singular verb with
inanimate plural, 4) after numbers, 5) generic predicate, 6) generic
singular vs. non-generic plural complexes, 7) generic vs. non-
generic direct objects, 8) noun-verb complexes; vocabulary;
drills; reading.

---

1) <u>OTHER USES OF ها </u>   (cf. p. 81)

   a) The English plural can also be used adverbially, as in
       'upstairs', 'thereabout<u>s</u>', etc. The same is found in
       Persian, in fact much more freely than in English, with
       adverbs to generalize, e.g.:

اینجا ها	hereabouts
بالا ها	somewhere up there
پائین ها	somewhere down there
امروز ها	these days (cf. p. 125)
این نزدیکی ها	somewhere nearby, in this vicinity
	(cf. p. 124)

b) <u>Such adverbial ها phrases</u> may also be connected by /-e-/
to nouns, e.g.:

اینجا های ِ کلاس	here somewhere in the class
بالا های ِ خانه	somewhere upstairs
نَزدیکی های ِ ظهر	somewhere near noon

c) <u>With the pronouns ما and شما</u> (only)
when 'we' and 'you' do refer to a group of people including the speaker or the addressee, e.g.:

ما ها آن کار را نمیکنیم.	We (people like us) do not do such things.
شما ها اینجا بنشینید.	You all sit down!

d) <u>With indefinite numbers, etc.</u>

کی ها	who (plural)
خیلی ها	many
دیگر ها	the others
بَعضی ها	several

e) <u>With mass nouns</u>

آبها را روی قالی ریخْت.	He poured all the water on the carpet.
دوستیها یت کجاست.	Where is all your friendship?
فِکر ها یش خیلی خوب است.	All his thinking (ideas) is very good.

2) **Plural in** ان ــ

a) **With nouns**

Nouns referring to humans, paired parts of the human
body, some animals and plants, may take the plural ending
ان ــ , e.g.:

Note /-y-/	آقا	آقایان	آقا ها	sirs
	بانو	بانُوان	بانوها	ladies
	چُشم	چشمان	چشمها	eyes
Note /-eg-/	مُژه	مژِگان	مژه ها	eyelashes
	اَسب	اسبان	اسبها	horses
	دِرَخت	درختان	درختها	trees
	دیگَر	دیگران	(دیگر ها)	the others
	هُزار	هزاران	هزارها	thousands

b) **Pluralized adjectives**

Whereas English does not usually use plural with independent adjectives, Persian mostly uses the plural
ending, usually ان ــ , e.g.:

خوب	خوبان	good - the good (people)
بزرگ	بزرگان	big - the great(s) (people)
ثَرْوَتْمَنْد	ثروتمندان	rich - the rich (people)
	زیبایان هالیوود	the beautiful/beauties of Hollywood

> ها does not always occur where the English equivalent
> has plural. (Some cases have already been discussed
> above.)

3) <u>SINGULAR VERB WITH INANIMATE PLURAL</u>

When the plural refers to <u>inanimate</u> items the verb may be
in the plural or singular; the plural tends to reiterate the
plurality of the items, e.g.:

plural: کتابهای درسی اینجا اند

The textbooks are (all) here.

singular: کتابهای درسی برای همه کس مفید است.

Textbooks are useful for everybody.

4) <u>AFTER NUMBERS</u>

There is no plural after numbers   (cf. p. 58), e.g.:

دارید؟	کتاب	تا	چند	How many books do you have?
دارم.	کتاب	دانه	یک	I have one book.
دارم.	کتاب	تا	ده	I have ten books.

5) <u>GENERIC PREDICATE</u>

    a) When the predicate identifies a characteristic (occupa-

        tion, etc.), no plural is used (c.f. p. 49) , e.g.:

او دانشجواست .   He is <u>a student</u>.

آنها دانشجو هستند .   They are <u>students</u>.

    b) 'Occupation' is only one class of nouns which, as predicates, identify

        a characteristic of persons or things; compare:

آنها چی اند؟   What are those?

آنها قالی اند .   Those are <u>carpets</u>.

آنها قالی کاشانی اند .   Those are <u>Kashani carpets</u>.

آنها کی هستند؟   <u>Who</u>/what are they?

آنها مهمان ما هستند .   They are our <u>guests</u>.

The reason for the use of the singular here is: the nouns
here identify a general characteristic common to one
or more persons, or things, i.e. the nouns are used in
their general <u>generic</u> sense, for which Persian uses
the singular, while English requires the plural with
countable nouns.

6) <u>GENERIC SINGULAR VS. NON-GENERIC PLURAL COMPLEXES AS PREDICATES</u>

However, whenever nouns (with or without descriptive adjectives

such as کاشانی etc.) are not used generically, ها must be

used. Compare the following pairs where those items making

a noun non-generic are underlined:

آنها قالی هستند . Those are carpets.

آنها قالی هایِ <u>من</u> هستند . Those are <u>my</u> carpets.

آنها قالی قرمز هستند . Those are red carpets.

آنها قالی های قرم<u>زی</u> هستند . Those are (<u>certain</u>) red carpets (which I bought etc.)

آنها مهمان هستند . They are guests.

آنها مهمان <u>ها</u> هستند . They are <u>the</u> guests.

Here, with the pronoun من , with selective ی , and the

implicit specifying <u>the</u>, the carpets are not (no longer)

'generic'; they are (become) '<u>my</u> carpets' or '<u>certain</u> carpets', etc.,

and thus clearly more than one, individual items and ها is obligatory. من ,

ی , and the implicit <u>the</u>, are only three of many contexts in

which a noun cannot be generic, including the items listed in

the 'shopping list' for specific direct objects.

7) <u>GENERIC VS. NON-GENERIC DIRECT OBJECTS</u>

The rules for the generic use of 'plain' nouns found in
equational sentences apply also elsewhere. Most conspicuous
is the generic use of nouns functioning as generic direct
objects. To recall, a noun as a direct object may identify:

a) either a <u>specific</u> item or items (then, of course, را
   is obligatory), or

b) a selected (certain or some) item or items (then, of
   course, ی is obligatory), or

c) the noun identifies <u>neither</u> a certain nor a specific
   item or items; in that case the noun is used generically
   and is used in its plain form, and may refer to one or
   more items, even where English uses the plural, e.g.:

a) specific   کار را میکنید؟ (آن)   You're doing <u>the</u> work?

b) selective   کاری میکنید؟   You're doing <u>some</u> work?

c) generic   کار میکنید؟   You're <u>working</u>?

a) specific   درس را میخوانم.   I study <u>the</u> lesson.

b) selective   درسی میخوانم.   I study <u>a/some</u> lesson.

c) generic   درس میخوانم.   I <u>study</u>.

8) <u>NOUN-VERB COMPLEXES</u>

Note the last two examples: When the noun is used generically
the English translation may be a <u>simple</u> verb (cf. p. 95,96):

'study' درس میخوانم 'work' کار میکنم

Like these two <u>noun-verb</u> complexes, there are many others
where a noun in its <u>generic</u> sense together with a verb in
English can usually be translated by a simple verb, though
not always (also in English not all actions can be expressed
by simple verbs), e.g.:

گوش میدهم	'listen'	سوال میکنم	'ask'
تلفن میکنم	'call' (on the phone)	جواب میدهم	'answer'
اِمتِحان میدهم	'have an exam'	امتحان میکنم	'examine' (teacher)

Thus, such noun-verb complexes express the general verbal
idea of the action: work-doing (کار میکنم), lesson-studying
(درس میخوانم). When, however, the noun is not generic
this <u>verbal</u> unit-meaning is broken, and verb and noun are
(become) separate units, e.g.:

کار میکنم	I do-work = work
کاری میکنم	I do/a work, some work (cf. p. 116)
نامه فرستادم	I letter-sent = wrote
نامه ای فرستادم	I sent a letter

(Note the change in translation in 'send-letter' = 'write').

VOCABULARY

لــغت

میٖنویسم /نوشتم	(نامه ــ کتاب ــ دیکته ــ انشاء ــ تمرین)
میخوانم /خواندم	(درس ــ کتاب ــ آواز ــ فارسی ــ فلسفه)
میگیرم /گرِفتم	(آپارتمان ــ عکس ــ بلیط ــ اجازه ــ دوش)
میزٖنم /زَدم	(حرف ــ پیانو ــ واکس)
رَوْشن میکنم/کردم	(ضبط صوت ــ تلویزیون ــ چراغ ــ ماشین ــ کولر)
خاموش میکنم/کردم	(ضبط صوت ــ تلویزیون ــ چراغ ــ ماشین ــ کولر)
میگُذارم/گُذاشتم	(عینک ــ ریش ــ سبیل)

speak, talk	حرف میزنم		letter	نامه
shoeshine	واکْس		dictation	دیکته
light	رَوْشن میکنم		composition	اِنْشاء
turn off, silence	خاموش میکنم		read, sing	میخوانم
tape recorder	ضَبْطِ صَوْت		song	آواز
lamp	چراغ		take	میگیرم
car	ماشین		picture	عَکْس
cooler	کولر		ticket	بلیط
put, place	میگُذارم		permission	اِجازه
glasses	عَیْنک		shower	دوش
beard	ریش		hit	میزَنم
moustache	سِبیل		word, letter	حَرْف

geography	جُغْرافیا	Iranian studies	ایرانْتِشناسی
physics	فیزیک	(Near) Eastern studies	خاوَرْشناسی
chemistry	شیمی	anthropology	مَرْدُمْشناسی
philosophy	فَلْسَفه	linguistics	زَبانْ شناسی
literature	اَدَبیات	sociology	جامِعِه شناسی
economy	اِقْتِصاد	psychology	رَوان شناسی
political science	عُلوم‌ِسیاسی	history	تاریخ
engineering	مهندسی	medicine	پزشکی

DRILLS تمرین

A) Question and answer drill:

Ask for the field of study of others and answer
according to the pattern:

چه رشته ای میخوانید ؟   من ایرانشناسی میخوانم .

B) In the following sentences indicate whether the nouns
are used generically or not, and then translate into
Persian, e.g.:

1) She is a student.

2) I have a blue car.

3) I buy a Persian book.

4) The room had a big window.

5) Do you need a taxi?

6) These are strange trees.

7) I have a brother.

8) Do you have tea?

9) I wrote you a letter.

10) I am reading a book.

(This drill is quite mechanical and should not be overdone.)

C) Practice the verbs given in the vocabulary above together with the nouns indicated in parentheses:

1) Use the nouns in the generic sense, e.g.:

letter

من نامه مینویسم .

حسن حرف میزند .

2) Use the nouns as specific items according to the
pattern:

آن نامه را نوشتم .

آن تلویزیون را روشن کردم .

3) Do the same by adding personal suffixes to the nouns
according to the pattern:

نامه ام را الان مینویسم .

picture

عکسش را الان میگیرم .

4) Make the nouns selective (Note: this is generally
impossible with languages, occupations, and fields
of study.

D) 1. Fill in the blanks with either ها or ان-, whichever is appropriate and translate.

2. Most sentences are perfectly good sentences without ها (or ان-), except two of them. Find these two sentences.

3. Compare the sentences where ها(and ان-) is optional and explain the difference between the presence and absence of ها/ان- :

invitation

۱) صد ـــــ نفر را دعوت‌کردند.

lazy

۲) شما ـــــ خیلی تَنبَل هستید.

۳) کی ـــــ از دانشگاه آپارتمان گرفتند؟

post office

۴) در نزدیکی ـــــ (ی) بانکِ ملی پُستخانه‌است.

above, up/expensive

۵) بالا ـــــ یِ شَهر آپارتمان‌ها خیلی گِران‌اند.

some-

۶) بَعضی ـــــ پیانو خیلی خوب میزنند.

wealthy

۷) ثروتمند ـــــ این شَهر در خیابانِ آرا زندگی میکنند.

۸) چشم ـــــ او را خیلی دوست دارم.

oil/pour (میریزم)

۹) رَوغَن ـــــ را روی میز ریخت.

(cf. p. 131)/sing.

۱۰) دیگر ـــــ با ما آواز میخوانند.

READING

خواندنی

وقتی دانشجوی زبانی یک متنی را به زبان خارجی میخواند و
چند لغت را نمیفهمد از لغت‌نامه استفاده میکند . مثلاً یکی از
این لغت‌نامه‌ها در زبان فارسی لغت‌نامهٔ "خیّم" است.استفاده
از لغت‌نامه در اوایلِ کار کمی مشکل است . چون در لغت‌نامه‌ها
معمولاً برای هَر لغتی چند تا معنی وجود داردکه با هم فـــرق
میکنند . پَس بَعْضی وَقْت‌ها پَیْدا کردنِ تَرجُمهٔ دُرُست اشکال بوجـــود
میآورد ولی با تمرین و تجربه به تدریج دانشجوی زبان ترجمهٔ
درستِ لغت را پیدا میکند .

Note the combination /-i-rā/ in the first line:'a certain, specific text'.

usually	معمولا	when	وقتی
meaning	مَعْنی	text	مَتْن
exists	وُجود دارد	foreign (stressed ی)	خارِجی
differ from from each other	باهم .. فَرْق میکند	word	لُغَت
some...	بَعْضی ... ها	understand	میفَهْمم/ فَهْمیدم
finding	پَیْدا کردن	dictionary	لُغَتْ‌نامه
difficulty	اِشْکال	use	اِسْتِفاده میکنم از
brings about	به وُجود میآورد/ آوردن	for example	مَثَلاً
but	ولی	towards the beginning	دَرّ اَوایِل
experience	تَجْرِبه	difficult	مُشْکِل
gradually	به تَدْریج	because	چون

fatherland مِیهَن

country

group

sea

mountains

cold

plains

میهن ما ایران است .

زَبانِ کشَورِ ما فارسی است .

گُروهی از ایرانیان در کنارِ

دریاها زندگی می کنند .

گُروهی دیگر در کوهستانهایِ

سَرد زندگی می کنند .

گُروهی دیگر در دشتهایِ

گَرم زندگی می کنند .

همه ایرانی هَستیم .

from a Persian
schoolbook

درس یازده

C O M P A R A T I V E   A N D   S U P E R L A T I V E

تَفْضیلی و عـــــالی

1) 'as --- as,' 2) the comparative, 3) از 'than,' 4) comparing
two clauses, 5) 'as...as/the...the,' 6) superlative, 7) numbers/
degrees; vocabulary; drills.

---

1) **'AS --- AS'**

There is no exact equivalent of 'as --- as.' Likeness
may be expressed by مِثْلِ 'like' or به ...ی (stressed ی),
e.g.:

a) پیراهَنت مِثْلِ بَرْف سِفید است .   Your shirt is white like
snow.

b) پیراهنت به سفیدیِ برف است .   Your shirt is of the white-
ness of snow, 'as white as
snow.'

2) **THE COMPARATIVE**

   a) The regular comparative ending is تَر , e.g.:

   خوب – بِهْتَر good-__better__   بزرگ – بزرگتر big-bigger

   خَیْلی – بیشتَر much-__more__   کوچک – کوچکتر small-smaller

   Note: 1) کَم و بیش 'more or less.' بیش از پیش 'more than before'

   2) بیشتر دوست دارم 'I like it __better__ (i.e. more)'

   3) تر is written separately after /e/, e.g.: خسته‌تر 'more tired'.

3) __از__ 'THAN'

    a) The comparative preposition is   از , e.g.:

       predicate: این کتاب <u>بزرگتر/از آن</u> است   This book is bigger than that.

       adverbial: حسن <u>تُندتَر/از جواد</u> حرف میزند.   Hassan speaks quicker than Javad.

    b) When the compared item or person is stressed it may

       occur __before__ the comparative, e.g.:

       این کتاب <u>از آن/بزرگتر</u> است .   This book is bigger than that.

       حسن <u>از جواد/تندتر</u> حرف میزند .   Hassan speaks quicker than Javad.

    c) از __may be omitted with__ کمتر / بیشتر

       (از) سه هفته بیشتر نیست .   It's not more than 3 weeks.

       (از) دو ماه کمتر است .   It's less than 2 months.

4) __COMPARING TWO CLAUSES__

When the compared part __follows__ the verb, تا   is used

(instead of از), e.g.:

       بیشتر میخورد/<u>تا</u> کار میکند .   He eats more than he works.

       این صندلی بزرگتر است/<u>تا</u> آن صندلی (است) .   This chair is bigger than that chair (is).

       او بیشتر به ژاله گوش میدهد/<u>تا</u> به من (گوش میدهد) .   He listens more to Zhale than (he listens) to me.

5) **'AS ... AS'/'THE ... THE'**

هَرْچه زودْتر .

<u>as</u> quickly as possible

هرچه تند تُر حرف میزند خَسْته تر/ بیشتر خسته میشود .

The quicker he talks, the more he gets tired, the tireder he gets.

هرچه (بیشتر) فِکْر میکنم بیشتر نِگَران/ نگران تر میشوم .

The more I think, the more concerned I become.

6) **SUPERLATIVE**

The superlative differs, depending on whether the adjective or adverb is independent, or precedes a noun.

a) <u>Independent superlative</u>

The superlative of an independent adjective or adverb is expressed by از همه ــ تر (literally 'more - than all'), e.g.:

غذای فرانسوی از همه بهتر است .

French food is <u>the best</u> (better than all)

حسن از همه تندتر حرف میزند .

Hassan speaks <u>the fastest</u> (faster than all).

b) <u>Superlative preceding a moun</u>

The superlative ending of an adjective preceding a noun is (stressed) ــ ترین . There is no connective /-e/, e.g.:

بهترین غذا ، غذای فرانسوی است .

The <u>best food</u> is French food.

بزرگترین شاهِ ایران داریوش بود .

The <u>greatest king</u> of Iran was Darius.

c) <u>the (great)est of the (plural)</u>

The superlative ـترین connected to the following plural

noun by /-e/ means: 'the ___est of the', e.g.:

<u>بزرگترین</u> شاهان	the <u>greatest of the</u> kings
<u>کوچکترین</u> کِشْوَرها	the <u>smallest of the</u> countries
<u>بزرگترینِ</u> ما	the <u>oldest of</u> us

7. NUMBERS/DEGREES

a) <u>many-more-the most</u>

<u>خیلی</u> دوست دارد	He has <u>many</u> friends.
(از دیگران) <u>بیشتر</u> دوست دارد.	He has <u>more</u> friends (than others).
از همه بیشتر دوست دارد.	He has the <u>most</u> friends, more friends than all others.

b) <u>very-more-the most</u>

<u>خیلی</u> راحت است	It's <u>very</u> convenient.
(از دیگران) <u>راحت تر</u> است.	It's <u>more</u> convenient (than others).
(از همه) <u>راحت تر</u> است.	It's <u>the most</u> convenient.

c) <u>much-more-the most</u>

<u>خیلی</u> کار میکند.	He works <u>much</u>.
(از دیگران) <u>بیشتر</u> کار میکند.	He works <u>more</u> (than others).
از همه بیشتر کار میکند.	He works the <u>most</u>.

d) <u>few-fewer-the fewest</u>

(خیلی) <u>کم</u> دوست دارد .   He has (very) <u>few</u> friends.

<u>کمتر</u> (از دیگران) دوست دارد .   He has <u>fewer</u> friends (than others).

از همه <u>کمتر</u> دوست دارد .   He has the <u>fewest</u> friends, fewer than <u>all</u> others.

e. <u>little-less-the least</u>

(خیلی) <u>کم</u> راحت است .   It's (very) <u>little</u> convenient.

(از دیگران) <u>کمتر</u> راحت است .   It's <u>less</u> convenient (than the others).

از همه <u>کمتر</u> راحت است .   It's <u>the least</u> convenient.

f) <u>little-less-the least</u>

<u>کم</u> کار میکند .   He works <u>little</u>.

(از دیگران) <u>کمتر</u> کار میکند .   He works <u>less</u> (than others).

<u>از همه کمتر</u> کار میکند .   He works <u>the least</u>.

<u>Note:</u>

بیشتر (اَغْلَبْ) کار میکند .   He works <u>mostly</u>.

کمتر کار میکند .   He works <u>rarely</u> (once in a while).

<u>بیشتر</u> دوستها   <u>most of</u> the friends

<u>بعضی اَز</u> دوستها   <u>some of</u> his friends

<u>بیشترِ</u> وقت   <u>most</u> of the time

بَعْضی وَقْتها   <u>sometimes</u>

VOCABULARY

لــــغت

sell	میفُروشم / فُروختم
buy	میخَرم / خَریدم
set out	راه میاُفْتم / راه اُفتادم
learn	یاد میگیرم / یاد گرفتم
tell, report	تَعْریف میکنم / تعریف کردم که
speak	حرف میزنم / حرف زدم
talk with	با ... صُحْبَت میکنم / کردم
explain	تَوْضیح میدهم / توضیح دادم
discuss	بَحْث میکنم / بحث کردم
get in, into (with /-e-)	سُوارِ... میشوم / سُوارِ ... شدم
get off	از... پیاده میشَوم / از ... پیاده شُدم
start (going), move	حَرَکُت میکنم / حرکت کردم
find	پَیْدا میکنم / پیدا کردم
rain	باران میبارد / باران بارید

---

quick/slow	تُنْد / یَواش
cold/mild/warm	سَرْد / مُلایم / گَرْم
high/low	بُلَنْد / کوتاه
long/short	دراز / کوتاه
dirty/clean	کثیف / تَمیز
near/far	نَزْدیک / دور
easy/difficult/hard	آسان / مُشْکل / سَخْت
expensive/cheap	گران / اُرْزان
late/soon	دیر / زود

old/young (person)	پیر / جَوان
old/recent/new (things)	کُهْنه / تازه/ نو
fat/slim	چاق / لاغَر
heavy/light	سَنْگین / سُبُک
good taste/bad taste	خوشْمَزه / بَدْمَزه
bitter/sour/salty/sweet	تَلْخ / تُرْش / شور / شیرین
industrious/clever/lazy	پُرْکار / زِرَنْگ / تَنْبُل
strong/weak	قَوی / ضَعیف
tidy/untidy	مُرَتَب / نا مُرَتَب

---

world	دُنْیا
state (of nation) /eyālat/	ایالَت
city	شَهْر
building	ساخْتِمان
factory	کارْخانه
carpet	قالی
carpet store	قالیفُروشی
travel	مُسافِرَت
family	خانِواده
in my opinion	به نَظَرِ مَن

DRILLS

تمرین

A) Translate the following into English:

۱) آیا این کلاس از آن کلاس بزرگتر است ؟

quick
۲) آیا من تند تر از شما فارسی حرف میزنم ؟

older
۳) پدرتان چند سال از شما بزرگتر است ؟

cold/or/heat
۴) سَرْما را بیشتر دوست داری یا گَرْما را ؟

winter/summer
۵) به نظر شما زمستان بدتر از تابستان است ؟

which
۶) کوچکترین ایالت در آمریکا کدام است ؟

۷) آیا شما بیشتر به کتابخانه میروید یا در منزل درس میخوانید ؟

۸) آیا خانوادهٴ شما تابستان ها بیشتر به مسافرت میروند یا زمستانها ؟

۹) شما چند تا برادر بزرگتر دارید ؟

۱۰) آیا شما خواهر کوچکتر دارید ؟

۱۱) کدام شهر را در آمریکا بیشتر از همه دوست دارید ؟

۱۲) غذای فرانسوی بهتر است یا غذای آمریکائی ؟

۱۳) آیا شما بیشتر دوستهای ایرانی دارید یا دوستهای آمریکائی ؟

۱۴) آیا میدانید بزرگترین شهر ایران کدام است ؟

۱۵) بهترین کارخانهٴ ماشین در آمریکا کدام است ؟

۱۶) بلند ترین ساختمان در دنیا کجاست ؟

۱۷) آیا شیکاگو از دیترویت قشنگتر است ؟

۱۸) آیا شیکاگو به دیترویت نزدیکتر است یا به نیویورک ؟

diligent, active
۱۹) پُرْکارترین ما کی است ؟

tall
۲۰) چند تا از همکلاسهای شما مثل شما قَدْ بِلَنْد هستند.

B) Answer the questions in Drill A.

C) Substitute any of the adjectives listed above for the
   adjectives in Drill A.

D) Fill in the blanks with the appropriate comparative
   or superlative adjectives:

۱) کلاس ما از کلاس شما ــــــ است .

۲) آیا خانهٔ پرویز به دانشگاه ــــــ است یا خانهٔ حسن ؟

۳) علی ــــــ دوستِ من است .

۴) هوای میشیگان از هوای تگزاس ــــــ است

۵) به نظر من ــــــ ایالت در آمریکا کالیفرنیا است .

۶) درسِ فلسفهٔ جواد خیلی ــــــ از درس تاریخ من است .

۷) خواهرِ حسن دو سال از او ــــــ است .

۸) حسن در آمریکا شهرِ نیویورک را از همه ــــــ دوست دارد .

۹) در کلاس فلسفه جواد ــــــ دانشجو است .

E) Compose sentences with the following set of words trying
   as many different verbs as possible:

۱) خانه ـ دورتر

۲) زمستان ـ سرد تر

۳) امتحان ـ آسانتر

۴) تمرین ـ مشکل تر

۵) خیابان ـ شلوغ تر

۶) گرمترین ـ بهار

۷) بهترین ـ ماه

۸) ملایم تر ـ هوا

۹) ماشین ـ قشنگ تر

F) Ask and answer questions about colors of parts of the
room, and of clothing. Draw a dressed figure of a woman
and a man for this drill:

shirt	پیراهَن	dress, clothes	لِباس
skirt	دامَن	jacket, coat	کَت
blouse	بُلوز	pants	تَنبان
put on tie	کِراوات میزنم/زدم	suit	کَت و تَنبان
overcoat	پالتو	pullover	پُلوور
hat	کُلاه	socks	جوراب
boot	چَکمه	shoe	کَفش
is wearing	پوشیده است	put on, wear	میپوشم/پوشیدم
(light) green	سَبز (رَوشَن)	(darkish) green	سبز (تیره)

In addition to the colors mentioned earlier (p. 79),
you probably will also use خاکی 'gray,' and خاکِستَری
(this last word also entered English!), e.g.:

حسن چه پوشیده است؟

حسن کَتِ قرمز رَوشَن پوشیده است.

Hassan is wearing a
light-red coat.

این میز چه رنگی است؟
کَتِ حسن چه رنگی است؟

G) LISTEN TO THE READING ON THE TAPE.

LESSON TWELVE

درس دوازده

ORDINAL NUMBERS

عَدَدِ تَرْتیبی

1) Ordinal numbers, basic forms, 2) ordinal numbers, focused
form; vocabulary; drills; reading; 3) temporal relations;
4) temperature

---

1) ### THE ORDINAL NUMBERS, BASIC FORMS

The ordinal marker is stressed م ـُ ; except اَوَل 'first'
and آخِر 'last:'

اَوَل ـ دُوُم ـ سِوُم   1st, 2nd, 3rd

بیستُم ـ بیست وُ یِکُم   20th, 21st

The question word is چَندُم 'which' ('the how many-th').

attributive:	کلاسِ چَندُم ؟	Class number what?
	کلاسِ دوم .	The second class/grade.
predicative:	حسن چندم است ؟	Hassan is number what?
	حسن دوم است .	Hassan is second.
adverbially:	اول نامه نوشتم .	First(ly) I wrote a letter.
	دوم درس خواندم .	Secondly, I studied.

153

(Note: For sequences like 'first, I have to...second, he is...,' etc., the Arabic adverbial form of numbers with the ending اً /-an/ may be used (especially for first and second), e.g.:

اُولاً به تو گُفتم... ثانیاً چرا زودتر نپرسیدی ؟ ثالثاً دروغ نیست .

Firstly, I have told you so; secondly, why didn't you ask sooner. Thirdly, it's not a lie.)

a) the first/second of

(روز) چندمِ مارس ؟ Day number what of March?

(روزِ) اولِ مارس . The first/second of March.

b) 'beginning of' اول / اوایل / 'end of' آخر / اواخر

اول تابستان the first/beginning of summer

آخرِ هفته the last/end of the week/ weekend

اوایل ماه /اول های ماه towards the beginning of the month

اواخر ماه /وسط های ماه towards the end of the month

اواسط ماه /آخرهای ماه towards the middle of the month

c) the first/second one

This is expressed by the stressed ending ی (مُ) , e.g.:

اولی رفت و دومی مُرد و سومی خَندید . 'The first one left, the second one died, the third one laughed.'

cooperation	همکاری
pal	اولی - رَفیق، کجائی؟ چکار میکنی ؟
older brother	دومی - زیر دست دادا شم، کار میکنم
	اولی - داداشت چکاره است؟
	دومی - بیکار .

2) ORDINAL NUMBERS, FOCUSED FORM

The ending of the focused ordinal is stressed مین ُ ' .

This focused form precedes the noun unconnected, e.g.:

چندمین سا لگَرد؟   anniversary <u>number what</u> (exactly)?

دو هَزار وپانصدمین سالگرد .   the <u>2500th anniversary</u> (exactly)

While the basic form of the ordinals identifies the position of an item in a series, always with a view on the series, this form is mostly used to focus on prominent positions, like '(very) first and last,' or (the particular) anniversary and similar 'highlights ' ; compare:

ا ین اولین اِمتِحا ن ما ست .   This is our very first/ <u>the first</u> exam.

ا ین دومین ا متحا ن ما ست .   This is already the <u>second</u> exam.

آخرین چا پ ا ین کتا ب .   the very <u>last/most</u> recent print of this book

چا پ آخِر ا ین کتا ب .   the <u>last</u> print of this book

اولین روز بهار   <u>the first</u> day of spring

روزِ اولِ بهار   the first day of spring

VOCABULARY

لغت

year	سال
season, chapter	فَصْل
month, moon	ماه
week	هَفْته
Saturday	شَنْبه
Sunday	یکشنبه
Monday	دوشنبه
Tuesday	سه شنبه
Wednesday	چهار شنبه
Thursday	پنج شنبه
Friday	جُمعه

نُوْروز = ۱ فروردین = March 21

رِمِسْتان	پائیز	تابِسْتان	بَهار
۱۰ – دَی	۷ – مِهْر	۴ – تیر	۱ – فَرْوَرْدین
۱۱ – بَهمَن	۸ – آبان	۵ – مُرْداد	۲ – اُردیبِهِشْت
۱۲ – اِسْفَنْد	۹ – آذَر	۶ – شَهْریوَر	۳ – خُرْداد

train	تِرِن / قَطار
term, semester	سِمِسْتِر / تِرْم
row	رَدیف
etc. /elā āxar/	اِلی آخَر

DRILLS   تمـــرین

A) Practice asking and answering days of the week and of

the month according to the pattern:

(unstressed ی , cf. p. 117)   ؟ امروز چه روزی است   Q

.امروز دوشنبه است   A

؟ امروز چندم دَیْ است   Q

.امروز سوم دی است   A

B) Fill in the blanks with ordinal numbers:

۱) جواد دانشجوی سالِ ـــــ زبانِ فارسی است ؟

۲) سه شنبه ـــــ روزِ هفته است ؟

this year   ۳) اِمْسال برادر شما در سالِ ـــــ دانشگاه است ؟

۴) ـــــ درسِ این کتاب خیلی آسان است .

۵) آگوست ـــــ ماهِ سال است ؟

۶) رِضا با اُتوبوسِ ـــــ میآید .

۷) چه روزی ـــــ روزِ فصلِ بهار است ؟

۸) مارچ ماهِ ـــــ سال است ؟

۹) آیا ـــــ روزِ کلاسِ فارسی خیلی مشکل است ؟

۱۰) ـــــ دسامبر روزِ کریسْمَس است ؟

C) **Translate** the following into Persian:

1) Today is the first day of the semester.

2) The 31st of December (دسامبر) is the last day of the year.

3) The last is not always the best.

4) The first one asks, the second answers, the third one asks again and so on (الی آخر).

5) First I did not see.

6) He goes to the second row.

7) Learn the 12th lesson.

8) I am second.

9) I want the first one.

10) He comes with the first train.

D) **Translate** the following into English:

۱) اولین روزتیر روز اول تابستان است .

۲) اول تابستان من و خانواده ام به یک مسافرت طولانی میرویم .   long

۳) دانشجو ها نزدیک امتحان خیلی بحث میکنند .

۴) هرچه پیر تر میشود بیشتر صحبت میکند .

۵) معلم آنها بیشتر توضیح میدهد تا تمرین میکند .   explain

۶) باران سه ساعت بیشتر نبارید .

۷) قالیفروش آن قالی کاشانی را بیست هزار تومان کمتر نمیفروشد .

۸) بلند ترین ساختمان در این شهر بیست و دو طبقه است .   building

۹) شما در دنیا ایالتی به خوبی این ایالت پیدا نمیکنید .

۱۰) هرچه زودتر سوار تاکسی میشویم .

READING

خــواندنی

این خواندنی قِسْمَتِ اول قِصهء "پِسَرَکِ لَبوفُروش" از صَمَدِ بِهْرَنگی است .

چند سال پیش در دِهی معلم بودم . مَدْرَسهء ما فَقَط یک اُطاق بود که یک پَنْجِره و یک دَرْ به بیرون داشت . فاصله اش با ده صد مِتر بیشتر نبود . سی و دو شاگرد داشتم . پانزده نفرشان کلاس اول بودند . هشت نفر کلاس دوم ، شش نفر کلاس سوم ، و سه نفرشان کلاس چهارم . مَرا آخِرهای پائیز آنجا فرستاده بودند . بچه ها دو سه ماه بی معلم مانده بودند و از دیدن من خیلی شادی کردند و قِشْقِرِق راه اَنْداختند . تا چهار پنج روز کلاس لنگ بود .

verbs	
send	میفِرِسْتم / فِرِسْتادم
remain	میمانم / ماندم
they had sent	فِرِسْتاده بودند
they had remained	مانده بودند
see	میبینم / دیدم
seeing	دیدَن
set in motion	راه میاندازم / انداختم
made a lot of noise for joy	قِشْقِرِق راه اَنْداختند

nouns	
part	قِسْمَت
little boy	پِسَرَک
sugarbeet-seller	لَبو فُروش
ago, before	پیش
village	ده
outside	بیرون
distance <u>from</u>	فاصِله با
student, pupil	شاگِرد
without	بی
be happy about	شادی کردن از
until, for	تا
lame, here: not going well	لَنْگْ

Note:

1) فاصله اَش با دِه صَد مِتْر بیشتر نبود .

   it was only 100 meters from the village

2) cf. p. 154b   آخرهای پائیز

3) TEMPORAL RELATIONS

a) Relationship of days

2 days <u>ago</u> دو روزِ پیش	2 <u>more</u> days <u>in</u> 2 days دو روزِ دیگر
2 days earlier قَبْل دو روزِ ('') پیش	2 days later بَعْد دو روزِ ('') دیگر

last
    Monday
 past   پیش دوشنبهٔ وَرَه گذشته
	<u>next</u>
	    Monday
	 coming دیگر دوشنبهٔ آئِنده

b) Day and year relationships

2 years ago پیرارْسال / دوسالِ پیش	2 days ago پَریروز 2 nights ago پریشب	پَریروز پریشب	-2
last year پارْسال/سالِ گُذَشته	yesterday دیروز last night دیشَب		-1
this year اِمْسال	today اِمْروز tonight اِمْشَب		0
next year سالِ دیگَر	tomorrow فَردا tomorrow night فردا شب		+1
2 years hence دوسالِ دیگر	day after tomorrow پَسْ فَردا		+2

Note: شَبِ شنبه = جُمْعه شَب   Friday evening = the night of/ before Saturday

Practice asking for years, days and nights, e.g.:

کَی به شیکاگو میروی /رفتی ؟   When will you/did you go to Chicago?

کَی این فیلم را میبینی / دیدی ؟   When will you/did you see this movie?

4) <u>TEMPERATURE (Persians use centigrade)</u>

Q-A

است ؟	چند دَرَجه	هَوا
است .	۲۵ درجه	
است .	۵ درجه	

How many degrees(دَرَجه) is the weather = What's the temperature?

(It's) 25 degrees.

(It's) 5 degrees.

Q-A

است ؟	چند درجه	امروز گَرّما
(بالای صِفر)است	۲۵ درجه	گرما
است .	گرم	خیلی
است ؟	چند درجه	امروز سَرّما
(زیرِ صِفر) است .	۲ درجه	سرما
است .	سرد	خیلی

What's the temperature (heat) today?

(The heat) is 25 (above zero).

(It's) very warm.

What's the temperature (cold) today?

(The cold) is 2 below zero.

(It's) very cold.

Practice asking and answering questions about temperature using adverbial phrases of time (season, months, days, including the charts of temporal relations) and of locale (بیرون ، در کلاس etc.), e.g.:

بیرون هوا چند درجه است ؟   What is the temperature outside?

زمستان پیرارسال هواچند درجه زیر   How cold was it during the win-
صفر بود؟   ter two years ago?

قا ل ی با ف ی

L E S S O N   T H I R T E E N

درس ســـــیزده

A D V E R B I A L   P H R A S E S

حُـــــروفِ إضـــافه
وعِبــا رّاتِ قَیـــــدی

1) Adjectives as adverbs, 2) prepositions, 3) some locational and
directional nouns and adverbs, 4) other prepositional expressions;
vocabulary; drills; reading 1, reading 2.

---

1) ADJECTIVES AS ADVERBS

Adjectives can function as adverbs:

او را خوب میشِناسم .	I know him <u>well</u>.
زود بـه هتل رفتم .	I went to the hotel <u>quickly</u>.
یَواش حرف بـزنید .	Talk <u>slowly</u>!
وَلی ایشان را بهتر میشناسم .	But I know him <u>better</u>.
زودتر بیا .	Come <u>quickly</u>, <u>sooner</u>!
از همه یـواش تر حرف میزند .	He talks <u>the slowest</u>.

163

2) <u>PREPOSITIONS</u>

Persian has very few prepositions. There is no single
English equivalent for any of them. The examples cited
illustrate the range in the meaning of the prepositions
to some extent.

a) <u>تا</u> <u>until</u>, <u>till</u> ('stretch' of time, distance)

تا تهران	<u>until</u> Tehran
تا فردا	<u>until</u> tomorrow
تا بِحال	<u>until</u> now
تا اَنُدازهای	<u>to</u> an extent/degree
تا ده دَقیقهٔ دیگر	<u>for</u>/within ten minutes

b) <u>از</u> 'from, by way of, than'

از من گرفت	took it <u>from</u> me
از تَرْس	<u>from</u>, <u>out of</u> fear
از راهِ رُم	<u>by way of</u> Rome
از آن لازِم دارم	I need <u>some of</u> that
از تهران میگُذَرم	we are passing <u>by</u> Tehran
از پِله بالا میرود	he goes (<u>along</u>) up the stairs
بهتر از من	better <u>than</u> I
دور از	far, away <u>from</u>

Note:

از آلِ اَحْمَد	<u>by</u> Al-e Ahmad
پُر از	full <u>of</u>
یکی از آنها	one <u>of</u>/<u>from among</u> them

c) با 'with, by means of'

با مِداد	<u>with</u> a pencil
با اتوبوس	<u>by</u> bus
با عَجَله	<u>with</u> haste, hastily
هَمْراه با تو	<u>together with</u> you
با هَم	<u>with</u> each other, together
Note: فاصِله اش با آنجا	<u>distance from</u> (there)
با آن فَرْق دارد	it is <u>different from</u> that one

d) بی 'without' (see also بدون below)

بی معلم	<u>without</u> teacher
بی کار	<u>without</u> work
بی زَحْمَت	<u>without</u> trouble

e) دَر 'inside, in' (see also توی below)

location:	در خیابان	<u>in</u> (on) the street
time:	در تابستان	<u>in</u> the summer
	در تلویزیون	<u>on</u> (in) television
other:	در جَواب	<u>in</u> answer
	در این صورَت	<u>in</u> this case
	در ضِمْن	<u>in</u> the meantime, by the way
Note:	یکی در میان	(one <u>in</u> between:) every other one
	دو در دو سانْت	two <u>by</u> two centimeters
	در بارهٔ	<u>in</u> matters of, about

f) ــِﺑﻪ 'to, in' (punctual)

direction: ﺑﻪ ﺗﻬﺮاﻦ   <u>to</u> Tehran

other: ﺑﻪ ﻓﺎﺮﺳﻰ   <u>in</u> Persian

                ﺑﻪ ﻣَﻮﻗﻊ   <u>in</u> time

                ﺑﻪ ﺗﻨﺪﻯ   quickly ('in quickness')

Note: ﺑﻪ ﻧَﻈَﺮِ (ﻣﻦ)   <u>in</u> (my) opinion

                ﺧﻮﺪ ﺑِﺨﻮﺪ   <u>by</u> itself, automatically

                ﺑﻪ (ﺳِﻔﻴﺪ) ﻯِ   as (white) as

g) <u>Note on ﺑﻪ and ﺪﺭ</u>

1) ﺑﻪ may be omitted when it refers to a <u>direction</u>, e.g.:

ﺁﻳﺎ ﺑﭽﻪ ﻫﺎﻳَﺖ (ﺑﻪ) ﻣَﺪْﺮَﺳﻪ ﻣﻴﺮﻮﻧﺪ؟   Do your children go to school?

2) ﺪﺭ may be omitted when it refers to <u>time or location</u>,

e.g.:

(ﺪﺭ)ﺗﺎﺑﺴﺘﺎﻦ ﭼﻪ ﻛﺎﺭ ﻣﻴﻜﻨﻰ؟   What do you do in the summer?

(ﺪﺭ) ﺗﻬﺮاﻦ ﺯﻧﺪﮔﻰ ﻣﻴﻜﻨﻨﺪ.   They live in Tehran.

h) ﺑَﺮ 'on, onto'

This preposition occurs mostly in fixed phrasing (see
list below). Today, 'on, onto' is generally expressed
by ﺮﻮﻯ , literally 'surface of.'

3) <u>SOME LOCATIONAL AND DIRECTIONAL NOUNS AND ADVERBS</u>

Besides prepositions, location and direction are expressed by nouns or adverbs which imply location or direction
such as '(the) inside of,' '(the) back of;' most of these
require the connective /-e-/; e.g.:

بالای ِ	above, up
پائین ِ	below, at the foot of
روی ِ	on, onto
روبروی ِ / مُقابِل ِ	opposite of
زیر ِ	under(neath)
توی ِ	in, into
جِلوی ِ	forward, in front of
پیش ِ	before, also: (go) <u>to</u> or (be) <u>with</u> persons
پُشت ِ	behind (back of)
عَقَب ِ / پَی ِ	behind, after (direction)
دُنبال ِ	after (direction)
کِنار ِ	side of, beside
پَهلوی ِ	beside, next to
دَم ِ	by (the window, etc.)
میان ِ / بَین ِ	between
طَرَف ِ	towards
اَطراف ِ	about, around
وَسَط ِ	middle
دور از	far from
بیرون / خارج از	outside of

نَزْدیک به		near to
Note:	سَرِ راه	on the way
	سَرِ کار	at, to work
	سرِ میز	at the table
	سرِ وَقْت	on time

4) OTHER PREPOSITIONAL EXPRESSIONS

شَبیهِ	similar to, like
طِیِّ	during
بَرْعَکْسِ	contrary, opposite to
بَرِ خِلافِ	contrary to
در بارهِ	about something
در حُدودِ	about, approximately
بِدونِ	without
بِوَسیلهِ	by means of
به جای	instead of
به إضافهِ	in addition to
به عَلاوهِ/ عَلاوه بَر	in addition to, besides
بَنا بَر	according to
راجِع به	concerning, about
مَرْبوط به	concerning, related to
قَبْل / پیش از	before
بَعْد / پَس از	after
بِجُز / غَیْرِ / گُذَشْته از	except for, besides

VOCABULARY لـــغت

go up	از ... بالا میروم / رفتم
cross	از ... عُبور میکنم / کردم
pass, go by, go along	از ... میگُذَرم / گُذَشتم
pass	از ... رَد میشوم / شدم
know about, of	از ... خَبَر دارم / داشتم
afraid of	از ... میتَرْسم / تُرْسیدم
ask (of)	از ... سوال میکنم / کردم
(I) like (it), fond of	از (آن) خوش (م) میآید / آمَد
take a picture of	از ... عَکْس میگیرم / گرفتم
talk about, of	از ... تَعْریف میکنم / کردم
apologize to	از ... مَعْذِرَت میخواهم / خواستم
ask of, request	از ... خواهِش میکنم / کردم
examine	از ... اِمْتِحان میکنم / کردم
be different from	با ... فَرْق میکند / کرد
be aquainted with	با ... آشْنا میشوم / شدم
talk with	با ... صُحْبَت میکنم / کردم
agree with	با ... مُوافِق هستم / بودم
disagree with	با ... مُخالِف هستم / بودم
meet with	با ... مُلاقات میکنم / کردم
need	به ... اِحْتیاج دارم / داشتم
have a good time (I)	به (من) خوش میگُذَرد / گُذَشت
help	به ... کُمَک میکنم / کردم
take, bring to	به ... میرِسانم / رساندم
invite to/for	به ... دَعْوَت میکنم / کردم
it seems/appears to (me) that	به نَظَرِ (من) میرسد / رسید
continue with	به ... اِدامه میدهم / داد

DRILLS   تمـریـن

A)   Draw a picture: a house, a tree, a street, a car, people
standing around, etc., all in proper position so that
you can write in all or nearly all locational nouns
and adverbial phrases. Practice explaining the relative positions in all possible variations, e.g.:

etc. / بچه دُنبالِ مَرد میرود/ ماشین کِنارِ خیابان/ مرد کَمِ درِ است .

Draw a picture of a classroom. Practice in the same way.

You may use the words

ایستاده است	is standing
نِشَسْته است	is sitting
خوابیده است	is lying/sleeping

B)   Fill in the blanks with the appropriate prepositions:

۱) تِرْمِ گذشته من و مَنوچِهر ــــ کلاس تاریخ داشتیم .

۲) امروز صبح ــــ ماشین پدرم ــــ مدرسه آمدم .

۳) ــــ اینجا ــــ دیترویت خیلی دور نیست .

۴) حسن زبانِ فارسی را بهتر ــــ من حرف میزند .

۵) کلاسِ فارسیِ تو ــــ کدام ساختمان است ؟

۶) خانهِ خواهرم ــــ دانشگاه زیاد دور نیست .

snow   ۷) زمستانها خیابانهایِ این شهر پُر ــــ بَرُف است .

always   ۸) عَباس هَمیشه ــــ کلاس ــــ من مینشیند .

party   ۹) دیشب ــــ منزلِ علی یک مِهمانیِ خیلی خوبی بود .

۱۰) کتابِ حسن ــــ میز است .

C) Fill in the blank as indicated:

(better than you) ‏۱) من او را ــــــ میشناسم .

(sooner than the others) ‏۲) ــــــ به هتل برگشتم .

(slower than this) ‏۳) لطفاً ــــــ حرف بزنید .

(the warmest) ‏۴) این تابستان ــــــ بود .

(the first of the month) ‏۵) پنجشنبهٔ گذشته ــــــ بود .

(last) ‏۶) در ــــــ ردیف مینشیند .

(until now/little cold) ‏۷) ــــــ پائیز ــــــ بود .

(fresher than these) ‏۸) پُرْتُقال ــــــ میخواهم .

(with/heavy) ‏۹) ــــــ چَمِدان ــــــ سوارِ تاکسی شد .

(in Persian) ‏۱۰) این ــــــ چی میشود ؟

(together/tasty) ‏۱۱) ــــــ خَرْبُزه ــــــ خوردیم .

(by that door) ‏۱۲) این دوچرخهٔ کُهْنه را کی ــــــ گذاشته است ؟

D) The following text is quite simple-minded but has the
   advantage of having a good number of prepositional phrases
   in it. Read the text, translate, underline the prepositional phrases and answer the questions listed below :

‏۱) بعد از دعوت آنها چه کردند؟

‏۲) آیا همه با حَرُکت در روز جمعه موافق بودند ؟

‏۳) چرا جاده ها خیلی شلوغ بود ؟

Then retell the story orally.

READING 1   خواندنـــی ۱

پشت خانهٴ برادرم کنار باغ شهر دوستم پرویز زندگی میکند .

پرویز با خواهرش در خانهٴ کوچکی نزدیک به دانشگاه زندگی میکند .

روز یکشنبه ساعت ۴ بعد از ظهر پیش آنها رفتم و برای ۶ ساعت در

منزل آنها بودم . تا ساعت ۶ با هم حرف زدیم و به موسیقی گوش

دادیم . خواهر پرویز ، سودابه ، خیلی خَسته بود . من و پرویز

با هم برای نیم ساعت توی باغ قدم زدیم . خیلی قشنگ بود . بعد به

خانه آمدیم . اَکبَر دوست پرویــز هم آنجا در خانه بود . کمی با هم

بازی کردیم . خواهر پرویز برای ما چای درست کرد . ساعت ۱۰ِ شب

من به آپارتمانم برگشتم . روزِ خوبی بود . چون خسته بودم خیلی

زود خوابیدم .

garden   باغ

house, apartment   مَنْزِل

walk up and down   قَدَم میزنم / زدم

Underline the prepositions and prepositional phrases and translate.
Don't forget to put in the connective /-e-/ wherever necessary!

READING 2   <u>خواندنی</u>

ما در شهر کوچکی در جنوب زندگی میکنیم . یکی از دوستان ما که اهل شمال است ، ما را برای چند روز به شمال دعوت کرد . هفتهٔ پیش تصمیم گرفتیم برای چند روز پیش او برویم . بهترین روز برای حرکت روز جمعه بود ولی همه موافق نبودند مخصوصاً پدرمان خیلی مخالف بود . او میگفت روز جمعه جاده ها خیلی شلوغ اند وبعلاوه او روز جمعه کمی کار دارد ، بهتر است روز شنبه حرکت کنیم . ما پنج نفر بیشتر نبودیم ولی ماشینمان پر از لباس و چمدان بود . البته از شلوغی توی ماشین نترسیدیم ولی من از شلوغی جاده ها میترسیدم . از شهر ما تا کنار دریا خیلی فاصله بود ، درحدود ۱۴۰۰ کیلومتر . دو روز در راه بودیم . شبِ اول در هتلی وسط راه خوابیدیم . روز دوم نزدیکی های بعد از ظهر ناگهان ماشین ما کنار جاده پای کوه بزرگی ایستاد .

(ادامه دارد)

South	جُنوب
North	شَمال
decide	تَصْمیم میگیرم / گرفتم
especially	مَخْصوصاً
highway, road	جاده
of course	اَلْبَتّه
were not afraid	نمیتَرْسیدیم
crowdedness (stressed ى)	شلوغی
sea, large lake	دریا
about	در حدودِ
road, way	راه
middle	وسط

(go to) sleep (silent و)   میخوابم / خوابیدم

suddenly   ناگهان

somewhere towards the afternoon   نزدیکیهای بعد از ظهر

foot of mountain   پای کوه

stop, stand up   می ایستم / ایستادم

continuation   ادامه

Note:

We decided to go..   تصمیم گرفتیم ... برویم .

He was saying   میگفت

It is better that we/
we better leave   بهتر است ... حرکت کنیم

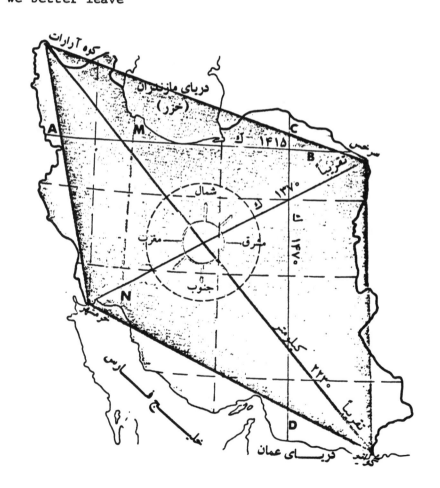

درس چهـــــا رده

ضَـــما یِر (ا دا مه)

1) Personal pronouns, 2) more on personal suffixes, 3) fronting
reference and emphasis, 4) indirect verbs, 5) خود 'self'; drills;
reading.

---

1) ## PERSONAL PRONOUNS

As a general rule, personal pronouns are used at the
first mention of the person; thereafter, their use implies
focus and emphasis, since the person is already identified
by the context (and the verbal ending when the person is
the subject), thus, at first mention:

subject: من ا مروز میروم .   I go today.

possessive: کتا ب من   my book

preposition: شما ا ز ا و گرفتید؟   Did you take it from him?

2) <u>MORE ON PERSONAL SUFFIXES</u>

As mentioned earlier, personal suffixes are the unfocused
partners of the independent personal pronouns. As such, they
can substitute for personal pronouns and آن ، این 'this,
that' in unfocused contexts (excepting, thus مالِ من 'mine'
etc.).

a) <u>with prepositions (از – به – با)</u> and adverbs

(از او) <u>ازش</u> میگیرم .	I take it from him.
(به او) <u>به‌اش</u> میدهم .	I give it to him.
(با این) <u>باش</u> ننویسید .	Don't write with this.
(از آن) <u>ازش</u> اطلاع ندارم .	I don't know about it.

   Note: Never * درش 'in it,'   * تاش 'until it.'

b) <u>replacing</u> اضافه

مُزاحِمِ شما شدم ← مُزاحِمِتان شدم .	I have bothered you.
میآمدم پیشِ تو ← میآمدم پیشت .	I would come to you.

c) 'the (its), for it'

پولِ آن زیاد است ← <u>پولش</u> زیاد است .	The (its) price is too much / The price for it is too much.
پولِ آن را بدهید ← <u>پولش را</u> بدهید .	Give its/the money/ Give the money for it.

d) replacing   را

The personal suffix is suffixed to the verb, or the pre-verbal

noun or the prefix, e.g.:

او را دیدم ⟵ **دیدمش**   I saw him.

آن را ترجمه کردم ⟵ **ترجمه اش کردم**   I translated it.

آنرا در آوردم ⟵ **درش آوردم**   I took it off.

Note: در   here is a preverb (not a preposition) and can

take the personal suffix.

e) replacing   به   (indirect object)

With a very few verbs the suffixes may replace the in-

direct object and   به   :

به شما نشان میدهم   I will show you.

⟵ **نشانتان میدهم**

به من کُمک کنید   Help me.

⟵ **کمکم کنید**

3)   FRONTING REFERENCE AND EMPHASIS

A pronoun or noun other than the subject of a sentence may

be put in front of the entire sentence for reference and

emphasis; it is then referred to within the sentence by

the corresponding personal suffix. This construction is

most frequent with the   اضافه   following the subject, e.g.:

اسمِ شما چیست ؟   What is your name?

⟵ شما اسمتان چیست ؟

پدرِ آن دختر سفیر است   The father of that girl
is an ambassador.

⟵ آن دختر پدرش سفیر است .

4) <u>INDIRECT VERBS</u>

There is a class of verbs which expresses an action or state
indirectly; the person is not the initiator of the action
but is 'overcome' by the action or the state. It 'happened
to him or her,' so to speak. With these verbs the person
affected is identified by the personal suffixes, e.g.:

a) از آن <u>خوشمان</u> میآید .
We like it. (It comes well to us from that.)

از آن <u>بدش</u> میآید .
He dislikes it.

<u>خوابم</u> میآید .
I am getting sleepy. (Sleep is coming to me.)

b) <u>mostly in informal speech</u>:

<u>گرمم</u> است .
I feel/am warm. (It feels warm to me.)

<u>سردش</u> است .
He feels/is cold. (It feels cold to him.)

چه <u>ات</u> است ؟ /céte?/
What is the matter with you?

هیچی <u>ام</u> نیست . /híci-m/
Nothing is the matter with me.

<u>گرسنه / تشنه اش</u> است .
He is (feels) hungry/thirsty.

بیست سال دارد = بیست <u>سالش</u> است

است describes a state; to express 'getting/becoming
cold or warm,' use میشود / شد , e.g.:

خیلی سردم میشود .
I am getting very cold.

کمی گرم شد .
I have become warmer now/
I am feeling warmer now.

5) خود 'self'

خود 'self, own' has three basic functions. In less formal speech
it is usually followed by the personal suffix for clarity, e.g.:

a) <u>reflexive - 'self'</u>

بیچاره خودش را کُشت . The poor fellow killed <u>himself</u>.

از خودتان بپرسید . Ask your<u>self/ves</u>.

با خود گفت . He said to <u>himself</u>

b) <u>emphatic</u>

در اینجا ما زندگی میکنیم .
←── در اینجا خودِ ما زندگی میکنیم We live here <u>ourselves</u>.

من دیدم ←── من خودُم دیدم . I saw it <u>myself</u>.

c) خود 'own'

This always refers to the subject of the sentence:

کتاب من است ←── کتابِ خودم است . It is my own book.

حسن کتابَش را گم کرد
←── حسن کتابِ خودش را گم کرد . Hassan lost his own book.

Note that ش in کتابَش را گُم کرد is ambivalent.
'his' may either refer to the subject, 'Hassan's book,'
or to somebody else's book 'his, the other's book.' To avoid
this ambiguity خود is used when referring to the subject,
but او is used when referring to somebody else, e.g.:

حسن کتابِ خود را گُم کرد . Hassan lost his (own) book.

حسن کتابِ او را گم کرد . Hassan lost his (the other's) book.

<u>DRILLS</u>   <u>تمریـــن</u>

A) In the following sentences transform the personal pronouns
    and/or demonstratives to their corresponding personal suffixes:

۱) قیْمَت آن برای من چقدر میشود ؟

۲) پول آنرا به کی دادید ؟

۳) دیروز پدرم به او یک کتاب داد .

۴) علی هر روز/روزی دو ساعت برای او کار میکند .

۵) فردا بعد از ظهر کتابمان را از او میگیریم .

rent   ۶) کرایهٔ آن خیلی برای ما گران بود .

۷) دوستان آمریکائی ما از او دو تا قالی قشنگ و بزرگ خریدند .

۸) پدرم همیشه از مسافرتش برای ما تعریف میکند .

۹) نامهٔ او را خواندم و جواب آنرا نوشتم .

discussion/use   ۱۰) من با او خیلی بحث کردم ، ولی فایده ای نداشت .

۱۱) حسن برای او یک پیراهن خیلی قشنگ خرید .

۱۳) آنرا ندیدم .

۱۳) او را کجا دیدی .

۱۴) آنرا آنجا پارک میکنم .

۱۵) لطفا آنرا دوباره تکرار کنید .

Note: For the personal suffixes after vowels see pp. 343,344.

B) Transformation drill:

Answer these questions by substituting the personal

suffixes for the object noun phrases according to the

pattern:

سوال : آیا او را دیروز دیدید ؟

جواب : بله ، دیروز دیدمش .

۱) آیا برنامهٔ دیشب تلویزیون را دیدید ؟

۲) آیا دوستان را خیلی خسته کردید ؟

۳) تمرین را کی نوشتید ؟

۴) آیا چراغ را روشن کردید ؟

۵) آیا آن شلوار قشنگتان را در مهمانی پوشیدید ؟

۶) آیا برای مهمانی شما را هم دعوت کردند ؟

۷) کی این خواندنی را به فارسی ترجمه کرد ؟

۸) مِثلِ اینکه شما غذا های ایرانی را خیلی دوست دارید ؟

۹) آیا این قالی را لازم دارید ؟

hat/ grey   ۱۰) آیا آن کُلاهِ خاکِسْتَری را خریدید ؟

C) Fill in the blanks with the appropriate خود 'self'

and the corresponding personal pronouns or suffixes.

Then indicate the type of خود used in the following

sentences, e.g.:

Type   Pattern

emphatic   دوستم دیروز (خود + ش) اینجا آمد .

‫- -‬

۱) کلاس فارسی ــــ خیلی خوب است .

party   ۲) در مهمانی جواد با ـــ صحبت کرد .

last/airport   ۳) پدرم هفتهٔ گذشته با ماشین ــــ به فرودگاه رفت .

۴) آنها ــــ را خیلی دوست دارند .

۵) ـــ فردا آن را برایتان میآورم .

۶) او فقط اسم ـــ را خیلی خوب میداند .

play   ۷) فردا بعد از ظهر شما ـــ با او بازی کنید .

۸) آن کتاب جغرافی مال برادر ـــ است .

۹) لطفاً هفتهٔ آیَنده دفتر ـــ را بیاورید .

tall   ۱۰) ما ـــ همه چیز را برای آنها تعریف میکنیم .

D) In this drill, a) translate, then b) use different persons
as subjects, e.g.:

وقتی تلویزیون تماشا میکنم همیشه خوابم میگیرد .

◄ —— وقتی آنها تلویزیون تماشا میکنند خوابشان میگیرد .

۱) وقتی که غذا را میبینم گرسنه ام میشود .

۲) این هم کلاسی شما چند سالش است ؟

۳) مثل اینکه امشب خوابم نمیآید .

۴) یادم میآید پولش را ندادم .

۵) وقتی پپسی میخورم بیشتر تشنه ام میشود .

۶) هیچوقت شما گرمتان نمیشود ؟

laughter   ۷) از این حرف ها خَنْده اَم میگیرد .

midnight   ۸) بچه ها نِصُفِ شَب خوابشان بُرْد .

polite behavior   ۹) ایرانیها از خارجی که تَعارُف میکند بسیار خوششان میآید.

۱۰) بچه های مدرسه از معلم تازه بدشان نیامد .

he did not remember   ۱۱) پسر پادشاه جوابِ درستی یادش نیامد .
("it did not come to his memory") ——

E) Using the basic sentence:

music ما از این موسیقی خوشمان میآید.

a) Substitute for این موسیقی :

mild زبان فارسی ــ این کلاس ــ تابستان ــ دیدنِ او ــ هوای مُلایم ــ

چای دارُجیلینگ ــ ماشین بنز آنها ــ ماست و پنیر ــ گفتگو با معلم ــ

این اطاقِ دونفره ــ زندگی در کنار دریا ــ این ساختمانِ بلند ــ

neat/tasty فصلِ بهار ــ خانواده ــ اطاقِ مُرَتّب ــ دنیای امروز ــ غذای خوشمزه

b) Substitute for ما :

من ــ آنها ــ شما ــ شما و دوستتان ــ من و جواد ــ تو ــ دختر برادرم ــ

پسر و دخترش ــ دانشجویان و معلم

c) Negate the sentences in both (a) and (b) using

either خوشم نمیآید or بدم میآید , etc.

۱ ماهیهای خاویار را
با تورهای مخصوص از
دریا میگیرند. آنها انواع
گوناگون دارند و بزرگ و
کوچک هستند.
در عکس بالای صفحه
مقابل یک ماهی خاویار
بزرگ را میبینید. طول آن
را با قد کارگری که در
کنارش ایستاده مقایسه
کنید!

خواندنی

READING

(بقیه) مسافرت به کنار دریا

همه از ماشین پیاده شدیم . چیز مهمی نبود . بنزین ماشین تمام شده بود . دَرِ ضِمْن هم به روغن اِحْتِیاج داشتیم . خوشبختانه بعد از چند دقیقه یک کامیون از جلوی ما رد شد و راننده تا ما را دید ایستاد . من به طرف او رفتم و از کمک خواستم . او ماشین ما را به راحتی با کامیونش به نزدیکترین پمپ بنزین رساند . او اهل شمال بود و آدم خوبی به نظر میرسید . گذشته از این او خیلی به ما کمک کرد . تا اندازه ای با او آشنا شدیم . از کمکش خیلی تشکر کردیم و پیشش ایستادیم از خودش و کامیونش عکس گرفتیم تا قسمت اول مسافرتمان را هیچ وقت فراموش نکنیم .

(پایان)

remainder	بَقِیه
important	مُهِم
come to an end	تمام می‌شود / شد
moreover	در ضِمْن
oil	رَوْغن
need of	اِحْتِیاج به
happily	خوشْبَخْتانه
truck	کامْیون

before, in front of	جِلَوْ
driver	راننده
as soon as he saw	تا ... دید
direction, side	طَرَف
help	کُمَکْ
take to	رساندن /میرسانم
person, man	آدم
appear to be	به نَظَر رسیدن
to an extent	تا اندازه‌ای
acquainted	آشْنا شدن
express thanks to	تَشَکُر کردن از
before	پیش
take picture of	عَکْس گرفتن از
part	قِسْمَت
never	هیچْ وَقْت
forget	فَراموش کردن
the end	پایان

زرتشتیان آتش مقدس را همیشه افروخته نگاه میداشتند

درس پا نـــــزده

W O R D   O R D E R ,   Q U E S T I O N S ,   A N D   ' F I L L E R S '

تَرْتیبِ جُمله ـ حُروفِ اِسْتِفْها می ـ قَیْد

1) A note on word order, 2) some major cases of reordering,

3) questions: overview; reading; review drill; drills; some use-

ful adverbial 'fillers'; drills

---

1) <u>A NOTE ON WORD ORDER: SUMMARY SURVEY</u>

There is what may be called a basic word order. Roughly, the

sequence of the main parts is: 1) subject, 2) time, 3) locale,

4) manner/circumstance, 5) direct object (D.O.), 6) indirect

object (I.O.)/direction, 7) (noun) verb. Of course, few sentences

contain all parts at once.

1	2	3	4	5	6	7
SUBJ.	TIME	LOC.	MANNER	D.O.	I.O.	(N)-VERB

Note: 1. When the <u>direct object</u> is not specific (i.e., no را),

it usually follows the indirect object, e.g.:

به او کتاب دادم .	I gave <u>him</u> a <u>book</u>.
کتاب را به او دادم .	I gave <u>the</u> book <u>to him</u>.

2. Directions, i.e. to a place, are often placed after the verb, e.g.:

امروز به مدرسه میروم .	Today I go to school.
امروز میروم مدرسه .	

2) SOME MAJOR CASES OF REORDERING

The two most prominent positions are the positions immediately preceding the verb and the beginning of the sentence:

a) Preverbal position

Basically all parts of a clause can be placed immediately before the verb for focusing and emphasis, e.g.:

امروز در خیابان معلم را ملاقات کردم .	Today I met the teacher on the street.
امروز معلم را در خیابان ملاقات کردم .	Today I met the teacher on the street.
معلم را درخیابان امروز ملاقات کردم .	I met the teacher on the street today.

b) Sentence initial position of locale, time, numbers

Usually, when sentences are answers to specific questions as to time or locale or when special distinctions are to be made in sequences like: 'today I do this (tomorrow...)' or 'first...(then)', 'here is...(there...)'. This part is placed at the beginning of the sentence, e.g.:

امروز من کار نکردم (ولی فردا حتماً کار میکنیم) .	Today I did not work but tomorrow I certainly will.
اینجا جان کار میکند و آنجا تام .	Here works John and there Tom.

3) QUESTIONS: SUMMARY OVERVIEW

  a) <u>Yes-no answer</u>

    The two general questions are: آیا 'I'd like to know whether...'

    مگر 'You don't mean...', e.g.:

آیا امروز کار میکند ؟	Does he work today?
مگر امروز کار میکند ؟	He works today!?

  b) <u>Why چرا</u>

      چرا امروز کار نمیکند؟   Why doesn't he work today?

  c) <u>Questions for parts of speech</u>

    Remember: question words are placed where their answer word
will be.

human:	کی	who	چه کسی	who	
	مال کی	whose	آقای کی	Mr. who	
inanimate:	چه / چی	what	چه چیزی	what (thing)	
	برای چی	what for	خیابان چی	what street	
do what:	چکار میکند ؟	what does he do?			
	چکار دارید ؟	what do you want, what?			
	چکاره است ؟	what does he do (occupation)?			
time:	کی	when			
	چه وقت	when, what time			
locale:	کجا	where	از کجا	from where	
	چه جائی	what place	از کجا میدانی	<u>how</u> do you know	
	کجائی	where from	اهل کجا	where from	

<u>manner:</u> (stressed) چطُوری	how (what manner)	چه جوری	how (what manner)
چطور	how about		
<u>how/what a...!/?:</u> چه‌خوب!	how good!	چه (مرد)ی	what a man!/?
<u>adjective:</u> چه طور(است)	how (is it)	چه جور ــی	what kind (of)
		چه طور ــی	what kind (of)
<u>color:</u> چه رنگی	what color		
<u>which:</u> کدام	which	کدام یکی	which one
<u>else:</u> دیگرِ کی	who else	دیگر چی	what else
دیگر به کجا	where else	دیگر به کی	to whom else
دیگر با چی	with what else	دیگر کجا	where else

d) <u>Measure</u>

چند تا	how many
چندْ ساعت	how many hours
ساعتِ چند	what time
چند وقت / چه مُدَتی	how long
چندُم / چندمین/ شماره‌ٔ چند	number what
چند است	how much is it
چقدر میشود	how much will it be

خواندنی

آقای هالو

آقای هالو وقتی صبح از خانه اش بیرون می آمد ، زنش یک نامه
به او داد و گفت :

"فراموش نکن ، این نامه را حتماً امروز پُست کُن .نامه خیلی
مُهمی است ."

ولی آقــــای هـــالـو با وُجودِ سِفارشِ زَنش فراموش کرد نامه
را به صندوقِ پست بیَندازد . وقتی از اتوبوس پیاده شد و دَوان دَوان
به طَرَفِ اِدارِه اش میرفت ناگِهان یک آقائی آهسته به شانه اش زد و گفت :
"نامه یادتان نرود ."

آقای هالو که خیلی متعجب بود نامه را به صندوق انداخت و به
طرف اداره اش برگشت . در راه ناگهان خانم خوشگلی به او گفت :
"آقا ، نامه تان را فراموش نکنید ."

این دفعه آقای هالو ایستاد و با تعجب فراوان گفت :
"خدایا ، این مردم از کجا میدانند که من باید نامه ای پست
کنم ، من خیلی وقت پیش آن را پست کردم ."

در جواب خانم که لبخندی بر لب داشت گفت :
"پس لطفاً این یادداشت را از پُشتِتان بردارید ."

روی یادداشت نوشته شده بود :
"خواهش میکنم به شَوْهرم بگوئید نامه یادش نرود ."

was coming	می‌آمد
forget (don't forget)	فَراموش می‌کنم / کردم (مکن)
order, instruction	سِفارِش
box	صَنْدوق
throw (that he should throw)	می‌اَنْدازم / انداختم (بیاندازد)
running	دَوانْ دَوان
office	اِداره
slow	آهِسْته
shoulder	شانه
may it not slip your mind	یادتان نرود
surprised	مُتَعَجِّب
beautiful	خوشگل
(this) time	(این) دَفْعه
stand (up), stop	می‌ایسْتم / ایستادم
surprise	تَعَجُّب
plenty	فَراوان
O God	خُدایا
people	مَردُم
I must... do	بایَد (به) کنم
smile	لَبْخَنْد
lip	لَب
then	پَس
note, reminder	یادْداشت
back	پُشْت
take off (take off!)	بَرمی‌دارم / برداشتم (بر دارید)
had been written	نوشْته شُده بود
husband	شَوهَر
(please) tell!	بِگوئید

Answer these questions:

۱) زنِ آقای هالو به او چه سفارشی کرد ؟

۲) برای اینکه آقای هالو نامه را فراموش نکند <u>so that not</u> زنش چه کار کرد؟

۳) آقای هالو چطوری فهمید که باید نامه را پست کند ؟

۴) آقای هالو چرا متعجب شد؟

۵) در آخرِ کار آقای هالو چه‌چیزی را فهمید ؟

۶) آقای هالو یک مردِ هالو است . معنیِ لغتِ هالو را از این قِصه پیْدا کنید .

REVIEW DRILL: ADVERBIAL PHRASES

a) translate, b) change into past or present, and vice versa, c) substitute other adverbial phrases wherever and however possible:

۱) غیْر از پیانو ویولُن هم میزند .

۲) من و همْ اُطاقی ام در باره‌ء امتحان خیلی صحبت کردیم .

۳) جامِعِه شِناسان راجع به ایران خیلی مینویسند .

۴) طالِبی تا اندازه ای شبیه به خُرْبزه است .

۵) گارسُن سیب زمینی ها را بِدون کَرِه برای ما آورد .

۶) یکی از همکلاسی های من تازه سِبیل گذاشته است .

۷) این زمستان بر خِلافِ زمستانهای پیش فقط باران میبارد .

۸) ورَقهایِ کاغذ و خودکارش را توی کیفش گذاشت و بدون حرف از کلاس بیرون رفت .

۹) در این صورت به وُکیل احتیاج دارید .

DRILLS

A) Reorder the phrases of time, location, and manner in the following
   sentences wherever possible as shown here:

بلیط را برای شما هر چه زودتر می‌فرستم .

هر چه زودتر بلیط را برای شما می‌فرستم .

بلیط را هر چه زودتر برای شما می‌فرستم .

١) بلیط را هر چه زودتر برای شما می‌فرستم .

٢) این لغت را با مداد قرمز می‌نویسم .

٣) در دانشگاه با چند تا از دوستانم درباره ادبیات بحث کردیم .

۴) معلم وقت نداشت ، پس او را فردا می‌بینم .

one-way   ۵) از این چهارراه رد می‌شوید ، و بعد وارد خیابان یکطرفه می‌شوید .

۶) جلوی خانهٔ ما بیمارستان بزرگی می‌سازد .

۷) دیروز در خیابان فردوسی دوست او را دیدم .

St. George   ۸) جرجیس کتش را به پیرزن فقیر داد .

۹) این روزها همه جا تند خانه می‌سازند .

۱۰) چند روز پیش من به شما نامه نوشتم .

مجسمهٔ برنزی اشکانی

B) Use Drill A of Lesson 14 (p. 180) to reorder the adverbial

phrases in the sentences of that drill; e.g.:

قیمتِ آن برای من چقدر میشود ؟

برای من قیمتِ آن چقدر میشود ؟

قیمتِ آن چقدر برای من میشود ؟

C) Focus the possessor of the following subjects according to

the pattern   (see p. 177 #3):

هوای پائیز معمولاً بارانی است .

پائیزهوایش   معمولاً بارانی است . ←

۱) تعطیلاتِ دانشگاه از دوشنبهٔ دیگر شُروع میشود .

۲) مُهندسِ این ساختمان یک نفر ایتالیائی است .

company ۳) کارمندانِ این شرکَت آخر این ماه پول نگرفتند .

passenger ۴) راننده‌ٔ این اتوبوس مُنتَظِر آخرین مُسافِر است .

۵) یادداشتِ مُهمِ زَنِ آقای هالو پشتِ آقای هالو بود .

۶) لغتنامه‌ٔ حَیّم یکی از بهترین لغتنامه ها در فارسی است .

۷) سَرِ این خیابان یک سینما است .

۸) غذا هایِ این رستوران ارزان است .

۹) اِتِفاقًا تلفظِ شما خیلی خوب است .

۱۰) قیمتِ ضَبطِ صَوتِ حسن چقدر بود ؟

D) Use as many question words as possible to ask for the parts of sentences in the sentences given in Drill A and B above, e.g.:

بلیط را برای شما هرچه زودتر میفرستم .

۱ـچه چیز را برای شما هرچه زودتر میفرستم ؟

۲ـبلیط را برای کی هرچه زودتر میفرستم ؟

۳ـبلیط را برای شما چطوری میفرستم ؟

۴ـبلیط را برای شما هرچه زودتر چکار میکنم ؟

4) SOME USEFUL ADVERBIAL FILLERS

Everyday language is full of adverbial expressions which identify the speaker's view of, and position about a statement. In Persian a good number of these are Arabic adverbs ending in the Arabic adverbial ending /-an/, orthographically written ً . The following is a list of some of those which will help to make speaking more personal. Evidently there is no way to put them in more than rough order.

a) <u>ARABIC ADVERBS IN</u> ـاً /-an/ (cf. لطفاً)

		source or origin	
relatively	نِسْبَتاً	relative to	نِسْبَت به
approximately, about	تَقْریباً	approximate	تَقْریبی
especially	مَخْصوصاً	special	مَخْصوص
usually	مَعْمولاً	usual	مَعْمول
accidentally, incidentally	اِتِفاقاً	incident	اِتِفاق
apparently, seemingly	ظاهِراً	evident	ظاهِر
really, truly	واقِعاً	real, true	واقِعی
immediately, directly	مُسْتَقیماً	direct, straight	مُسْتَقیم
immediately (time)	فَوْراً	immediate(ly)	فَوْری
certainly, by all means	حَتْماً	certain	حَتْمی
seriously	جِدّاً	serious(ly)	جِدّی
possibly	اِحْتِمالاً	possibility	اِحْتِمال
never (with negated verb)	اَصْلاً (نه)	root, source	اَصْل
continuously	دائِماً /دائِماً	continuous	دائِم
completely	کامِلاً	complete	کامِل
lately	اَخیراً	last, recent	اَخیر
afterwards, later	بَعْداً	after	بَعْد
previously, earlier	قَبْلاً	before	قَبْل
for instance	مَثَلاً	it seems as if	مِثْلِ اینکه
at least	اَقَلّاً	at least	لااَقَل

b) OTHER 'FILLERS'

fortunately	خوشبُخْتانه	under no cir- cumstances /-vajh/	به هیچ وَجْه (نه)
unfortunately	مُتأسِّفانه	that's it!	هَمین (است)
perhaps	شاید	completely	به کُلّی
it's possible, possibly (with /be/ form of verb	مُمْکن است(به)	to an extent, partially	تا اَنْدازه ای
it's obvious, obviously	مَعلوم است	in reality, actually	در واقع
admittedly, it's true	درُست است	in fact	در حقیقَت
apparently, in my opinion	به نَظر من	finally /bel-āxare/	بالآخَره
in any case	به هَر حال	immediately, without hesitation /be-lā-fāsele/	بِلافاصِله
at most	حَدِاکْثَر	of course	اَلْبَته
at least	حَدِاقَل	in short	خلاصه
		altogether /ruye ham rafte/	رویِهَمْرَفته

These fillers should not be learned all at once but
learned gradually by using them in drills and
compositions.

DRILLS   تمرین

A) Try to fill in the blanks with one of the 'fillers'

    which you assume will fit, and check with the instructor,

    or a speaker of Persian:

۱) من ——— صبح ها ساعت ۸ به مدرسه میروم .

۲) از اینجا تا شیکاگو ——— با ماشین ۴ ساعت راه است .

intelligent   ۳) جواد ——— دانشجوی باهوشی است .

۴) ——— فردا شب با دوستان خواهرم به سینما میروم .

۵) پَرویز این شَهْر را ——— دوست ندارد .

۶) ——— حسن کتابش را پُیْدا کرد .

driving ·   ۷) ——— بعد از یک روز رانَنْدِگی با ماشین به منزل آنها رسیدیم .

۸) فردا ——— ساعت ۹ صبح لطفاً به من تلفن کنید !

۹) این نامه را ——— برای دوستم علی مینویسم .

literature   ۱۰) کلاسِ اَدَبیاتِ انگلیسی ——— کلاس خوبی است .

The Coral   ۱۱) ——— دیروز در رستورانِ مَرْجان او را دیدم .
(name of restaurant)

B) Substitute and add as many other fillers as possible in the

    sentences of Drill A above, e.g.:

fortunately   خوشبختانه شما فارسی خوب حرف میزنید .

obviously   ظاهراً   شما فارسی خوب حرف میزنید .

seriously   جداً   شما فارسی خوب حرف میزنید .

نَفت

oil

نَفت دَر زیرِ زمین پیدا می شَوَد .

earth, ground

چه خوب است وَقتی که بُزرگ شُدیم

how   good

it were(is)

for us

to dig ...

زمین را بِکَنیم .

نفت را دَر بیاوریم .

اَز نفت بِنزین بگیریم .

بِنزین را دَر ماشین و تراکتور

and

to pour

بِریزیم .

با آنها کارکنیم .

from a Persian
schoolbook

LESSON SIXTEEN

درس شـــــانزده

THE PERSIAN VERB SYSTEM,
INDICATIVE MOOD

فِعْل، وَجْهِ اَخْباری

1) The basic verb system, 2) notes on the verb forms, 3) present and past perfect, 4) differences, 5) notes on the perfect and distanced past; vocabulary; drills

---

1) THE BASIC VERB SYSTEM

	Present	Past
incomplete:		
habitual	میرود he (always) goes	میرفت he used to go
ongoing (progressive)	میرود he is going	میرفت he was going
complete:		
just now/then (past)	رفت he (has) just left	رفت he left (then)
by now/then (perfect)	رفته است he has left	رفته بود he had left

201

2) <u>NOTES ON THE VERB FORMS</u>

<u>The مـی - past</u>

In the basic verb system of Persian there is no difference
between habitual and progressive action; both are expressed
by the prefix مـی (cf. p. 93). This prefix also expresses
habitual or progressive action in the past; e.g.:

كار كردم   I worked

كار مـیكردم
$$\begin{cases} \text{I used to work} \\ \text{I was working (when...)} \end{cases}$$

Thus, when encountering a past form with مـی, only the context
will tell whether the action was habitual or progressive. On
the other hand, this makes things somewhat simple for the
speaker (and learner): irrespective of whether the action
was habitual or progressive, the use of مـی will do in both cases.

What is important to know is whether the action was <u>incomplete</u>
at the point in the past you are talking, or writing about, or not.

<u>Complete Action</u>

In fact, in order to understand, and learn, the Persian verb system
well, it is important to recognize that the basic distinction is
not so much whether an action happens in the present or happened
in the past, but whether it is seen, and described, by the speaker
as <u>incomplete</u> or <u>complete</u> at one point.

Because of this fact, there are interesting differences when
comparing the Persian forms with their English translations.
This is especially the case when comparing the Persian 'preterit'
and 'perfect' with the English 'preterit' and 'perfect' forms; they
are <u>not</u> the same, although there are obvious similarities.

The Persian 'preterit' ('simple past')

The Persian preterit is basically <u>not</u> a form to express a complete past action, but to express a complete action at any point in time. This is, of course, very often, even most frequently the case when we talk about an action that happened, at one point, and was completed , in the <u>past</u>, e.g.:

دیروز رفتم بازار .	Yesterday I <u>went</u> to the bazaar.
روزی از روزها پادشاهی به جنگل رفت .	One of those days a king <u>went</u> in the woods.

a) <u>The 'preterit' in the present</u>

Here there is no evident difference from the use of the English 'preterit'. But an action can also be (seen or described as) complete at the present, that is at the point of speaking. Here Persian quite 'logically,' also uses the form for complete action, i.e. the misnamed 'preterit', whereas English usually uses the perfect; e.g.

حسن کجاست ؟ <u>آمد</u> .	Where's Hassan? He <u>has just come.</u> = There he is.

incomplete	این را خوب می‌فهمم .	I (always) understand this well.
complete	این را خوب <u>فهمیدم</u> .	I <u>understand</u> this (now) (have understood just now),

incomplete	به مدرسه می‌روم .	I am going/ I go to school:
complete	خداحافظ. من رفتم .	Goodbye, I leave right now/ am on my way.

(In fact, the last sentence may be said while the speaker is still sitting.)

Such present complete function is, of course, exemplified by such standard phrases as:

خوش آمدید .   Welcome! = you <u>are</u> well-come

خوشحال شدم .   Nice to meet you = I <u>have just</u> become happy = I am happy.

d) <u>Use with first person:</u>

من پَریدم ، تو هم بِپَر .   I <u>will jump right now,</u> you jump
یک ــ دو ــ سه .   too.   1 - 2 - 3 !

The use of this form in the first person with verbs of movement usually comes as a surprise, e.g.:

حسن بیا . آمدم .   Hassan come! - I <u>am coming</u> (as good as there).

Here آمدم cannot mean 'I have just come' since the persons 'I/we' are still in their place. before the movement, thus these forms with the first person generally can be rendered 'as good as here', etc., 'will come immediately', etc.

b) <u>'As soon as'</u>

Most striking is the difference between Persian and English in contexts like 'as soon as'. This, and similar phrases, imply that an action will happen only after,'as soon as' another action happens first,and is completed before the action that follows.

Accordingly, Persian again uses the complete (past) 'preterit' verb form whereas English generally uses the <u>present</u>! ,e.g.:

وقتی <u>آمد</u> به او بگوئید.   As soon as he comes tell him.

اگر <u>آمد</u> به او بگوئید.   If/the moment/when he <u>comes</u> tell him.

c) <u>Past to present point</u>

Following this 'logic' of the verb system, when an action in the past is complete at the point of speaking, i.e. in the present, the 'preterit' is used in Persian and the 'perfect' in English, e.g.:

تا حالا سه ساعت تمرین <u>کردم.</u>   I <u>have worked</u> three hours until now.

d) **'have ... for '**

On the other hand, when an action began in the past but is not
completed yet at the moment of speaking it follows that in Persian
the می - form must be used, as opposed to the 'perfect in English.
The time the action has been going on is indicated by

(...) است که ...   literally: it is (TIME) that...

or   <div dir="rtl">(...) میشود که ...</div>   literally: it is about/ will be (TIME) that...

Taking a present and a past point of reference, an example wpuld be:

۵ سال است/میشود که اینجا زندگی میکنم .   I have lived here for 5 years
(and still do).

۵ سال بود/میشد که آنجا زندگی میکردم .   I had lived there for 5 years
(and still did then).

Summary of differences

	Persian	English
Preterit	**Preterit** <div dir="rtl">وقتی آمد ...</div>	**Present** as soon as he arrives...
	Preterit <div dir="rtl">الان آمد .</div>	**Perfect/Present** has just arrived/is here
	Preterit <div dir="rtl">الان پنج ساعت کار کردم .</div>	**Perfect** I have worked five hours until now
Present	**Preterit** <div dir="rtl">پنج سال است اینجا زندگی میکنیم</div>	**Perfect** We have lived here for five years.

3) PRESENT PERFECT AND PAST PERFECT

The Persian 'present perfect' and 'past perfect' are formed
from the 'perfect' participle, i.e. for all verbs, the preterit
stem with the stressed ending /-e/, to which forms of 'to be'
are added, e.g.:

Present perfect		Past perfect	
رفته ام	I have left	رفته بودم	I had left
رفته ای	You have left	رفته بودی	You had left
رفته است	He/she has left	رفته بود	He/she had left
رفته ایم	We have left	رفته بودیم	We had left
رفته اید	You have left	رفته بودید	You had left
رفته اند	They have left	رفته بودند	They had left

The negative نـ precedes these forms:

نرفته ام	I have not left	نرفته بودم	I had not left
نرفته ای	You have not left	نرفته بودی	You had not left

Never نیست or هست .

These two perfects describe a) an action that has/had been com-
pleted <u>before</u> <u>the</u> <u>present/past point</u> and b) a <u>state</u> <u>at</u> <u>the</u> <u>present/</u>
<u>past</u> <u>point</u> resulting from a prior action. As such there is a certain
similarity between the Persian and English 'perfects', but there are
major differences (cf. the next lesson).

4) <u>NOTES ON THE PERFECT AND DISTANCED PAST</u>

(for information only)

<u>Distanced past</u> refers to a mode of expression not found in English. In contrast to the non-distanced past, which describes an action directly, the distanced forms express actions and situations indirectly, i.e., the speaker: a) <u>reports on</u> them from second-hand knowledge, or b) <u>assumes</u> or concludes from information that they have happened, or c) <u>recalls</u> from his distant past and reminisces about them after having forgotten about them.

The three forms of distanced past are:

<u>Distanced</u>	<u>Non-distanced</u>
رفته است	رفت
میرفته است	میرفت
رفته بوده است	رفته بود

In English there are no special verb forms for distanced past. Thus the 'distanced past' corresponds to an English past, progressive past and past perfect. Note especially the distanced form رفته است , the most frequently found of the three: it appears as if an English past corresponds to a Persian perfect, but it must not be confused with the present perfect, e.g.:

a) <u>Reporting</u>

<u>Fact</u>:

دیروز در یک تَصادُف ده نفر
<u>کشته شدند</u> .

Yesterday ten people <u>were killed</u> in a single accident.

<u>Distanced (second hand)</u>:

(میگویند) دیروز در یک تصادف

ده نفر <u>کشته شده اند</u> .

<u>(They say)</u> yesterday ten people

were killed in a single accident.

b) <u>Knowledge</u>

<u>Fact</u>:

معلوم است زودتر <u>آمده بود</u> .

It is evident that he <u>had come</u> earlier.

<u>Distanced (assumption,
conclusion)</u>:

معلوم شد زودتر <u>آمده بوده است</u> .

It became evident (from what he said), that he <u>had already come</u> earlier.

c) <u>Memory</u>

<u>Fact</u>:

در بارهٔ این خیلی <u>مُطالِعه
میکردم</u> .

I <u>used to study</u> this intensively.

<u>Distanced (reminiscence)</u>:

اَلان یادم میآید سالها پیش
در بارهٔ این خیلی <u>مطالعه
میکرده ام</u> .

I <u>remember now</u> that years ago I <u>used to study</u> this very intensively.

VOCABULARY

لغت

hand, arm	دَسْت	head	سَر
elbow	آرَنْج	hair	مو
wrist	مچ	face	صورَت
finger	اَنْگُشْت	forehead	پیشانی
fingernail	ناخُن	eye	چِشْم
arm	بازو	brow	اَبْرو
fist	مُشْت	eyelashes	مُژه
foot, leg	پا	eye-lid	پِلْک
leg	لِنْگ	nose	دَماغ / بینی
knee	زانو	cheek	گونه
shin	ساقِ پا	mouth	دَهان / دَهَن
heel	پاشْنه	lip	لَب
knucklebone	قوزکِ پا	tooth	دَنْدان
toe	انگشتِ پا	chin	چانه
sole, palm	کَفِ پا / دست	ear	گوش
throat	گُلو	neck	گَرْدَن
vein	رَگ	back	پُشْت
blood	خون	shoulder	شانه
heart	قَلْب / دِل	chest	سینه
liver	کَبَد / جِگَرِ (سیاه)	breast	پِسْتان
lungs	شُش / جِگَرِ سِفید	stomach, belly	شِکَم
stomach	مَعْده	waist	کَمَر
intestines	روده	navel	ناف
kidneys	کُلیه	pelvis	باسَن

doctor's office	مُطَبّ	not well	کِسِل
physician	پِزِشْک / دُکْتِر	feel dizzy	سَر (م)گیج میرود/رفت
nurse	پُرَسْتار	pain (hurt)	دُرْد میکند
get a doctor's appointment	از دکتر وقت میگیرم /گرفتم	headache	سَرْ دَرْد
visit	ویزیت	sick	مَریض / بیمار
examine	مُعایِنه میکنم/ کردم	disease	مُرَض / بیماری
treat	مُعالِجه میکنم / کردم	fever	تَب
blood pressure	فِشارِ خون میگیرم / گرفتم	effusion	خونْریزی
inject.	آمْپول میزنم / زدم	wound, injury	زَخْم
bandage	پانْسْما میکنم / کردم	sore spot, infection	وَرَم
hospital	بیمارِسْتان	diarrhea	اِسْهال دارم / داشتم
hospital bed	تَخْتِ (بیمارستان)	vomit	اِسْتِفْراغ میکنم / کردم
surgery	جَراحی میکنم/ کردم	drugstore	داروخانه / دواخانه
surgeon	جَراح	have prescription filled	نُسْخه میپیچم /پیچیدم
operate	عَمَل میکنم / کردم	take a pill	قُرْص میخورم / خوردم
		cough	سُرْفه

disobedient/ parents	عاقِ والِدَیْن
breath	حاج سَمَنْدَرقُلی ، وقتی آخرین نَفَس را میکشید،
	برای صدمین بار به پسرش سمندرزاده میگفت :
child/turn one's back :	فَرْزَنْد، همیشه به این سه تا پُشت کن :
liquor/playing card/. secret,alchemy/happiness	عَرَق، وَرَق، زَن . کیمیای سَعادَت همین است .

<u>DRILLS</u>   تمرین

A) Draw one or two pictures of a person and add the names of the
   parts of the body.

B) Change the following sentences to the present tense, using the
   'filler' معمولا 'usually':

۱) من روزهای سه شنبه و پنجشنبه کلاس فارسی داشتم .

۲) خواهر کوچکم صبح ساعت ۸ از خواب بیدار شد .

per month/once   ۳) مادرم ماهی یکبار به دیدن من میآمد .

۴) برادر او سینما را بیشتر از تآتر دوست داشت .

fast   ۵) در اینجا اتوبوسها سَریع تر از ترنها میرفتند .

۶) دوستم هفته ای یک نامه برای من مینوشت .

۷) خانوادهٔ جواد لباسهایشان را از این فروشگاه نخریدند .

lunch   ۸) من و علی هر روز بعد از نهار برای نیم ساعت در این باغ قدم
   میزدیم .

cigarette   ۹) پدرم روزی ۱۰ تا سیگار میکشید .

۱۰) در این دانشگاه کلاسها از ساعت ۸ صبح شروع میشد.

C) Translate the following into English:

۱) پنج سال است که پیشِ این دکتر میروم .

during   ۲) در طّیِ این پنج سال مریض نشده ام .

۳) آیا قرصتان را خوردید ؟ بله خوردم .

۴) دکتر کجاست ؟ آه ، آمد !

۵) دیروز دستم زخم شده بود . رفتم بیمارستان پیشِ پرستار ، پانسمان کردم .

۶) دکتر مَرا معاینه کرد ولی معلوم نشد چه مرضی دارم .

۷) دیشب خیلی تب داشتم و استفراغ میکردم .

۸) وقتی دکتر فشارِ خونم را گرفت این نسخه را بمن داد .

۹) از دیشب تا حالا همین جور سرم گیج میرود .

۱۰) مادرش را برای معالجه به بیمارستان بُرده بود ولی تخت خالی نبود .

D) Complete the following sentences with the appropriate verb
forms. Use the verbs in parenthesis:

(to go)   ۱) خوب ، خیلی دیر شد . من ____ ____ .
it got late

(to arrive)   ۲) دیشب متاسفانه ما به مهمانی آنها خیلی دیر ____ .

(to write)   ۳) آیا اخیراً برای ایرج نامه ____ ؟

(to come)   ۴) دوست علی با خواهرش فردا از نیویورک ____ .

(to like)   ۵) ترمِ گذشته من کلاس تاریخِ ادبیات را خیلی ____ .

(to study)   ۶) چند سال است در این دانشگاه ____ .

(to understand)   ۷) شما خوب توضیح دادید . من خیلی خوب ____ .
explain

(to live)   ۸) چند ماه است در این شهر ____ .

(to go)   ۹) فردا صبح زود من و ژاله به بازار ____ .

(to see)   ۱۰) قبلا من او را در کلاس فلسفه ____ .
again   ولی بعد دیگر او را ندیدم .

E) Fill in the blanks:

۱) چند سال است در تهران زندگی ـــــ ؟

۲) تقریباً سه سال میشود اینجا زندگی ـــــ .

(arrives) ۳) وقتی نامه اش ـــــ فوراً به او تلفن میکنم .

(you have not come) ۴) چرا زودتر ـــــ ؟

(have worked) ۵) تمامِ روز کار ـــــ .

(work/will be working) ۶) متاسفانه ساعتِ نه ـــــ .

(we lived) ۷) آنجا سی سال زندگی ـــــ .

(had written) ۸) نامه ـــــ ولی جواب نفرستادند .

(have come) ۹) تا حالا فقط سه نفر ـــــ .

(did you do) ۱۰) امروز چه کار ـــــ ؟

F) Composition

Write a short composition about your visit to the doctor.
You make an appointment; the nurse takes your blood pressure;
the doctor examines you. You tell him what your problem(s)
is (are)(any part of your body). The nurse gives you an
injection, gives you pills; you take them; the nurse makes
a bandage, etc.; you feel dizzy; at the drugstore you have
your prescription filled out; you get better. Or: afterwards
you go to the hospital for treatment; get a bed; the surgeon
operates on your...; you leave after one week....

G) LISTEN TO THE READING ON THE TAPE.

LESSON SEVENTEEN

درس هفـــده

SOME ADDITIONAL NOTES ON VERBS

فعل (ادامه)

1) Three verb classes which behave differently when compared to
English, 2) focused ongoing action, 3) focused future; vocabulary;
drills; dialogue.

---

1) **THREE VERB CLASSES WHICH BEHAVE DIFFERENTLY WHEN COMPARED**
   TO ENGLISH

a) **The two stative verbs 'have' and 'be'**

They don't have می - forms (except in certain noun-
verb complexes), e.g.:

پول دارم .   I have money.

دانشجو هستم .   I am a student.

(Of course, English 'have' in its meaning of 'possession'
and 'be' in its meaning of 'existence' do not have incomplete
forms either; there is no *'I am having money,' *'I am being
a student.')

b) <u>Simple past in English -</u> مـی <u>- form in Persian</u>

There are verbs which imply a continuous, and thus

incomplete, situation (e.g. physical, mental or emotional

verbs like 'can,' 'want.' 'know,' 'fear' and verbs

like 'be worth.') In the past tense, these appear as

simple past in English, but in Persian, because the situation

they describe is usually incomplete they have مـی .

Only in specific contexts <u>where a single 'once' activity</u>

is implied, they occur, of course, without مـی , e.g.:

<u>Incomplete</u>

میخواستم از شما بپرسم .

I <u>wanted/would like</u> to
ask you.

<u>Complete</u>

در آن‌مَوقِع خواستم بروم
ولی ...

At that moment, I <u>wanted/
intended</u> to leave <u>but</u>....

_____

<u>Incomplete</u>

میدانستم (میفهمیدم)

I <u>knew (all along)/under-
stood</u> that wasn't true.

درست نیست .

<u>Complete</u>

در آن موقع دانستم (فهمیدم)
چه جورْ آدمی است .

At that moment, I <u>knew/
recognized</u> what kind of
person he is.

Note the changes in translation, which reflect this once-

activity:

want : intend/know : understand/know : recognize

c) Further notes on the 'perfect'

As mentioned in lesson 16, the 'perfect' in Persian describes a) an action that happened prior to a point in the present or past, and b) a state at a point in the present or past that resulted from a prior action. Both are more or less two sides of the same coin. Only, in English they are expressed differently.

For example, take the verb 'sit': the sentence ' He has sat (down)' implies an action prior to the present; in Persian this is

نشسته است . Now , the result of this action at the present point of speaking is 'He is sitting', which is no longer a 'perfect' but looks like a present progressive form;in Persian, however, the same 'perfect' form is used: نشسته است . Or, take the verb 'put on (clothes)': the action prior to the present is in English: 'He has put on his clothes'; however, the result of this action is quite different; not only is the progressive -ing form used, but even a different verb, i.e.: 'He is wearing clothes.' Persian uses for both the same 'perfect' form: لباس پوشیده است . With other verbs, English uses 'is' plus perfect participle; e.g. take the verb 'break': the action prior to the present is the 'perfect': ' It has broken.', whereas the result is expressed as : 'It is broken.'

Verbs where this difference between English and Persian is most evident are those which describe a change into a new state (from standing to sitting, putting on to wearing, from breaking to being broken etc.). In any case, in Persian the 'perfect' form fits both.

A random list of such verbs is:

خوابیده است	has gone to sleep/	is sleeping-asleep
ایستاده است	has stood up /	is standing
نشسته است	has sat sown /	is sitting-seated
افتاده است	has fallen /	is fallen-lying
مرده است	has died /	is dead
آمده است	has come /	is here
رفته است	has gone /	is gone
(سرد) شده است	has <u>become</u> /	<u>is</u> (now cold etc.)

Note that the Persian 'perfect' describes a <u>state</u> which <u>continues</u>
at a point in time. It does <u>not</u> describe a state which <u>repeats</u> ,
since in that case not only is the sitting etc. interrupted by
getting up and sitting down, and so on, but the matter becomes, in
fact is, habitual; and accordingly, the 'logic' of the Persian
system requires the use of می . English, however, often uses the
same form for both continuing state and interrupted state. This may
be exemplified by a somewhat drastic example:

۵ سال میشود اینجا نشسته است .	He has been sitting here for 5 years (and never got up).
۵ سال میشود اینجا مینشیند .	He has been sitting here for 5 years (has been coming here every day).

2) FOCUSED ONGOING ACTION

As mentioned earlier, می is used for <u>both</u> ongoing action and habitual action. To indicate that <u>ongoing</u> action is meant, the verb دار/داشت, is placed before the می -forms, e.g.:

<u>Present:</u>

             کار میکنم .   a.   I always work/am working.

<u>focus:</u>   دارم کار میکنم.   b.   <u>in progress</u>: I am working (don't you see).

<u>Past:</u>

            کار میکردم .   a.   I used to work/was working.

<u>focus:</u>   داشتم کار میکردم .   b.   <u>in progress</u>: I was working (at that moment).

Note: There is <u>no negation</u>. If the action is/was <u>not</u> ongoing now/then, there is <u>no</u> reason to focus at all. Thus there is no دارم میروم .

With verbs which imply <u>once-activity</u> like 'leave,' 'die,' 'come to an end,' and 'begin,' this formation mainly indicates immediate action '<u>about to</u>,' e.g.:

      دارم میروم .   I am about to leave/leaving now.

    دارد تمام میشود.   It's about to end/ending now.

    دارد شروع میشود.   It's about to begin/beginning now.

3) <u>FOCUSED FUTURE</u>

Compare:

<u>English</u>	<u>Persian</u>
a. I go (tomorrow).	‫ا ـ (فردا)میروم .‬
b. I'll go (tomorrow).	‫ب ـ (فردا) میروم .‬
c. I will go (tomorrow). (intend to)	‫ج ـ (فردا) خواهم رفت .‬

As you notice, the 'focused', stressed future 'will' has an
equivalent in Persian: it uses the verb ‫خواه‬ 'want, will'
(stress usually on the personal endings) followed by the <u>endingless</u>
past form of the verb. Focusing on 'will' does allow for negation:
Note that there is no ‫می‬; e.g.:

I will (not) write a letter.	‫نامه (نه)خواهم نوشت .‬
You will (not) write a letter.	‫نامه (نه)خواهی نوشت .‬
He/she will (not) write a letter.	‫نامه (نه)خواهد نوشت .‬
We will (not) write a letter.	‫نامه (نه)خواهیم نوشت .‬
You will (not) write a letter.	‫نامه (نه)خواهید نوشت .‬
They will (not) write a letter.	‫نامه (نه)خواهند نوشت .‬

a) <u>Position</u>

‫دار ـ/داشت‬ can be, and often are separated from the main verb/
almost like fillers such as ‫حالا،فعلا‬ but ‫خواه‬ has to
precede the verb immediately, almost like ‫می‬ , e.g.:

‫دارم برای برادرم نامه مینویسم .‬	I am just writing to my brother.
‫به زودی با یران بر خواهم گشت‬	I will soon return to Iran.
‫برای او کار نخواهم کرد .‬	For him I will not work.

VOCABULARY

لغت

oven	اُجاق
refrigerator	یَخْچال
knife	کارْد
spoon	قاشُق
fork	چِنْگال
plate	بُشْقاب
saucer	نَعْلْبَکی
cup	فِنْجان
small glass	اِسْتِکان
glass	لیوان
bowl	کاسه
salt cellar	نَمَکْدان
tray	سینی
samovar	سَماوَر
teapot	قوری
kettle	کِتْری
dining cloth	سُفْره
breakfast	صُبْحانه
lunch	ناهار
dinner	شام

<u>Bed and living room</u>	<u>اطاق خواب و نشیمن</u>
bed	تَخْتِخواب
blanket	پَتو
bedsheet	لِحاف
mattress	دُشَک
pillow	بالِش
curtain	پَرده
furniture	مُبْلُمان
couch	کاناپه
heater	بُخاری
central heating	شوفاژ
<u>Bath</u>	<u>حَمام</u>
tub	وان
shower	دوش میگیرم
faucet	شیرِ آب
mirror	آیِنه
soap	صابون
towel	حَوْله
comb	شانه میکنم
toothbrush	مِسْواک میزنم
toothpaste	خَمیرِ دَنْدان
W.C.	مُسْتَراح / توالِت
sink, washroom	دَسْتشوئی

Verbs implying continuous situation (cf. p. 216) (می - past):

(Some of these require the بـ form in dependent verbs)

want/wanted (to go)   میخواهم / میخواستم (بروم)

can/could (go)   میتوانم / میتوانستم (بروم)

know/knew (acquainted with)   میشناسم / میشناختم

know/knew (something)   میدانم / میدانستم

think/thought   فِکر میکنم / فکر میکردم

feel/felt   حس میکنم / میکردم

be/was afraid (to go)   میترسم /میترسیدم (بروم)

is worth/was worth   میأرزد / میارزید

Verbs implying both state and change of state (perfect

for -ing forms):

stand (up)/stood (up)/am standing   میأیستم/ایستادم/ایستاده‌ام

sit (down)/sat (down)/am sitting   مینشینم/نشستم/نشسته‌ام

lie (down)/lay (down)/am lying; sleeping   میخوابم/خوابیدم/خوابیده‌ام

put on/put on/am wearing (clothes)   میپوشم/پوشیدم/ پوشیده‌ام

put on/put on/am wearing (beard)   (ریش)میگُذارم/گذاشتم/ گذاشته‌ام

stick/stuck/is sticking to   میچسبد/ چسبید/ چسبیده است

Verbs implying change of state (perfect = is + participle):

tie/tied/is tied, closed   میبَندم / بَستم / بسته ام

cut/cut/is cut   میبُرم / بُریدم / بریده ام

break/broke/is broken   میشِکَنم / شِکَستم / شکسته است

die/died/is dead   میمیرم / مُردم / مرده است

fall/fell/is fallen, lying   میاُفتم / اُفتادم / افتاده است

come/came/has come, is here   میآیم / آمَدم / آمده است

leave/left/is gone   میرَوم / رفتم / رفته است

pour/poured/is strewn, poured   میریزم / ریختم / ریخته است

cook/cooked/is cooked   میپَزم / پُختم / پخته است

stretch out/stretched out/am stretched out, relaxing   دراز میکِشم / دراز کشیدم / دراز کشیده‌ام

gets cloudy/got cloudy/is clouded   (هَوا) میگیرد / گرفت / گرفته است

gets cold/got cold/is cold   (سَرد) میشَود / شُد / شده است

DRILLS

تمرین

A) Draw pictures of rooms with the items listed above in them.

B) Change the following sentences to the past tense:

(Note that the tense of the verbs in the dependant clauses

remains unchanged; thus change only the tense of the main verb.)

۱) من میخواهم برای شما یک سماور بخرم .

۲) من نمیتوانم در یخچال را باز کنم .   open

۳) من یک پزشک خوب در این بیمارستان میشناسم .   physician

۴) من میدانم در این نمکدان بجای نَمَک فِلْفِل است .   pepper

۵) من فکر میکنم بخاری منزل شما خیلی گرم باشد .

۶) من از آمپول خیلی میترسم.

۷) این مبلِ ایتالیائی خیلی میارزد.

۸) من فکر میکنم مسواک و خمیر دندان هم لازم داریم .

۹) متاسفانه من نمیتوانم سر وقت به مطب دکتر برسم .

For this drill, and the 'options', cf. p. 216!

1. Find different persons as subjects of the sentences of

    Drill B. Use the past tense, e.g.:

پدرشما میخواست برای من یک سماور بخرد .

2. Change all sentences of Drill B to the negative past, e.g.:

or vice versa, e.g.:

پدر شما نمیخواست برای من یک سماور بخرد .

C) **In the following sentences** describe a present state:

(stand)	۱) الان جواد دم پنجره ———
(wear) moustache	۲) به به ، چه قشنگ شدی با این سبیلی که ———
(wear)	۳) امروز هوا خیلی سرد است همه پالتو ———
(sleep)	۴) زیاد شلوغ نکنید بچه ها ———
(sit)	۵) همهٔ خانواده سر میز صبحانه ———
(stick)	۶) یادداشت پشت آقای هالو ———
(stand)	۷) بچه های مدرسه کنار بخاری ———
(wear)	۸) وَکیلِ ما کُلاه ———
(wear)	۹) پدر بزرگ من تازگیها عَیْنک ———
(sit) passengers	۱۰) مُسافِرین همه در اتوبوس ———

Check the verb lists for the different Persian equivalents of 'wear' (hat, glasses, etc.)

1. Change the sentences in Drill C to the past perfect

('was ...ing').

2. Change the sentences in C to the present and past

progressive with داشتم / دارم .

D)   **Change the following sentences** to describe a present state, according to the pattern:

بچه لیوان را میشکند	The child breaks the glass.
لیوان شکسته است	The glass is broken.
سوار اتوبوس میشود	He got on the bus.
سوار شده است	He is riding the bus.

۱) غذا برای شام میپزد

۲) مریض میمیرد

۳) دستش را برید

۴) فوراً در را ببندید

fall to ground   ۵) پرده زَمین میافتد

۶) مهمانِ ما الان میآید

۷) چای را روی قالی ریخت

۸) روی کاناپه دراز میکشد

1. Having completed the changes in Drill D, put the changed sentences in the past.

2. Put the sentences in D in the present and past progressive.

3. Put the sentences in D⁻ into the focused future with خواه .

E) Translate the following. Explain why you have chosen the
particular verb form by referring to the explanations given
in this lesson:

1. I thought the Kashani carpets were the best.

2. I knew that was not right.

3. I wanted this very much.

4. He was afraid of (از) the hospital.

5. Did you not know that he was busy?

6. I realized (understood) that the program was interesting.

7. Tehran used to be a very small city.   (شهر)

8   Where do you sit in the class?

9. Hassan is sitting by the window.

10. Careful, the child is asleep.

11. What will you wear/be wearing at the party?

12. I thought the child was afraid (fearing).

Note that after verbs of observation ('know, think, realize')
the verb of the 'observed' dependent sentence is usually in the
present (cf. p. 312), e.g.:

میدانستم آنجاست .   I knew it was ('is') there.

گفتگو

DIALOGUE

While somewhat forced, this dialogue is rather moderately polite,
but still has plenty of polite formulae; note especially the
reference to 'giving trouble'.

A) ببخشید خانم ، رضا هست ؟

B) نه خَیر ، الان میآید . بفرمائید تو .

A) خیلی‌متشکرم . مزاحم نمیشوم .

B) اِختیار دارید ، چه مزاحمتی ، بفرمائید تو،رضا رفت تا سر کوچه،الان برمیگردد . من مادرش هستم .

A) قرار بود امشب با هم به کتابخانه برویم .

B) بله ، به من گفت ، چند دقیقه تشریف بیاورید تو الان پیدایش میشود .

A) بسیار خوب ، امیدوارم که مزاحمتان نشوم .

B) بفرمائید ، تا رضا بیاید فِعلاً یک چای میل کنید .

A) خانم ، اینکه اسباب خجالت شد ، چقدر زحمت میکشید .

B) اختیار دارید . این حرفها چیست . قابلی ندارد .

A) ما پَس فردا یک امتحان داریم که امتحان آخری‌ماست . بعدش دیگر راحت میشویم .

B) میدانم رضا این روزها خیلی درس میخواند . معمولاً تا نصف شب بیدار است . بفرمائید خواهش میکنم . چایتان یخ میکند .

A) چشم .

B) انشاء‌الله بعد از امتحانات یک روز ناهار تشریف بیاورید اینجا .

A) اختیار دارید ، امروز به اندازهٔ کافی‌مزاحم شدم .

B) چه مزاحمتی ، منزل خودتان است . شما هم برای‌من مثل رضا هستید .

A) چشم، با کمال میل خدمتتان میرسم .

B) مثل اینکه رضا آمد . بله خودش است .

please come in	بِفرمائید تو
I won't trouble you	مُزاحِم نِمیشوم
no trouble at all	چه مُزاحِمَتی
We are supposed <u>to go</u>.	قَرار اِست / بود برویم
please come in	تَشریف بیا ورید تو
he will appear	پِیْدا یش میشود
I hope not <u>to bother</u> you.	اُمیدوارم مُزاحِم نشوم
until he comes	تا ... بیا یَد
have some...	مَیْل کنید
matter of shame	اَسْبا بِ خِجالَت
take the trouble	زَحْمَت میکِشَم / کِشیدم
don't mention it	قابِلی ندارد
midnight	نِصْفِ شَب
gets cold (ice)	یَخْ میکند
fine! ('by my eyes')	چُشْم
I hope you come	اِنْشاء اَللّه تشریف بیا ورید
enough	کافی
I gave you trouble	مُزاحِم شدم
with pleasure	با کَمالِ مَیْل
will come to see you	خِدْمَتِتان میرسم

LESSON EIGHTEEN

درس هجده

THE SUBJUNCTIVE MOOD

وَجْهِ اِلْتِزامى

1) The subjunctive prefix بـ , 2) the subjunctive after modals,

3) the subjunctive elsewhere, 4) suggested action, 5) the imperative;

drills; reading.

---

1) <u>THE SUBJUNCTIVE PREFIX</u> بـ

The <u>indicative</u> mood (the forms discussed so far) implies that
an action has actually happened or will happen, or is happening.
The <u>subjunctive</u> mood implies that an action is possible, or
suggested, i.e. <u>may or should happen (or have happened)</u>. The present
subjunctive is indicated by the (stressed) prefix بـ in the
positive, by نـ in the negative, e.g. 'I arrive':

میرسم	I arrive
بِرسم	that I arrive
نَرسم	that I don't arrive

(For بـ and نـ before verbs beginning with a <u>vowel</u>, see p. 345).

231

In many cases, the subjunctive, and thus the prefix بـ , is
the equivalent of an English infinitive, e.g.:

میتُواند برود   is able <u>to go</u>

میخواهد برود   wants <u>to go</u>

بهتر است برود   is better for him <u>to go</u>

The prefix بـ is <u>omitted</u>:

    a) <u>optionally</u> in noun-verb complexes with   میشوم / شدم

    میکنم / کردم , e.g.:

کار (به) کنم (نکنم)   I should work (not work)

بلند (به) شود (نشود)   He should get up (not get up)

    b) <u>obligatorily</u> by the <u>verbal prefix</u> بر , e.g.:

بر گردد (برنگردد)   He should return (not return)

and in the subjunctive forms of the two stative verbs

<u>'to be' and 'to have,'</u> which are:

(نه) باشد.   It should be (not be)

(نه) داشته باشد.   He should have (not have)

2) <u>THE SUBJUNCTIVE AFTER MODALS: 'CAN, WANT, MUST'</u>

All modals imply that the action modified is possible,

thus the use of the subjunctive. Note that the subjunctive

form stays the same whether the modal is in the present or the

past or any other form.

a) <u>میخواهم / خواستم</u> 'want to'; 'like to'

Present

میخواهم   فارسی یاد بگیرم .   I want to learn Persian.

میخواهی   فارسی یاد بگیری .   You want to learn Persian.

میخواهد   فارسی یاد بگیرُد .   He/she wants to learn Persian.

میخواهیم   فارسی یاد بگیریم .   We want to learn Persian.

میخواهید   فارسی یاد بگیرید .   You want to learn Persian.

میخواهند   فارسی یاد بگیرند .   They want to learn Persian.

Past

میخواستم   فارسی یاد بگیرم .   I wanted to learn Persian.

میخواستی   فارسی یاد بگیری .   You wanted to learn Persian.

میخواست   فارسی یاد بگیرد .   He/she wanted to learn Persian.

میخواستیم   فارسی یاد بگیریم .   We wanted to learn Persian.

میخواستید   فارسی یاد بگیرید .   You wanted to learn Persian.

میخواستند   فارسی یاد بگیرند .   They wanted to learn Persian.

Note: In both present and past, the بـ form is the same.

This modality can also refer to others than the subject, e.g.:

میخواهم حسن یاد بگیرد .   I want Hassan to learn.

میخواستم زود تر بیائی .   I wanted you to come earlier.

b) میتوانم/توانستم 'can, able to; allowed to'

Present

میتوانم فارسی حرف بزنم .	I can speak Persian.
میتوانی فارسی حرف بزنی .	You can speak Persian.
میتواند فارسی حرف بزند .	He/she can speak Persian.
میتوانیم فارسی حرف بزنیم .	We can speak Persian.
میتوانید فارسی حرف بزنید .	You can speak Persian.
میتوانند فارسی حرف بزنند .	They can speak Persian.

Past

میتوانستم فارسی حرف بزنم .	I could speak Persian.
میتوانستی فارسی حرف بزنی .	You could speak Persian.
میتوانست فارسی حرف بزند .	He/she could speak Persian.
میتوانستیم فارسی حرف بزنیم .	We could speak Persian.
میتوانستید فارسی حرف بزنید .	You could speak Persian.
میتوانستند فارسی حرف بزنند .	They could speak Persian.

Note: Both in present and in past, the ب form is the same.

Note: نمیتوانم که نخندم   I cannot help laughing.

c)   میشود / شد   'can, it is possible'

(cf. p. 253)

The third singular of شد / میشود 'become, come about' may also express modality 'it is possible that...'. Its use is more restricted than میتوانم/توانستم and implies some impersonal 'outside force' that permits, or prevents (if negative), e.g.:

نمیشود اینطوری حرف بزنی .	It is not possible for you to/ you cannot talk like this.
چرا نشد به آمریکا بروی ؟	Why was it not possible for you to/ could you not go to America?

d) باید 'must/have to (had to)'

The equivalent of 'must' is باید 'it is necessary.' Similar to 'must', باید has three basic meanings:

1. obligation (must go = have to go),

2. suggestion (must go = should/ought to go),

3. assumption or conclusion   (must be there = ought to be there).

In the present tense it is followed by the present subjunctive. (For the past tense see lesson 20); e.g.:

Present

باید کار بکنم .	I must, have to work/should work.
باید کار بکنی .	You must, have to work/should work.
باید کار بکند.	He/she must, have to work/should work.
باید کار بکنیم .	We must, have to work/should work.
باید کار بکنید.	You must, have to work/should work.
باید کار بکنند.	They must, have to work/should work.

A variety of adjectives may be used for the notion of 'must'; e.g.:

مَجْبورم کار بکنم .

I am forced to/must work.

ناچارم کار بکنم .

I cannot help working/must work.

لازم است کار بکنم .

It is necessary for me/I have to work.

بهتر است بروی .

It is better that/you better go/leave.

These should be used for the past tenses until reaching lesson 20.

e) **Negation of modals**

The negative prefix نـ usually precedes the modals and not the subjunctive, since usually the modality is negated, not the possibility; thus, e.g.:

نمیخواهم بروم .

I do not want - to go.

نمیتوانم بروم .

I cannot - go.

نمیشود بروم ؟

Can I not - go?

نباید بروم .

I must not - go.

Of course, some logical twistings allow the negation of the possibility, but those are rare, e.g.:

میتوانم نروم .

I can - not go.

3) <u>THE SUBJUNCTIVE ELSEWHERE</u>

There are many expressions besides the modals which also modify

an action as a hope, a possibility, an intent, etc., e.g.:

اُمیدوارم امروز بیا ید .   I hope that he comes today.

مَیْل دارم بیا یم .   I am inclined - to come.

دوست دارم بیا یم .   I like - to come.

میتَرسم امروز نیا ید .   I am afraid - that he may not come
          today.

بهتر است امروز بیا ید .   It is better - that he come today.
          = He better comes today.

مُمکن است امروز بیا ید .   It is possible - that he come today.
          = He may come today.

قَرار است امروز بیا ید .   It is agreed that we come.
          = We are supposed to come.

کاش امروز بیا ید .   I wish he comes today.

آمدم شما را ببینم .   I came - to see you.

4) <u>SUGGESTED ACTION</u>

The suggestive function of the subjunctive is most evident

when: (a) following (ید) بِگذار 'let ---' (ید for polite address)

and (b) in questions equivalent to: 'shall---?', e.g.:

'shall I?' etc.   'let me' etc.

بروم ؟   shall I go   بِگذار (ید) بروم   let me go

___   ___

برود ؟   shall we go   بگذار (ید) برود   let him go

برویم ؟   shall we go   بگذار (ید) برویم   let us go

___   ___

بروند ؟   shall they go   بگذار (ید) بروند   let them go

5) **THE IMPERATIVE**

The forms بگذار and بگذارید are actually imperatives:
'let!' (you, singular), 'let!' (you, plural). The ending of
the second singular is <u>zero</u>, that of second plural (or the
polite form of the singular) is بد , e.g.:

<u>Polite</u>

please listen	لطفا گوش (به) کنید .
please answer	لطفا جواب بدهید .
please come	لطفا بیائید .
please say	لطفا بگوئید .
please go there	لطفا آنجا بروید .
please/will you?	بفرمائید .
please <u>stay</u> here	لطفا اینجا باشید .
please <u>keep</u> your book	لطفا کتابتان را داشته باشید .

<u>Familiar</u>

listen		گوش (به) کن .
answer	/bedeh/	جواب بده .
come	/biyā/	بیا .
say	/bogu/	بگو .
go there	/boro/	برو آنجا .
<u>stay</u> here		اینجا باش .
<u>keep</u> your book		کتابت را داشته باش .

The <u>negative</u> is نه : please, don't talk; لطفا حرف نزنید .

don't talk حرف نزن .

239

DRILLS تمرین

A) Review

Fill in the blanks in the following sentences with prepositions,
prepositional phrases (cf. p. 164) را or ی . (Note: some blanks remain blank).

۱) کتاب ـــــ میآورم .

high school   ۲) ـــــ دَبیرستان میروم .

۳) ـــــ ماشین ـــــ تهران میروم .

۴) حسن ـــــ ناراحت نکنم .

۵) نامه ـــــ روی میز میگذارم .

elementary school   ۶) امروز ـــــ دَبستان نمیروند .

۷) ماشین ـــــ میخرم .

۸) یک جواب ـــــ میدهم .

۹) اینجا خانه های بزرگ ـــــ میسازند .

۱۰) ـــــ مادرم نُسخه میپیچم .

۱۱) منتظرِ حسن ـــــ هستم .

۱۲) درس ده ـــــ یاد میگیرم .

۱۳) این درس ـــــ میخوانم .

۱۴) یک فیلم ـــــ تماشا میکنم .

۱۵) ـــــ رادیو ـــــ گوش میدهم .

۱۶) یک آواز ـــــ میخوانم .

۱۷) دو چرخه سوار ـــــ میشوم .

۱۸) امشب استاد ـــــ ـــــ ملاقات میکنم .

۱۹) راحت ـــــ نیستم .

۲۰) او ـــــ دوست دارم .

B) Having filled in the blanks in Drill A, change each sentence to:

1. Imperative

2. Suggestive , either first or third person plural

3. Add بـایـد to each sentence.

4. Add (نه) میخواهم to each sentence.

5. Add (نه) میتوانم to each sentence.

6. Add بـهتر است (نیست) to each sentence.

7. Change the sentences created by Drills B3 through B6 to the past.

8. Change all sentences created to the negative. At least two examples for each of Drills B1 through B7.

9. Change the persons in the examples, at least two examples for each of Drills B1 through B8.

Note: Remember , once you understand the pattern of each drill, go on to the next one.

C) In the following sentences (1) fill in the verbs in the subjunctive , (2) fill in as many fillers as possible (such as فوراً ، معمولاً).

(speak)   ۱) ـــــ ـــــ میتواند فارسی حرف ـــــ .

(teach)   ۲) ـــــ رفت سرِ کلاسِ درس ـــــ .

(work)   ۳) دانشجو ها ـــــ مجبورند نزدیکِ امتحان خیلی کار ـــــ .

(be)   ۵) ـــــ ترجمهٔ من باید درست ـــــ .

D) **Translate the following dialogue into Persian:**

(Note: You <u>can do</u> the translation; don't translate word for word, literally, but look for a word you know with approximately the same meaning.)

A) Excuse me, sir, could you tell me where I can find a chelo kebabi?

B) Sure, there is one in this vicinity. You go straight ahead ('direct'). But if you want a really good restaurant, you must go to Tajrish.

A) I am afraid I will not be able to find it.

B) Well, you better take a taxi and ask the driver. He will take you there directly.

A) Thank you very much.

E) **Translate the following dialogue into Persian:**

A) What is your field (of study)?

B) Iranian studies.

A) That is interesting. Mine (مال) is Iranian studies, too. Are you Iranian?

B) Yes. Are you American? I noticed the script of your book.

A) Yes.

B) Where did you learn Persian?

A) In America, at...

B) Your Persian is very good.

A) Thank you. It is not that good. (خیلی هم ...)

B) How long have you been here? (Note: Pay attention to

the tense.)

A) Only a week (never یکدانه with time).

B) Who is your professor?

A) Professor.... He is a good professor.

B) Let me see, do you like Iranian food?

A) I had (ate) some.

B) You must have some. Will you have time tonight?

Would you like (want) to come (use polite expression) to my house
for dinner?

A) Yes, fine (thank you). I think I can come tonight. But I must
leave (= go) at 9:30 p.m.

B) Is it possible (could you) for you to stay until 10:00?

I want to fix a good dinner. That needs (wants) time.

A) That's alright (= be it).

B) Fine (very good), let's go now. I'll see you at 8:00.

A) See you. (Note: Add a polite expression.) Wait,

sorry, where do you live? What's your address?

B) I will wait for you in front of the university.

Bye.

A) Bye.

243

READING خواندنی

دیشب در حدود ساعت ده میخواستم پیش دوستم بروم . نمیتوانستم تاکسی پیدا کنم .
فراموش کرده بودم که آن وقت شب خیابانها معمولاً شلوغ است . ترافیک خیلی بد
بود . به دوستم تلفن کردم و گفتم متاسفانه ممکن است دیر برسم . بعد از تلفن
دوباره به خیابان رفتم . خوشبختانه توانستم یک تاکسی خالی پیدا بکنم . خیلی
شانس آورده بودم .

درست وقتی وسط میدان وَنَک رسیدیم ، دیدیم چرخ ماشین پنجر شده است . خیلی دیر
شده بود . ولی لازم بود پیاده بشویم و ماشین را به کنار میدان هول بدهیم .
به هیچ وجه نمیتوانستم به موقع به منزل دوستم برسم . قضیه به اینجا تمام
نمیشود . وقتی ماشین را به کنار میدان هول دادیم یکدفعه چرخش توی جوب رفت .
خیلی ناراحت شده بودم . بالاخره بعد از یک ساعتِ تمام ماشین درست شد و در حدود
ساعت ده و ربع به منزل دوستم رسیدم .

this time	این دَفْعه
am lucky	شانس میآورم / آوردم
wheel, tire	چَرْخ
flat tire	پَنْجَر
push (short /o/)	هول میدهم / دادم
matter, case	قَضیه
all at once	یکْدَفْعه
small ditch along street	جوب
full, complete	تَمام

سکینه: من زن انتر نمیشم به این چیزا خر نمیشم....

چند دفعه گفتم نمیخوام!؟   بازمیگم من نمیخوام

حاجی اعیون نمیخوام   مرغ و فسنجون نمیخوام

لباس نو میخوام چیکار؟   مرغ و پلو میخوام چیکار؟

پول و پلاس میخوام چیکار؟   خونه و اثاث میخوام چیکار؟

من زن انتر نمیشم   باین چیزا خر نمیشم

از : سید ابوالقاسم انجوی شیرازی

بازیهای نمایشی . تهران : امیر کبیر
۱۳۵۲/۱۹۷۴

L E S S O N   N I N E T E E N

درس نوزده

T H E   V E R B شُـــدَن

1) 'Become' میشُوم/شُدم , 2) 'become-make become,' 3) 'kill-get killed,' 4) English passives and their Persian equivalents, 5) where also not to use شدن , 6) a note on literary Persian, 7) 'it is possible'; vocabulary; drills; dialogue; giving directions.

---

1) __'BECOME'__ میشوم/ شدم

میشوم / شدم is a very useful verb to know. Its basic meaning is the process of becoming or getting to be something or someone, as opposed to the state of being something or someone, for example, the notorious aunt asking her nephew:

عَمِه : عَزیزم وقتی بزرگ شُدی میخواهی چه بِشَوی ؟

Aunt: My dear when you have grown up, what do you want to be(come)?

پسرِ برادر: میخواهم دکتر بشوم، عَمِه جان.

Nephew (confidently): I want to be(come) a doctor, auntie.

245

Note the difference between process and state in:

تا هتل چقدر میشود ؟	How much will it be(come) to the hotel?
این چند است ؟	How much is this?
من یُواش یُواش خسته میشوم .	I am slowly getting tired.
من خسته هستم .	I am tired.

Some frequent combinations

acquainted:	آشْنا
با خانم فُلانی آشْنا بشوید .	Become <u>acquainted</u> with Mr. X.
tall:	بُلَنْد
از صندلی بلند میشوم .	I am <u>getting up</u> from the chair.
pedestrian:	پیاده
از ماشین پیاده شد .	He <u>got off</u> the car.
rider:	سُوار
سوارِ ماشین میشوم .	I am <u>getting into</u> the car, etc.
face to face:	روبرو
ناگهان با جادوگری روبرو شد .	Suddenly he <u>met</u> a witch.
happy:	خوشحال
خیلی خوشحال شدم .	Very <u>happy</u> (to meet you).

الان چی میشود؟/ اینجا چی شد؟	What will happen now?/What happened here?
حالش خوب میشود ./ حالش خوب شد .	She <u>will be(come)</u> fine./She got well.

2) 'BECOME-MAKE BECOME'

a) **With adjectives**

These two verbs are most frequently used with adjectives,
e.g.:

awake:	بیدار
او را بیدار کرد .	He woke him up.
او بیدار شد .	He woke up.
tired:	خسته
او را خسته کرد .	He made him tired.
او خسته شد .	He got tired.
alright:	درست
آنرا درست کردم .	I repaired it.
درست شد .	It turned out alright.

With adjectives ميشوم / شدم indicates a change of
state 'get, become'; ميكنم / كردم indicates the
causation of a change of state 'make (it become).'

b) **With nouns**

Besides adjectives, a number of nouns with شدم / كردم
indicate change of state and causing change of state,
e.g.:

آنرا ترجمه کردم .	I <u>translated</u> it.
ترجمه شد .	It <u>got/was translated</u>.
او را دعوت کردم .	I <u>invited</u> her.
او دعوت شد .	She <u>got/was invited</u>.

Note that in English the forms with شدن are often translated as passives ('was translated, was invited'); this is only a matter of translation, as there is no passive in Persian; forms with شدن simply indicate change of state ('got translated, got invited').

c) <u>With Arabic participles</u>

Similarly, شدن with Arabic participles, especially so-called 'passive' participles like معلوم 'known, evident' (see Appendix II, p. 351) are often translated as passives, but only indicate change of state, e.g.:

known: مَعْلوم	
آنرا <u>معلوم کردم</u> .	I <u>found out</u> about it.
<u>معلوم شد</u> .	It <u>became evident</u>.
forced: مَجْبور	
او را <u>مجبور کردم</u> .	I <u>forced</u> him.
او <u>مجبور شد</u> .	He <u>was forced</u>.
accepted: قَبول	
او را <u>قبول کردند</u>.	They <u>accepted</u> him.
او <u>قبول شد</u> .	He <u>was accepted</u>, <u>passed</u> (an examination).

3) **'KILL-GET KILLED'** كُشْت ـ كُشْته شد

'Kill' is one of the causative verbs which indicate causing a change of state. There are not many of these in Persian. (Just as there are not too many simple verbs in general in Persian.) The change of state form is expressed by the verbal participle and شدن .
The causation form is the verb itself, as كردن is already implied. Compare:

او را خَسْته کردم / کرده‌ام	I <u>made him tired</u> /have made
او خسته شد / شده‌ام	He <u>got tired</u> /has gotten
او راكُشْتم / کشته‌ام	I <u>killed</u> him /have killed
او کشته شد / کشته شده است	He <u>got/was killed</u> / has been killed

Again, in English, such forms as كشته شد are usually translated as passives: 'he was killed,' but there is no passive in Persian, only change of state: 'got/became killed.'

The <u>negation</u> is usually attached to شدن :

او در جُنْگ کشته نشد . He was not/did not get killed in the war.

4) <u>ENGLISH PASSIVES AND THEIR PERSIAN EQUIVALENTS</u>

English has a complex system of passives, and passives
are used frequently. There is no passive in Persian,
as indicated. There is only <u>one</u> well defined context
where شدن appears to be the equivalent of an English
passive: when the agent is unmentioned. This is
illustrated in the following table:

<u>Persian</u>	<u>English</u>

a) <u>Agent known (no شدن)</u>

دانشجو   نامه فرستاد.   The student sent a letter

دانشجو   نامه فرستاد.   A letter was sent by the student.

b) <u>Agent is 'someone/some people' (no شدن)</u>

نامه فرستادند.   They/someone sent a letter.

نامه فرستادند.   A letter was sent by someone/them.

c) <u>Agent unmentioned (only here شدن)</u>

نامه فرستاده شد .   A letter was sent.

<u>i.e. in Persian</u>

a) Agent is known: use regular ('active') sentence
whether English has passive or not;

b) <u>Agent is 'someone, some people'</u>: use regular
('active') sentence, <u>3rd plural</u> (ـند);

c) <u>Agent is unmentioned</u>: use participle and شد / شو .
Thus, use the شدن formation only when the agent of
the killing/sending, etc. is unmentioned (i.e. when
there is no 'by him/someone etc.').

5) <u>WHERE ALSO NOT TO USE شدن</u>

a) In English, there are also passives with the dative/
receiver as subject. Again, in Persian, use the
active form:

برای من کتاب فرستاد.   He sent me a book.

برای من کتاب فرستاد.   I was sent a book by him.

b) <u>No change of state implied</u>

Many English passives do not imply a change of state.
Again, Persian does not use شدن in these
instances, e.g.:

<u>Persian</u>	<u>English</u>
به من گفتند.	I was told.
میگفتند.	It was said.
او را دیدند.	He was seen.
فهمیدند.	It was understood.
او را دوست داشتند.	She was loved.
او را صِدا کردند.	He was called.
از آنها پرسیدند.	They were asked.
ادامه دارد.	To be continued.

6) A NOTE ON LITERARY PERSIAN

The use of participles with شدن is most frequently
found in formal and/or written Persian in expository and
argumentative prose. 'Change of state' on that level of
language implies not only physical change (like 'kill')
and movement (send, bring, take), but also observation
(show, call somebody something). Note that sensory
observation (see, hear) often implies 'can' (get to be
seen--can be seen). Some examples are:

نویسنده خوانده میشود .	(Such a person) is called a writer.
مَعْنیِ آن اینجا نِشان داده شده است .	Its meaning has been shown here (that).
خیلی کتاب نوشته شده است .	Many books have been written (about this).
خیلی شِنیده شده است .	It has often been heard/one can often hear that.
در امتحانات بخوبی دیده میشود .	Especially during the examinations it is/can be observed quite well (that).

7) <u>'IT IS POSSIBLE'</u>

میشود / شد   has also the meaning and function of 'it

is possible' (derived from its basic meaning 'become,

get' ⟶ 'get off the ground, it goes' ⟶ 'it is possible').

This meaning is exemplified in the following conversation:

Still   ده حسن ، هَنوز اینجا هستی ؟ فکر میکردم آمریکا رفتی .   (A

نشد .   (B

چرا نشد ؟   (A

نشد دیگَر .   (B

چی نشد ؟   (A

همه چی ، اول گفتند اَصلاً نمیشود . بعد گفتند امسال نمیشود .   (B
آخر گفتند بسیار خوب بعد از اِزدِواجِتان میشود . ازدواج یعنی چه ؟

A) What's that? Hassan, you're still here? I thought

    you went to America.

B) It was not possible. (I couldn't)

A) Why couldn't you?

B) It just wasn't possible.

A) What wasn't possible?

B) Everything. First they said it isn't possible (you

    can't); then they said it isn't possible (you can't)

    this year; finally they said, 'very well, it's possible

    (you can) after your marriage.' What has marriage (got to do with

    it?)

    Note that as indicated by the parentheses, the meaning

    'can' is also implied.

VOCABULARY

لـغت

begin/begin	شروع میکنم / میشود
let off/get off	پیاده میکنم / میشوم از ـ
pick up/get on	سَوارِ میکنم / میشوم
wake up/wake up	بیدار میکنم / میشوم
translate/is translated	ترجمه میکنم / میشود
both polite forms of 'I say,' 'I remark'	عَرْض میکنم / میشود
make (un)comfortable/get (un)comfortable	(نا)راحت میکنم / میشوم
accept, pass/gets accepted, pass (exam)	قَبول میکنم / میشوم
reject, fail/gets rejected, fail (exam); (if 'pass by'	رَد میکنم / میشوم (اَز)
light-switch on/gets light	رَوْشن میکنم / میشود
extinguish-switch off/is extinguished	خاموش میکنم / میشود
find/is found	پَیْدا میکنم / میشود
lose/gets lost	گُم میکنم / میشود
fill/gets full	پُر میکنم / میشود
empty/gets empty	خالی میکنم / میشود
open/opens	باز میکنم / میشود
make ready/gets ready	حاضِر میکنم / میشود
change/changes (a thing, plane, but not 'money')	عَوَض میکنم / میشود
discuss/is discussed	بَحْث میکنم / میشود
prepare, repair/gets alright	دُرُسْت میکنم / میشود
destroy/is destroyed	خَراب میکنم / میشود
add/is added	اِضافه میکنم / میشود به ـ
end/(come to) end	تمام میکنم / میشود

<u>DRILLS</u>   تمرین

A. Construct sentences with the words indicated, using

either   شدم /میشوم or کردم /میکنم .   Note that compounds

with شدن often express cause by از :

I got tired from work(ing).   از کار خسته شدم .

۱) مسافر ــ ترن ــ پیاده

۲) سوارِ هواپیما ــ   airplane

۳) تلفن ــ من ــ صبحِ زود ــ بیدار

۴) از درس خواندن ــ خسته

۵) شاگِرْد   مجبور ــ امتحان بدهد

۶) خواندنی ــ به انگلیسی ــ ترجمه

۷) سرما ــ مرا ــ ناراحت

۸) چراغ را ــ ناگهان ــ روشن

۹) توریست ــ نمیتوانست ــ راه را ــ پیدا(subjunctive)

۱۰) اُمیدوارم ــ کم   (negative subjunctive)

۱۱) اتوبوس ــ از مسافر ــ پر

۱۲) کیف ــ خالی

۱۳) چمدان ــ باز

۱۴) چند لُغَت ــ درس ــ اضافه

۱۵) صبحانه ــ حاضر

۱۶) هواپیما ــ عوض

۱۷) درس بیستم ــ کلاس ــ بحث

۱۸) نظر ــ شما را ــ قبول

۱۹) از پارکِ شهر ــ رد

۲۰) ماشینم ــ خراب

۲۱) غذا ــ درست

B. The sentences as given in Drill A are very short. Using
the completed sentences of Drill A, add fillers like
(امیدوارم ، بهتراست ، خوب است etc.), and/or phrases like (معمولا
ممکن است ، قرار است etc.) which require the following subjunctive.

C. Some forms with شدم/میشوم have already occurred in the
previous lessons. Copy ten sentences with شدن
from the previous lessons.

D. Fill in the blanks in the following sentences:

۱) سوارِ ماشین ـــــ .

۲) ببینم اینجا چی ـــــ ؟

۳) راحت باشید ، حالش خوب ـــــ .

۴) ببخشید من اینجا ـــــ .

۵) امروز صبح زود ـــــ .

۶) از اینجا تا فرودگاه ـــــ ؟

۷) با خانم میلر ـــــ .

۸) من از دیدنِ شما خیلی ـــــ .

۹) حسن میخواهد استاد ـــــ .

۱۰) امروز ساعت چند ـــــ .

۱۱) شما باید فورا ـــــ .

DIALOGUE

گفتگو

(A) شنیدید که جواد از دبیرستان فارغ التحصیل شده است .

(B) نه ، جای تعجب است . تا یادم است جواد هیچوقت شاگرد خوبی نبوده است . فکر کنم این آخر سری ها هم یکسال تجدید شد ، بعدش هم رفوزه شد .

(A) اختیار دارید ، تا آنجا که بنده میدانم جواد هیچوقت رفوزه نشد . تازه امسال هم در امتحانات نهائی با معدلِ هفده قبول شد .

(B) بارک الله ، پس مثل اینکه شاگرد زرنگی شده است . خوب الان میخواهد چکار کند ؟ دانشگاه میرود ؟

(A) نه ، اول میخواهد یک مُدتی در شرکتِ تِلفن کار کند .

(B) چرا ؟

(A) والله ، بنظرم پول برای دانشگاه ندارد . اول میخواهد پول جمع کند .

(B) یادم میآید من وقتی دانشجو بودم هم درس میخواندم و هم کار میکردم .

(A) بله ، مثل اینکه این روزها آدم نمیتواند بدون پول پدر تحصیل کند .

hear	میشنوم / شنیدم
graduate	از ـــ فارغ التحصیل میشوم
surprise	تَعَجُب
as far as I remember	تا یادم است
pupil, student	شاگِرد
lately	این آخرْ سَری ها
it seems to me ('I should think')	فکر کنم
take exam over	تَجدید میشوم
after that	بعدش
I am flunked	رفوزه میشوم
I ('your slave')	بَنده
the finals	امتحانْ نِهائی
grade point average	مُعَدِل
excellent!	بارک اَلله
clever	زَرَنگ
period of time	مُدَت
both ... and	هم ... هم

collect	جَمع میکنم
comes to mind, remember	یادم میآید
man, person, one	آدَم
study (university)	تَحصیل میکنم

Note: The highest grade point in Iran is 20.

GIVING DIRECTIONS

In the following, some sample questions are given which ask for directions. These are followed by sample answers. (Note that this type of dialogue generally uses the subjunctive.)

After studying these questions and answers, draw a map, or find a map, that allows you to play through most, or all of them.

Questions

ممکن است لطفا بفرمائید این آدرس را چطوری پیدا کنم ؟

ممکن است لطفا پستخانه را به من نشان بدهید؟

آیا میدانید پستخانه کجاست ؟

ببخشید آقا ، این نزدیکی ها پستخانه کجاست ؟

Could you please tell me how I can find this address?

Could you please show me the post office?

Do you know where the post office is?

Excuse me, sir, is there a post office nearby?

Answers

The following are sequences of three sets of possible answers:

(. . . . .)   (بعد . . .)   (اول . . .)

These can be combined with each other freely.

I	**First I**
اول از بانکِ ملی رد بشوید	Pass by the bank (Melli)
اول دستِ راست بپیچید	Turn right
اول از این خیابان یکطرفه بروید	Go along this one-way street
اول تا تهِ این خیابان بروید	Go down this street
اول از چراغ راهنمای دوم رد بشوید	Pass the second traffic light
II	**then II**
بعد مستقیم بروید	go straight ahead
بعد دستِ چپ وارد خیابان دوم بشوید	enter the second street on the left
بعد از میدان عبور کنید	cross the square
بعد به یک سه راهی میرسید	you reach a سه راهه
بعد به یک کوچه میرسید.	you reach a small street
III	**the post office is III**
پستخانه نزدیک تعمیرگاهِ بنز است	near the garage (Mercedes Benz)
پستخانه روبروی بیمارستان مِهر است	opposite the مهر hospital
پستخانه آنطرفهاست	there(abouts)
پستخانه جَنبِ سینما است	by the movie theater
پستخانه بَغَلِ شرکتِ خاوَر است	next to the Khavar Company

VOCABULARY

لغت

turn	میپیچم / پیچیدم	straight	مُستَقیم
cross	عُبور میکنم / کردم از۔	right here	هَمین جا
pass, go along	رد میشوم / شدم از	hereabouts	این طَرَفها
show	نشان میدهم / دادم به ۔	further over there	آنطرفها
find	پَیْدا میکنم / کردم	further (forward)	جِلوتر
enter	وارد ِ میشوم / شدم	top, end of street	سَر ِ خیابان
left (hand)	دست ِ چَپ	bottom end of street	تَه ِ خیابان
right (hand)	دست ِ راست	middle	وَسَط
behind	پُشت	store	فُروشگاه
near	نَزدیک	small store	مَغازه
opposite	روبروی	repair shop	تَعْمیرگاه
next to	جَنب	gas station	پُمپ ِ بنزین
next to	پَهْلو	lane, alley	کوچه
next to	بَغَل	bank	بانک
map	نَقشه	company	شِرْکَت
street	خیابان	post office	پُستخانه
square	مَیْدان	movie theater	سینِما
intersection	چهار راه	market	بازار
street leading into another	سه راه	address	آدْرِس
one-way	یک طَرَفه	station, stop	ایستگاه
traffic light	چِراغ ِ راهنما	hospital	بیمارستان
traffic sign	عَلامَت ِ راهنمائی		

L E S S O N   T W E N T Y

درس بیست

M O O D ,   C O N T I N U E D

وجهِ التزامی (ادامه)

1) The complete subjunctive, 2) the conditional, 3) the past
tense with باید , 4) generalized modals; drills; dialogue.

---

1) <u>THE COMPLETE ('PERFECT') SUBJUNCTIVE</u>

   a) The <u>complete subjunctive</u> is expressed by the participle
      and the <u>subjunctive</u> of 'be':

رفته باشم	I should/may have gone.
رفته باشی	You should/may have gone.
رفته باشد	He/she should/may have gone.
رفته باشیم	We should/may have gone.
رفته باشید	You should/may have gone.
رفته باشند	They should/may have gone.

Compare the complete subjunctive with the incomplete subjunctive:

باید برود.	He must go.
باید رفته باشد.	He must have gone/be gone.
ممکن است بیاید.	It is possible that he comes.
ممکن است آمده باشد.	It is possible that he has come/ is here.
اُمیدوارم زود بیدار بشود.	I hope he wakes up soon.
امیدوارم بیدار شده باشد.	I hope he has woken up/is awake.

b) **Transitional verbs**

The perfect forms of verbs of change express either the completion of the change or the result of the change (as discussed earlier). Similarly, the subjunctive expresses both, e.g.:

باید آنجا نشسته باشد.	He must <u>have sat down</u> there.
باید آنجا نشسته باشد.	He must <u>be sitting</u> there.
امیدوارم لباس خوبی پوشیده باشد.	I hope he <u>has put on</u> nice clothes.
امیدوارم لباس خوبی پوشیده باشد.	I hope he <u>is wearing</u> nice clothes.

c) **Negation**

The negative precedes the verb form, e.g.:

ممکن است نیامده باشد.	It is possible that he has not come yet.
امیدوارم گم نشده باشد.	I hope it has not gotten lost.

2) THE CONDITIONAL

The subjunctive indicates a (good) possibility; the
conditional indicates a remote possibility, a conjecture
or impossibility. Just as there are two forms of the
subjunctive, there are two forms of the conditional: an
incomplete and a complete conditional. Wishes are among
the typical contexts for the conditional, e.g.:

كا ش ميآ مد .	If only/I wished he came/would come.
كا ش آ مده بود .	If only/I wished he had come/would have come.

(Another typical context is conditional clauses, 'if he would,'
etc., which are discussed in Lesson 27.)

In terms of form (but not of function!), the two conditionals
are identical with forms you already know; compare:

Incomplete

past:	ميآ مد	he was coming/used to come
conditional:	ميآ مد	he would come/if he came

Completed-by

past:	آ مده بود	he had come
conditional:	آ مده بود	he would have come/had he come

In everyday usage, the distinction between incomplete and
complete conditional is not always strictly upheld, i.e.
the incomplete conditional may be used instead of the
complete conditional.

3) <u>THE PAST TENSE WITH</u> باید (cf. p. 235)

باید has two past formations: when <u>assumption</u> is implied, باید is followed by the perfect (complete) subjunctive; when <u>obligation</u> or <u>suggestion</u> is implied, باید is followed by the می -past or the past perfect, e.g:

<u>assumption (past)</u>

باید رسیده باشم .	I must have arrived.
باید رسیده باشی.	You must have arrived.
باید رسیده باشد.	He/she must have arrived.
باید رسیده باشیم .	We must have arrived.
باید رسیده باشید.	You must have arrived.
باید رسیده باشند.	They must have arrived.

<u>obligation or suggestion (past)</u>

باید کار میکردم / کرده بودم .	I had to work <u>or</u> should have worked.
باید کار میکردی / کرده بودی .	You had to work <u>or</u> should have worked.
باید کار میکرد / کرده بود.	He/she had to work <u>or</u> should have worked.
باید کار میکردیم / کرده بودیم .	We had to work <u>or</u> should have worked.
باید کار میکردید / کرده بودید .	You had to work <u>or</u> should have worked.
باید کار میکردند / کرده بودند .	They had to work <u>or</u> should have worked.

Note: In literary Persian میبایست / میبایستی/ بایستی are also used, mainly for 'should/should have'.

4) <u>GENERALIZED MODALS</u>

With باید and میشود whenever the person is <u>not identified</u>

('<u>one</u> has to,' etc.), the verb form is the endingless past

stem; compare:

باید بگویم .	I must say it.
باید <u>گفت</u> .	One must say it/it has to be said.
نمیشود بروم ؟	It is not possible/can't I go?
نمیشود <u>گفت</u> .	One cannot say that!

Similarly, after impersonal modal phrases, the generalized

modality is expressed by the past stem, e.g.:

لازم است این چیز ها را یاد بگیریم .	It is necessary for us to learn these things.
لازم است این چیز ها را یاد <u>گرفت</u> .	It is necessary /one must learn these things.
ممکن است این چیز ها را یاد بگیرید .	It is possible for you to learn these things.
ممکن است این چیز ها را یاد <u>گرفت</u> .	It is possible/one can learn these things.

Note: In literary Persian the same is possible with 'can', میتوان

which then has no ending, e.g.:

میتوان <u>گفت</u> .	it can be said
میتوان <u>تَصَوُّر کرد</u> که ...	one could imagine that...

DRILLS
تمرین

A) Change the following sentences to the subjunctive
according to the pattern:

الان جواد دمِ پنجره نشسته است .

باید الان جواد دم پنجره <u>نشسته باشد</u> .

۱) الان جواد دم پنجره ایستاده است .

۲) بچه راحت خوابیده است .

۳) شَوهرم ریش گذاشته است .

۴) همهٔ خانواده سرِ میز نشسته اند .

۵) یادداشت پشت آقای هالو چُسبیده است .

۶) وکیل ما کلاه گذاشته است .

۷) همه در این سرما پالتو پوشیده اند .

۸) بچه های مدرسه کنارِ بُخاری ایستاده اند .

recently ۹) پدر بزرگ من <u>تازگیها</u> عَیْنَک گذاشته است .

۱۰) مسافرین همه در اتوبوس ایستاده اند .

B) Change the sentences in Drill A above according to
the pattern:

الان جواد دم پنجره ایستاده است .

باید الان جواد دم پنجره <u>ایستاده بود</u> .

C) Use the sentences of Drill A to make wishes according
to the pattern:

غذا برای شام می‌پزد .

⟵ کاش غذا برای شام می‌پُخت (پخته‌بود)

D) Change the following sentences to generalized modals
according to the pattern:

شما میتوانید از اینجا با ماشین عبور کنید .

⟵ از اینجا میشود با ماشین عبور کرد .

or:

شما میتوانید بلیط را از اینجا بخرید .

⟵ بلیط را باید از اینجا خرید .

sentence/easily

۱) این جُمله را میتوانم به آسانی ترجمه کنم .

۲) این بیماری را میتوانم بخوبی معالجه کنم .

۳) این ماشین را میتوانم بخوبی تعمیر کنم .

۴) این آدرس را میتوانید بدون زحمت پیدا کنید .

۵) این در را نمیتوانید به راحتی باز کنید .

۶) این لغت را نمیتوانید به فارسی بگوئید .

۷) این خواهش را نمیتوانید رد کنید .

۸) این نقشه را میتوانید بخوبی بخوانید .

۹) از این بیشتر نمیتوانیم صَبر کنیم .

گفتگو

DIALOGUE

Another example of polite formulae:

A) سلام آقای خطیبی .

B) سلام ، قربان شما ، بفرمائید ، چه عجب ازاین طرفها ؟

A) اختیار دارید ، ما که هرچند وقت یکدفعه مزاحمتان میشویم .
راستی،ایشان آقای نادری از دوستان بسیار با صفای ما هستند.

B) خیلی خوشوقتم .

A) دوست ما آقای نادری عَقَبِ یک خانهٔ خوب و ارزان میگردند . من
به ایشان گفتم با لطف شما یک خانهٔ خیلی خوب میشود پیدا کرد .

B) تقاضا میکنم . خانه برای خریدن یا برای اجاره ؟

C) برای اجاره .

B) عرض کنم حضورتان، این روزها در این محلهٔ خانهٔ اجاره ئی خیلی
کم پیدا میشود.

A) بهر حال آقای خطیبی یک فکری برای دوست ما بکنید که با شما
همسایه بشوند.

B) استدعا میکنم ، باعث افتخار بنده است .

A) یادم میآید چند هفته پیش شما میگفتید یک دوست مکانیک دارید
که میخواهد خانه اش را اجاره بدهد.

B) بله ، غُلامرضا خان را میگوئید . درست است . به من گفت ولی
نمیدانم تا الان اجاره داده است یا نه .

A) ممکن است یک جوری باش تماس بگیرم ؟

B) بله ، اِتِفاقًا شمارهٔ تلفن مغازه اش را به من داده است و
ضرری ندارد به ش یک تلفن بکنیم . اجازه بفرمائید الان به اش
تلفن بکنم .

(ادامه دارد)

thank you ('sacrifice for you')	قُربان ِ شما
what surprise	چه عَجَب
being around here	از این طَرَفها
ever so often, once in a while	هَرْچَند وقت
pleasant, good friend	دوست ِ با صَفا
your kindness	لُطف ِ شما
please ('I beg you')	تقاضا میکنم
rent - for rent	اِجاره ــ اجاره ئی
well ('let me remark')	عَرض کنم
(to) you ('your presence')	(به) حُضورِتان
neighborhood, area	مَحَله
think of something for...	یک فکری ... میکنم
neighbor	هَمْسایه
please ('I implore you')	اِسْتِدْعا میکنم
honoring ('cause of honor')	با عِثراِفْتِخار
I ('your servant')	بَنْده
Mr. ('honorable...')	خان
I <u>mean</u>	... را میگویم
get in contact with	با .. تَماس میگیرم
shop	مَغازه
there's no harm in...	ضَرَری ندارد
let me ('give permission')	اجازه بفرمائید

اختیار دارید ما که که in... is a contrastive particle, difficult to render in English, here approximately 'I beg you, we <u>do</u> come...' (cf. p. 273)

(B) الو ، غلامرضا خان ، سلام عَلَیکُم ، خسته نباشید .

(D) ببخشید ، جنابعالی را بجا نیاوردم .

(B) من خطیبی هستم .

(D) به به ، آقای خطیبی ، حال شما چطور است ؟

(B) از مُحَبَتتان ، شما چطورید ؟

(D) قربان شما ، بد نیستم .

(B) غلامرضا خان تلفن کردم ببینم آن خانه را اجاره داده اید یا نه .

(D) بله هفتهٔ پیش اجاره شد دادم . اتفاقا به برادر خانم اجاره دادم .

(B) بسیار خوب ، بسلامتی . من میخواستم ببینم اگر اجاره نداده اید من
یک مستاجر داشتم . خوبه امری نیست ؟
                    if

(D) خواهش میکنم ، خیلی خوشحال شدم .

how is it going ('don't be tired')	خسته نباشید
you ('your high side')	جنابعالی
recognize	بجا میآورم ...
fine ('for your graciousness')	از مُحَبَتتان
here: my wife's brother	برادر خانم
well ('with health')	بسلامتی
tenant	مستأجر
anything else ('any other order')	امری نیست ؟

LESSON TWENTY-ONE

درس بیست و یک

COORDINATE CLAUSES

جُمْلاتِ هَمْپا یه

1) Coordinate conjunctions, 2) three idiomatic connectives,

3) Coordinating pairs; reading; grammatical review drill; drill;

dialogue

---

1)   COORDINATE CONJUNCTIONS

Series of actions often follow each other without

conjunction, e.g.:

در را باز کرد ، کتاب را   He opened the door, took the
گرفت ، رفت .   book and left.

Note that English here requires 'and' before the final

clause (verb).

a) و 'AND' (/(v)o/ or /va/)

Stressed /va/, or unstressed /(v)o/, are used similar to English

'and', e.g.:

كتاب را باز كرد و شروع كرد   He opened the book and began to
به خواندن .   read.

b) يا 'OR'

كار ميكنى يا وقت دارى ؟   Are you working or do you have
                               time?

وقت دارى يا نه ؟   Do you have time, or not?

c) ولى 'BUT/THOUGH' اما 'HOWEVER'

فِعلا وقت ندارم ، ولى بعدا ميآيم .   I have no time now, but I will come
                                         later/ I will come later, though.

من ميآيم اما اول بايد كار كنم .   I will come; however, first I have
                                         to work.

d) مگر 'UNLESS'

من نميآيم مگر تو هم بيائى .   I will not come, unless you come,
                                   too.

e) زيرا '(THIS IS) BECAUSE, FOR'

دانشگاه تعطيل است زيرا بَرق نيست .   The university is closed for/because
                                          there is no electricity.

f) پس 'THUS, THEREFORE'

نيامد ، پس برويم .   He didn't come, so let's go.

2) <u>THREE 'IDIOMATIC' CONNECTIVES</u>

These connectives are idiomatic to Persian; they do not

have any one particular English equivalent; the nearest

may be 'though.' Note the pause between the clauses.

Try to use them; they will make your Persian more 'native.'

Learn by trial and error.

a) <u>هم</u> 'also,' 'and,' 'though,' etc.

Always attached to the first part of a clause.

استاد وارد شد ، دانشجویان هم مُتَوَجّه نشدند .
The professor came in; and the students didn't notice.

b) <u>که</u> 'though,' 'as for', etc.

Always attached to a noun phrase, usually the first part

of a clause:

تو برو ، من که وقت ندارم .
You go; I, though, have no time/ as for me, I have no time.

c) <u>دیگر</u> 'after all,' 'you know,' 'though,' etc.

Usually after the first part of a clause:

تو برو ، من دیگر خیلی کار دارم .
You go; I have lots of work to do, you know/after all.

In fact, these three can be lined up almost pleonastically

in the following sequence:

من هم که دیگر نرفتم .
And me, I didn't go either, you know.

3) <u>COORDINATING PAIRS</u>

هم – هم / و	both..., ...as well
یا – (و) یا	either...or
نه – نه	neither...nor
چه – چه	whether...or
خواه – خواه	whether...or (literary)

Note that خواه ... خواه and چه ... چه require the subjunctive.

هم درس میخواندهم درس میدهد .	He both studies and teaches.
یا درس میدهد (و) یا درس میخواند .	He either teaches or studies.
نه درس میدهد نه درس میخواند .	He neither teaches nor studies.
چه درس بدهد چه درس بخواند ، در هر صورت کارش خوب است .	Whether he teaches or studies, in both cases he does it well.
خواه سُلطان اراده کند خواه اراده نکند ، وُزیر اِطاعَت نمیکند .	Whether the Sultan wants, or doesn't want it to be done, the vazir will not obey.

منظره‌ای از رامسر

READING   خواندنی

دوسال پیش وقتی که به این کشور آمدم   فصل زمستان بود و هوا هم خیلی

سرد بود . من هم کسی را در اینجا نداشتم و کسی را هم نمیشناختم .   (cf. p. 105)

اول با هواپیما از شهر خودم به لُنْدَن پَرْواز کردم و بعد هم به

نیویورک آمدم . وقتی به فرودگاه نیویورک رسیدم ساعت هشت شب بود .

از آنجا میخواستم به کلمبوس در اُها یو بروم ولی بلیط من برای روز

بعد ساعت یازده و پنج دقیقه   صبح بود . من دیگر مجبور بودم شب را

در نیویررک بمانم و شِنیده بودم شهر نیویورک خیلی خطر ناک است ،

مخصوصا برای آنها که زبان انگلیسی را خوب نمیدانند . بهر حال مجبور

بودم آن شب را در نیویورک بمانم زیرا بلیطم برای روز بعد بود . به

قسمت اطلاعات فرودگاه رفتم . یک دختر خانم نسبتا جوانی آنجا کار

میکرد . از او خواهش کردم یک اطاق برای من در هتلی رزرو کند و او

هم به چند جا تلفن کرد ولی متاسفانه همه جا پر بود . بالاخره بعد از

چند تلفن یک اطاق در هتلی نزدیک فرودگاه برای من پیدا کرد . او گفت

خودِ هتل ماشین دارد که مسافر ها را به آنجا ببرد و فردا صبح هم   (cf. p. 179)

دوباره مسافر ها را از هتل به فُرودْگاه میآورد . از او پرسیدم قیمت

آن اطاق برای یکشب چقدر میشود ، او گفت تقریبا سی و پنج دولار .

خیلی گران بود . او برای چند مسافر دیگر هم در همان هتل اطاق

رزرو کرده بود . چاره ای نداشتم مگر اصلا نخوابم . ماشین هتل بعد از

نیم ساعت همهء ما را به هتل برد ، ولی میدانی بعد چه شد ؟

young lady	دختر خانم
(no اضافه)	
young	جَوان
(like English)	رِزِرْو
take away, carry	میبَرم / بُردم
I had no choice ('way out')	چاره‌ای نداشتم مگر نخوابم
but ('unless') not to sleep	
country	کِشوَر
one, a person	کَس
dangerous	خَطَرْ ناک
those who	آنها که
information	اِطِّلاعات

GRAMMATICAL REVIEW DRILL

For the reading above:

1) Underline the coordinating conjunctions and give the
   approximate English equivalents.

2) Underline the fillers and translate them in their context.

3) Underline the subjunctive phrases (like میخواستم ··· بروم)
   and translate.

4) Underline the remaining verb forms (نمیشناختم/ آمدم)
   and explain their use (why می , why not می , etc.) by
   referring to the discussion in the earlier lessons.

5) Underline the occurrences of را and indefinite ی and
   explain their use by referring to the discussion in
   earlier lessons.

<u>DRILL</u>   تمرین

1) Complete the following sentences with the appropriate

   coordinators (pp. 272-274) and then translate into English:

۱) امروز دو تا کلاس دارم ــــ فردا یک کلاس بیشتر ندارم .

۲) دیروز کتابم را روی میز گذاشتم ، مدادم را ــــ همانجا گذاشتم .

۳) لطفا یک کمی تو رانندگی بکن ،من ــــ خیلی خسته شدم .

۴) امروز متاسفانه وقت ندارم ــــ فردا حتما میآیم .

۵) جواد ــــ درس میخواند ــــ کار میکند .

۶) ماه آینده دانشگاه تعطیل میشود ــــ ترم تمام میشود .

۷) من نمیآیم ــــ او هم با دوستش بیاید .

۸) آیا دوست داری برای شام به رستوران برویم ــــ همینجا در منزل بمانیم؟

۹) دیشب به او تلفن کردم ــــ گفتم حتما بیاید .

۱۰) من خوشبختانه فردا ــــ کلاس دارم ــــ کار میکنم .

villager   دهاتی

sheep/landlord/gift   دهاتی یک گوسْفَنْد برای اَرْبابش هَدیه آورد

order/donkey   و ارباب دَسْتور داد اُلاغی در عَوَض به او بدهند .

simply   دهاتی با سادگی گفت : ارباب جان، اختیار دارید،

worth   شما خودتان برای ما صدتا الاغ بیشتر اَرْزِش دارید .

DIALOGUE

گفتگو

In the carpet store:

در قالی فروشی :

A) سلام

B) سلام آقایان ، بفرمائید . چه‌فرمایشی داشتید ؟

A) ایشان دوست آمریکائی من آقای دکتر میلر هستند . مثل اینکه
دیروز هم برای دیدن فرش های شما اینجا آمده بودند .

B) بله ، میشناسمشان ، سلام حال شما چطور است ؟

C) مرسی ، شما چطورید ؟

B) الحمدالله . شکر . بفرمائید چه نوع قالی میخواستید ؟ این
کرمانی است ، آن اصفهانهاست ،آن یکی قَشْقائیست وا ینهم تبریزی است

A) من از آن اصفهانی خیلی خوشم میآید . شما از کدام خوشتان میآید ؟

C) چه بگویم آنقدر اینجا فرش و قالیاست که آدَم گیج میشود . به نظر
من آن‌ها ولی قشنگ است .

A) گفتید کرمانی است ؟

B) نه خیر ، اصفهانی است . آن وسطی کرمانی است .

C) به نظر من از همه قشنگ تر است .

B) درست است . ولی گرانتر هم هست . هرچه قشنگ تر گرانتر .

A) مثل اینکه بافتش هم خیلی ریز است .

B) درست است . معمولا این نوع قالیهای اصفهانی خیلی ریز بافتند .

(ادامه دارد)

gets dizzy   گیج میشوم / شدم

the one in the
middle   وَسَطی

weft   بافْت

ریز   fine (structure, consistency)

چه فَرْمایِشی داشتید ؟   may I help you? (what order would you have?)

فَرْش ، قالی   carpet

شُکْر   thanks (to God)

نَوع (اضافه no)   kind of

C) من شنیده بودم قالی های کاشانی پر ارزش تر و گرانتر هستند .

B) وُالله ، ارزش قالی بستگی به طرح و رنگ و بافت قالی دارد . فرق نمیکند مال کجا باشد . مثلا آنرا ببینید، کاشانی است .

C) این یکی ؟

B) نه ، آن دومی ــ آن طرفتر .

C) این را میگوئید ؟

B) نه ، یکی زیر تر از آن . ببینید حاشیه اش خیلی باریک است . با اینکه کاشانی است ولی طرحش زیاد جالب نیست .

A) آقای میلر، آنرا ببینید خیلی قشنگ است .

B) آن قالی کار مشهد است . بافتش خیلی ریز است و خوش رنگ هم هست .

C) پشمی است یا ابریشمی ؟

B) پشمی است . اگر این قالی ابریشمی بود قیمتش سه برابر قیمت فعلیش میشد .

C) بسیار خوب ، قیمتش چند است ؟

B) ۱۰٬۰۰۰ تومان .

A) یک کمی به دوست ما تخفیف بدهید .

B) بسیار خوب . صد تومان هم برای شما تخفیف .

C) خیلی گران است .

B) بسیار خوب دویست تومانش را هم ندهید .

narrow	باریک
although	با اینکه
(of) wool	پَشْمی
(of) silk	اَبْریشُمی
three times as much	سه بَرابَر
present	فِعْلی
reduction	تَخْفیف
valuable	پُر اَرْزِش
depends on	بَسْتِگی دارد به
pattern	طَرْح
difference	فَرْق
further over there	آن طَرَفْتَر
margin	حاشِیِه

L E S S O N   T W E N T Y - T W O

درس بیست و دو

T H E   R E L A T I V E   C L A U S E

جُمْلهٔ وَصْفی

1) Restrictive and non-restrictive clauses, 2) pronouns and
names, 3) sequence of suffixes, 4) the repetitions,
5) generalized relative clauses, 6) playing with the verb
forms, 7) focusing; drills.

---

1) RESTRICTIVE AND NON-RESTRICTIVE CLAUSES

a) Relative clauses are generally introduced by که
   (basically 'that'), e.g.:

تهران (که بزرگترین شهر ایران است) ، خیلی شلوغ است .	Tehran, which is the largest city in Iran, is a busy city.
من (که وقت ندارم) ، باید آنجا بروم .	I, who have no time, must go there?
خاویار (که در ایران و شَوَرَوی به فُروش میرسد) ، خیلی گران است .	Caviar, which is sold by Iran and the U.S.S.R., is very expensive.

281

In all the examples above, the relative clause (put in brackets here) in English as well as in Persian is set off by pauses. These are <u>non-restrictive</u> clauses which describe and give information, or some after-thought or emphasis ('as you know, I may add, as you mentioned'). The non-restrictive relative clause may also follow an indefinite noun with indefinite ی , e.g.:

یک دختری (که خیلی خوشگِل بود)، وارد شد .	A/some girl, who was very pretty, came in.
با یک پیرزنی (که جادوگربود)، روبرو شدِ	He met a/some old woman, who was a witch.

b) Many relative clauses, however, are not non-restrictive, but 'restrictive': they <u>select</u> persons or things <u>from among others</u>, e.g. compare:

<u>Non-restrictive</u>

خاویار(که در ایران و شوروی به فروش میرسد)، خیلی گران است .	Caviar, which is sold by the U.S.S.R. and Iran, is expensive.

<u>Restrictive</u>

خاویار(ی که در شوروی به فروش میرسد)، گران است .	(That) caviar which is sold by the U.S.S.R. is expensive. (<u>not caviar sold elsewhere</u>)

Non-restrictive

دختر (که خیلی زیبا بود)،   The girl, who was very beautiful,
وارد شد.   entered.

Restrictive

دختر(ی که خیلی زیبا بود)،   The girl who was very beautiful
وارد شد.   entered (<u>not the other one</u>).

Thus, the formal sign of a restricted relative clause

is ی . The function of ی here is different from

the ی of an indefinite noun phrase. Compare:

دختر (که خیلی خوشکل   The girl, who was very pretty,
بود)، وارد شد.   entered.

دختر(ی که خیلی زیبا بود)   The (that) girl who was pretty
وارد شد.   entered.

یک دختری (که خیلی خوشکل   A/some girl (ی), who was very
بود) وارد شد.   pretty, entered.

Thus:

non-restrictive (with pause): که (or ی که)

restrictive (no pause) : ی که

(For the orthography of ی after vowels, see p. 344.)

2) <u>PRONOUNS AND NAMES</u>

As mentioned above (Lesson 9), ی <u>selects</u> an item
or items from among others. Pronouns and names refer to
individuals; thus the relative clause, after these,
should be only non-restrictive, since one can only
select from more than one. Thus, no ی after pronouns
and names. Yet occasionally even individuals may be
made 'more than one.' Such instances clearly illustrate
the selective function of ی and the restrictive relative
clause; e.g.:

<u>تهران که</u> پایْتَخُْترایران است .

Tehran, which is the capital of Iran.

<u>تهرانی که</u> میشناختم .

The (that) Tehran which I knew (not the one I see now).

<u>آنها که</u> دوستمان هستند .

They, who are our friends.

<u>آنهائیکه</u> دوستمان هستند .

Those who are our friends (not the other ones).

Note: ی after plural ها is written هائی ; e.g.:

<u>کتابهائی که</u> دارم .

The books I have.

<u>مهمانهائیکه</u> دیشب داشتیم .

The guests we had last night.

3) <u>SEQUENCE OF SUFFIXES</u>: ی را که

As mentioned above, the basic sequence of nominal affixes is:

را	ئی	ها	noun
را	personal suffix	ها	noun

The same sequence is followed with relative clauses:

که	را	ئی	ها	noun
که	را	suffix	ها	noun

i.e. when the 'head' - noun of a relative clause is
itself a specific direct object it takes را which
follows the entire noun phrase including ی , e.g.:

کتاب را پیدا کردم .   I found the book.

کتابی را (که پارسال گم
کرده بودم) پیدا کردم .   I found the book which I had lost last year.

کتابهائی را (که پارسال
گم کرده بودم) پیدا کردم .   I found the books which I had lost last year.

There is no ی after personal suffixes. With restrictive
relative clauses the head noun phrase is instead expressed
by آن یکی از

compare:

دوستان که همین الان رفت ...   Your friend, who just left...

آن یکی از دوستهایتان که
همین الان رفت .   <u>That friend (of yours) who</u> just
left (not the other one).

4) <u>THE REPETITIONS</u>

The که in Persian does not mean 'who(m)' or 'which'; it is
a <u>dummy</u>, something like 'that.' Have you noticed Persians
speaking English say:

> The man <u>that</u> I got the book
> from <u>him</u>.

> The man <u>that</u> I talked to <u>him</u>.

That's how to do it in Persian (and in substandard American
English). A pronoun referring back to the noun thus has to
be in the relative clause, e.g.;

a) <u>Prepositions and 'whom'</u>:

مردی که با او صحبت کردی /
حرف زدی

The man that you talked <u>with</u>
(<u>him</u>) = the man <u>with whom</u> you
talked.

مردی که از او کتاب گرفتی .

The man that you got the book
<u>from</u> (<u>him</u>) - the man <u>from whom</u>
you got the book.

مردی که برای او بلیط خریدی .

The man that you bought a ticket
<u>for</u> (<u>him</u>) - the man <u>for whom</u>
you bought a ticket.

مردی که <u>به او</u> پول دادی .

The man that you gave money
<u>to (him)</u> = the man <u>to whom</u>
you gave money.

دختری که <u>پدرش</u>دیروز اینجا آمد .

The girl <u>that her father</u> =
<u>whose</u> father came here yesterday.

b) <u>Who is/whom you</u>:

However, when 'who' is subject and 'whom' is direct object,

<u>no repetition</u> is required, although one could do so, e.g.:

دختری که (او) دیروز آمد .

The girl <u>who</u> came yesterday.

دختری که (اورا) دیروز دیدی .

The girl <u>whom</u> you saw yesterday.

<u>Summary</u>:

a) Use ی when the relative clause is restrictive.

b) <u>No</u> repetition when <u>who(m)</u> is subject or direct
object of the relative clause.

c) Obligatory repetition elsewhere (with prepositions
'for/with/from' etc.)

دختری که برایاو / با او / از او / پدرش / بزرگترشان

5) <u>PLAYING WITH THE VERB FORMS</u>

Similar to other subordinate clauses, the verb forms

in relative clauses, besides indicating a fact, may

indicate a possibility or suggestion. Note the following

subjunctives:

اینجا کسی نیست که <u>کار بکند</u> .

There is no one here <u>to work</u>.

ماشینی میخواهم کهِ گران <u>نباشد</u> .

I want a car that <u>(hopefully)
is not</u> expensive.

قالی هرچه پر ارزشتر <u>باشد</u> ،
گرانتر است .

The more valuable a carpet <u>is
(may be)</u>, the more expensive it is.

6) <u>FOCUSING ('SUCH A...WHO')</u>

Focusing on the head-noun ('such a...who') is marked by

moving the relative clause into final position:

حسن همان معلمی است که دیروز
<u>اینجا بود</u> .

Hassan is the same teacher
<u>who was here yesterday</u>.

من کسی را میشناسم که <u>میتواند
آنرا ترجمه کند</u> .

I know someone (such one) <u>who
can translate it</u>.

کارهائی پیش آمده که <u>لازم است
فورا انجام بدهم</u> .

Some (such) work has come up
<u>that I have to do immediately</u>.

7) <u>GENERALIZED RELATIVE CLAUSES - 'EVER'</u>

Generalized relative clauses are <u>not</u> introduced by که ,

and ی is optional. The equivalent of 'ever' is هر .

Compare the following pairs of generalized and

restrictive clauses:

<u>هرکس (ی)</u> معلم بوده .   <u>Whoever</u> has been a teacher.

هر <u>کسی که</u> معلم بوده .   <u>Anyone who</u> has been a teacher.

هرجا <u>(ئی)</u> راحت هست ، بمان.   <u>Wherever</u> it is comfortable, stay.

هرجائی <u>که</u> راحت هست ،بمان .   Stay at <u>any place</u> that is comfortable.

هر <u>کار (ی)</u> آسان است .   <u>Whatever</u> is easy to do.

هر <u>کاری که</u> آسان است .   <u>Anything that</u> is easy to do.

Most frequently, generalized clauses are introduced by:

person:	هر کس (ی) / هر که	whoever
thing:	هر چیز (ی) / هرچه	whatever
place:	هر جا (ئی)	wherever
time:	هر وقت (ی)	whenever
manner:	هر طور (ی)	however
(degree:	هرچه	however, the more)

DRILLS

Isolated sentences with relative clauses in drills like these are often odd without a larger context. Thus try to imagine a context where the sentence may be said.

A) Translate the following sentences:

۱) ماشینی که دیروز جلوی دانشگاه دیدیم خیلی قشنگ بود.

۲) پسری که کتابش اینجا روی‌میز است دانشجوی سال دوم فلسفه است.

۳) معلمی که به ما فارسی درس میدهد آمریکائی است.

۴) پیراهنی که دیروز خریدی کمی بزرگ است.

۵) شیراز که در جنوب ایران است یکی از شهر های بزرگ است.

۶) کارمندی که ازش سوال کردی اصلا بی اِطلاع بود.

۷) چیزی که از همه برای من جالب‌تر بود کتابی بود که دوستِ دخترم به من داد.

۸) معلوم است که باید خواندنیهائی را که نسبتا دراز است پیش از کلاس یکبار بخوانیم.

B) Re-read the readings in previous lessons. Collect at least 5 relative clauses.

C) Write a composition (a letter):

Before you came to Iran, you decided to study Persian at/with.... While you studied, you studied hard. From the time you started studying until now you have finished twenty-two lessons. It is only five months now that you have been studying. Since you have vacation now, and some time, write a letter in Persian for the first time. As soon as you finish the class, you'll go to Iran.

D) Complete these sentences and translate:

  a) 1. That girl who just left is Iranian.

       2. The carpet dealer who sold you the carpet....

       3. That man who gave you the ticket....

       4. The man who works a lot....

       5. The car which works....

       6. The beautiful girl who just left...

  b) 1. The carpet (which) you bought....

       2. The lessons (which) we read....

       3. The man (whom) you saw....

       4. The sentences (which) you translated....

       5. This friend whom you like....

       6. The big carpet which you bought....

  c) 1. The students whom you gave the ticket....

       2. The man   whom you telephoned....

       3. The person (شَخْــص) to whom you said (it).

  d) 1. The girl with whom you went to the movies....

       2. The men for whom you bought the tickets....

       3. The man from whom you took the tickets....

       4. The doctor <u>to</u> whom you go (Careful!)

       5. The beautiful girl with whom you went to the movies....

  e) 1. The student whose parents were here yesterday.

       2. This carpet the price of which (Careful!) I don't know.

E) LISTEN TO THE READING ON THE TAPE.

کعبهٔ زردشت در نقش رستم

درس بیست و سه

SUBORDINATE CLAUSES

جمله های فرعی

ADVERBIAL CLAUSES

جمله های قیدی

1) Some basic observations, sequence and tenses, 2) چون

3) وقتی 4) other temporal conjunctions; drills.

---

1) **SOME BASIC OBSERVATIONS**

   a) There are only four basic conjunctions: چون 'because,'

     وقتی 'when,' اَگَر 'if,' تا 'until, as long

     as,' etc.

چون من پول ندارم نمیروم .	Since I have no money, I won't go.
وقتی من پول ندارم نمیروم .	When I have no money, I won't go.
اگر من پول ندارم نمیروم .	If I have no money, I won't go.
تا من پول ندارم نمیروم .	As long as I have no money, I won't go.

b) <u>The dummy</u> که

If the context is clear enough, there is an even simpler
way: the 'dummy' که . که is a 'dummy' and jack-of-all-
trades. که is inserted <u>after the first part</u> of the
clause, e.g.:

من که پول ندارم نمیروم.   Since/when/as long as/if I have
no money I won't go.

c) <u>Sequence and tenses</u>

   <u>Sequence of clauses</u>

   As a <u>general</u> rule in Persian, adverbial clauses that
   describe actions which logically or temporally precede the
   action of the main clause precede the main clause, whereas
   in English one has more of a choice:

وقتی وارد اطاق شدی ترا ندیدم.   When you entered the room
I didn't see you.
Or: <u>I didn't see you</u>.
when you entered the room.

d) <u>Use of Tenses</u>

Whether the tense of the adverbial clause is indicative or
subjunctive depends on whether it describes a fact or a
possibility/suggestion. Thus cause is usually a fact that
causes something, while condition indicated by اگر 'if' is
often a possibility which may result in something.

2) 'BECAUSE' چون

Cause is generally stated as a fact; thus the verb forms

are in the indicative, e.g.:

چون کار میکنم ، نمیتوانم بیایم . Because I <u>work</u>, I cannot come.

چون هنوزنرسیده است ،بایدبمانیم . Because he <u>has not arrived</u> yet, we must stay.

3) 'WHEN' وقتی

Time varies, and the view of the action varies; it may be

a fact or a possibility, e.g.:

<u>Fact</u>

اووقتی کار میکندخیلی جدی میشود . When he <u>works</u>, he becomes very serious.

وقتی آمد همه رفته بودند . When he <u>came</u>, all had left.

<u>Possibility</u>

وقتی بیاید ما رفته ایم . When he <u>should come/comes</u>, we will be gone.

<u>'When = as soon as, once'</u>

وقتی آمد به او بگو . When he <u>comes</u>, tell him I am here.

وقتی تمام کردی به من تلفن کن . When you <u>finish/have finished</u>, call me.

Here the forms آمد and تمام کرد are the just-completed

form of the verb: 'tell him, as soon as/once he's arrived,'

and 'once he has finished.' The main action presupposes the

completion of the action preceding it.

4) OTHER TEMPORAL CONJUNCTIONS

While there are only four simple conjunctions, there are
a host of conjunctional phrases. This may be illustrated
with conjunctional phrases relating to time, which are
the most numerous. Note that most conjunctional phrases
must have کﻪ :

phrasal conjunctions

a) / ——ی کﻪ / with nouns of time and or prepositions, e. g.:

وقتی کﻪ   at the <u>time</u> that --- when

مٌوﻗﻌﯽ کﻪ   at the <u>moment</u> the --- when

از وقتی کﻪ   from the time that --- since

از موﻗﻌﯽ کﻪ   from the moment that --- since

تا وقتی کﻪ   until the time that --- until, as long as

تا موﻗﻌﯽ کﻪ   until the moment that --- until

b) / اﯾﻦ کﻪ – / with prepositional phrases

پس از اﯾنکﻪ   after this that --- after

قبل از اﯾنکﻪ
پیش از اﯾنکﻪ   before this that --- before

c) <u>Some others</u>

هر وقت که   each time that = whenever, as soon as

هر گاه که   each point in time that = whenever, as soon as

همین که   the very same (time) that = just as

Note: قبل از اینکه / پیش از اینکه   'before'
require the subjunctive since the action has not
happened yet and is not a fact yet when the other
main action happens; for example, in the sentence:

پیش از اینکه بروی به من تلفن کن .   Before you <u>leave</u>, call me,

the leaving has not happened yet at the time of
calling.

DRILLS   تمرین

A)   Translate the following sentences into English:

hit against
۱) چون چراغ روشن نبود و اطاق تاریک بود پایم به میز خورد .

۲) پَرَستار قبل از اینکه آرنج دستم را پانسمان بکند مرا آمپول زد .

۳) بعد از اینکه دکتر گَلویم را معاینه کرد به من چند تا قرص داد .

۴) وقتی شوفاژ خراب شد ما مجبور شدیم پالتو بپوشیم .

۵) قبل از اینکه حمام بروید این حَوله تازه را با خودتان ببرید .

water/cool
۶) متاسفانه یخچال که کار نکند ما آبِ خُنَک نداریم .

۷) چون که هفتهٔ آینده خیلی مهمان داریم مجبوریم فردا بشقاب و

چنگال و کارد و لیوان اضافی بخریم .

۸) وقتی بخاری کار بکند میتوانیم به اطاق نشیمن برویم .

۹) وقتی آب کتری گرم شد لطفا دوتا چای برای ما درست کن .

۱۰) وقتی که بَرق آمد شام را حاضر میکنم .

B)   Fill in the blanks with the appropriate conjunction:

۱) ـــــ مرا دید از اطاق خارج شد .

۲) ـــــ برود باید برای او لباس نو بخرم .

۳) ـــــ ماشین خراب است مجبورم پیاده به دانشگاه بروم .

۴) ـــــ تلفن کرد فورا پیش او رفتم .

۵) ـــــ خیلی خسته هستم بهتر است زودتر بخوابم .

۶) ـــــ به کلاس رسیدم معلم درس را شروع کرده بود .

۷) —— به کتابخانه بروم با جواد میروم.

۸) —— رسیدیم آنها رفته بودند.

۹) —— فردا کتابخانه تعطیل است من نمیتوانم به آنجا بروم.

۱۰) —— همسایهٔ ما با مشت به دیوار زد مجبور شدیم صدای رادیو را
یواش کنیم.

C) Fill in the blanks with the proper tenses:

(was singing,
were sitting)
۱) موقعی که آواز —— همهکا ملا ساکت ——.

(not arrive,
live)
amount
۲) تا وقتی که برایم پول —— مجبورم با همین مِقْدار
پول ——.

(they invite,
go)
try
۳) هروقت شما را به مهمانی —— سَعی کنید سروقت ——.

(got, started)
۴) همین که هوا روشن —— ما حَرَکَت ——.

(got, have
not seen)
times
۵) از موقعی که با او آشنا —— تابحال او را سه مَرْتَبه
بیشتر ——.

(come,
standing)
stairs
۶) همین که از پلِکان پائین —— او را دیدم کنار در ——.

(set out,
close)
۷) قبل از اینکه راه —— بهتر است پنجره را ——.

(go, take)
۸) هروقت برای خرید قالی به بازار —— حتما یک دوست
ایرانی همراه ——.

(has left,
have)
۹) از وقتی که از اینجا —— از او اصلا خبری نه ——.

(get, buy)
additional
۱۰) قبل از اینکه باطری های این ضَبْطِ صَوْت ضَعیف ——
بهتر است چندتا باطری اِضافی ——.

D) Translate the following sentences into Persian:

1) When she comes, tell her I want to see her.

2) As soon as he came, he went to the bathroom.

3) When I got home, it was very dark.

4) Since I am very busy, I cannot come to your house.

5) Talk to him before he leaves.

E) LISTEN TO THE READING ON THE TAPE.

زندگی بعضی قبیله‌های امروزی نمونهٔ تکامل‌یافتهٔ زندگی چادرنشینان پیش از تاریخ است

LESSON TWENTY-FOUR

درس بیست و چهــار

ADVERBIAL CLAUSES (CONTINUED)

جمله های قَیْدی (ادامـــــه)

1) Some conjunctional phrases, 2) focused form of conjunctional phrases,

3) the 'complete' form after conjunctions; drills; reading.

---

1) SOME CONJUNCTIONAL PHRASES

Some fairly frequent conjunctional phrases are:

برای اینکه	because (for this, that)
به عِلَتِ اینکه	because (the reason of this, that)
گُذَشته از اینکه	besides the fact (passing by this)
غَیْرِ از اینکه	besides (except for this)
به عُلاوهِ اینکه	besides (in addition to)
همینطور که	as, while (in this way)
طوری که	as, the way in which

برای اینکه پول ندارم، به ایران نمیروم.

Because I have no money?
will not go to Iran.

گذشته از اینکه خوب میخواند، نوشتنش هم خیلی خوب است.

Besides the fact that she reads
well, her writing is also very good.

با وجود اینکه ایرانی نیست، از تلفظش معلوم نیست آیا ایرانی است یا نه.

Although he is not Iranian it is not
evident from his pronunciation whether
he is Iranian or not.

Some conjunctional phrases imply that the action or situation
is not a fact or did not take place (yet). These always
require the <u>subjunctive</u>; they are:

قبل / پیش از اینکه <u>برود</u>.

1) before he left/leaving (cf. p.297)

بدونِ اینکه <u>حرف بزند</u>.

2) without <u>saying a word</u>

بجای / در عَوَضِ اینکه <u>تلفن کند</u>.

3) instead of <u>calling by phone</u>

A number of these conjunctional phrases are derived from
adverbs. In English, adverbs may function as conjunctions
unchanged, but in Persian, adverbs introducing <u>full sentences</u>
<u>require</u> اینکه , e.g.:

بعد از ناهار

<u>after</u> lunch

بعد از اینکه ناهار خورد

<u>after</u> (this, that) he ate/lunch
<u>having lunch</u>

بدونِ خداحافظی

<u>without</u> good-bye

بدونِ اینکه خداحافظی کند

<u>without</u> (this, that) <u>saying</u>
good-bye

These two examples also show that in many cases English

uses the participle here: <u>after having</u> - <u>without saying</u>.

In Persian, the conjunctional phrase with اینکه is required

<u>and</u> a full verb form, as in the examples above.

بعد از اینکه <u>خورد</u>   after he ate

بدون اینکه <u>بخورد</u>   without that he ate/eating

It is possible to use the verbal noun (but avoid such at this stage), e.g.:

بعد از <u>خوردنِ</u> شام   after eating dinner

بدونِ <u>خوردن</u>   without eating

2) <u>FOCUSED FORM OF CONJUNCTIONAL PHRASES (FOR INFORMATION ONLY)</u>

With conjunctional phrases, it is possible to emphasize and

focus on the reason, the time, etc. (Similar to focused relative

clauses, cf. p. 289).

Focus on the noun is indicated by the fact that the

subordinate clause is final position. In this case, که

is obligatory, e.g.:

موقعی که رسید هیچکس نبود.	When he arrived, no one was there.
موقعی رسید که هیچکس نبود.	He arrived at a moment when no one was there.
طوری که گفت درست نبود.	The way he said it was not correct.
طوری گفت که درست نبود.	He said it in a way which is not correct.
برای اینکه اصلا دوستش ندارم نیامدم.	Because I simply don't like him I didn't come.
برای این نیامدم که اصلا دوستش ندارم.	I didn't come because I simply don't like him.

3) **THE 'COMPLETE' FORM AFTER CONJUNCTIONS**

As mentioned in Lesson 16   above, forms like آمد

express a complete action either present or past:

a) he arrived (just then), b) he has just arrived,

is here (now).

 This same form is used in subordinate clauses to express

an action that is complete and a given fact at the time

another action follows,and has the connotation of 'as

soon as' or 'once.'

In these cases, the verb is usually the equivalent of an

English <u>present</u> (cf. p. 205), e.g.:

وقتی آمد بهاش بگو بیا ید .	When he <u>comes</u> (as soon as he has arrived), tell him to come here.
وقتی آمد میتوانیم از خودش بپرسیم .	When he <u>comes</u> (as soon as he has arrived), we can ask himself.
وقتی آمد عمل میکنیم .	As soon as he <u>comes</u>, we'll operate.
اگر نیامد تلگرام بفرست .	If he <u>doesn't arrive</u> by then, send a telegram.
اگر نبود برگرد اینجا .	If he <u>is</u> not there, come back.
اگر نداشتند برو کتابخانه .	If they <u>don't have</u> it, go directly to the library.
همینکه آمد به فرودگاه میرویم .	As soon as he <u>comes</u>, we'll leave for the airport.

DRILLS   تمرین

A) Select conjunctions and conjunctional phrases for the following

  sentences. In most cases there are several possibilities.

۱) ــــ ــــ من ــــ دید از اطاق بیرون رفت .

۲) ــــ ــــ برود باید برایش این لباس را بخرم .

۳) ــــ ــــ او ــــ دیدی بگو من اینجا منتظرش هستم .

۴) ــــ ــــ تلفن ــــ فوراً پیش او رفتم .

۵) ــــ ــــ دیر برسیم جا ــــ ــــ برای نشستن پیدا نمیکنیم .

۶) ــــ ــــ به موقع برسد باید ــــ ــــ او بگویم امتحان کی شروع ــــ شود .

۷) ــــ ــــ نیاید ما اصلاً نمیتوانیم درس ــــ شروع کنیم .

۸) ــــ ــــ ــــ خواهی درس بخوانی به من بگو ــــ مزاحم نشوم .

۹) ــــ ــــ به کتابخانه بروم ــــ ــــ جواد صحبت کردم .

۱۰) ــــ ــــ رسیدم آنها رفته بودند .

B) Fill in the blanks with the appropriate verb forms.

  The verb in the main clause will give you the clue.

۱) اگر او را ــــ لطفا به او بگو بیاید اینجا .

۲) دیروز وقتی به کلاس ــــ معلم درس را شروع کرده بود .

۳) تا به ایستگاه اتوبوس ــــ اتوبوس را افتاد .

۴) اگر ــــ به مهمانی بیائی پس چرا نیامدی ؟

۵) بدون اینکه به من ــــ کتاب مرا برداشت .

۶) پیش از اینکه ــــ لطفا چراغ را روشن کن .

۷) پس از اینکه به منزل ــــ خواهش میکنم بمن تلفن کن .

۸) موقعی که به سینما ــــ فیلم شروع شده بود .

۹) با وجود اینکه آن قالی خیلی گران ــــ ولی آنرا خریدم .

۱۰) اگر وقت ــــ میتوانیم با هم قهوه ای بخوریم .

C) Translate the following sentences:

(Don't forget اینکه and the full verb!)

1) After having dinner in the nice restaurant, we went to the theatre.

2) After getting tired from (از) studying, I decided to go to bed.

3) Without braking, the truck ran the traffic light. (رد شد)

4) Instead of turning right, I turned left.

5) In addition to studying Persian, she also studies Arabic.

6) In spite of seeing the policeman, he did not stop.

7) Because he was very hungry, he went into the nearest sandwich shop. (ساندویچی)

8) As I was driving, I suddenly saw the police behind me.

9) In addition to the fact that the (its) music was very good, the (its) food was not bad either.

10) Before you translate this sentence, read the grammar.

READING خواندنی

مارْگیر

از کتابِ : آینه —— نوشتهٔ : محمد حِجازی

وقتی در کنارِ شهر منزل داشتیم ، روزی در خانه تنها مانده بودم ،
از صندوقخانه صِدائی آمد ، آهسته گوشهٔ پرده را کنار زدم و دیدم
هیولائی مشغولِ اسبابِ جمع کردن است .

بخیالِ اینکه بیصدا از خانه بیرون بروم ، پا برهنه خود را بــــه
ایوان انداختم ، چیزی مهیب‌تر از دزد بچشمم خورد ، بــــی اختیار
فریاد زدم : " آی مار"

همین قدر یادم هست که شنیدم یکی گفت کجاست ؟ آمدم ! دیدم گرفتارِ
دزد و مارم ، زانوهایم لرزید ، افتادم و از حال رفتم .

(ادامه دارد)

veranda	اَیْوان	snake	مار
throw	میاَنْدازم / انداختم	(guess!)	مارگیر
frightful	مُهیب	pantry	صَنْدوقچه
thief	دُزْد	noise, sound	صِدا
'hit my eye'	به چشمِ خورد	corner	گوشه
helplessly	بی اختیار	curtain	پَرْده
shout, scream	فَریاد میزنم/ زدم	lift, pull aside	کنار میزنم
be caught by	گرفتارِ - بودن	monster	هیولا
shake	میلَرْزم /لرزیدم	busy with	مَشْغولِ
(guess!)	ازحال میروم	things	اَسْباب
		gather	جَمْع میکنم
		thinking, intending (subjunctive)	به خیالِ اینکه
		barefoot	پا بَرَهْنه

Note !آمدم (cf. p.203)

فرامرز پایور ـ سنتور   حسین تهرانی ـ تنبک

از مشهورترین هنرمندان موسیقی سنتی ایران

LESSON TWENTY - FIVE

درس بیست و پنـــج

SUBORDINATE CLAUSES

جمله های فَرْعـی

COMPLEMENT CLAUSES

جمله هـای مُتَــمِم

1) Complement clauses with subjunctive, 2) complement clauses with
indicative, 3) indirect questions ; drills; dialogue

---

1) COMPLEMENT CLAUSES WITH SUBJUNCTIVE

Whenever a verb or expression describes a possible or

suggested action, it is followed by a subordinate clause

with the subjunctive; که is optional, e.g.:

امیدوارم (که) زود برگردی .	I hope (that) you return soon.
ممکن است (که) امروز نیایـد .	It is possible that he won't come today.
اجازه دادند (که) درکلاس شرکت کند .	They permitted him to participate in the class.

Some of the verbs and expressions requiring the subjunctive
are:

intending to	به خیال اینکه
it is possible	ممکن است
it is likely	اِحْتِمال دارد
I doubt	شک دارم
it is necessary	لازِم است
I have to	مجبورم
I like to	دوست دارم
I like to, am inclined to	مَیْل دارم
I ask (you) to	خواهش میکنم
I better	بهتر است
am/are supposed to	قَرار است
planning to	در این فکر هستمکه
expect to	منتظرم که
hope that	اُمیدوارم
am afraid that	میترسم
let, allow to	میگذارم
instruct, recommend	سِفارِش میکنم
order	دَسْتور میدهم
forbid	مَمْنوع / قَدَغَن میکنم
allow, permit	اِجازه میدهم
decide	تَصْمیم میگیرم

2) <u>COMPLEMENT CLAUSES WITH INDICATIVE</u>

a) <u>General observations</u>

The verbs and phrases cited above are followed by
subordinate clauses in the subjunctive since they
describe a possibility or suggestion.

There are verbs and expressions which basically
describe a fact. They are, therefore, followed by
subordinate complement clauses in the indicative.
Again after such phrases, که is optional. Some of
these factual phrases are:

it is obvious	معلوم است
it is clear	پیْدا است
it is evident	واضح است
it is apparent	آشْکار است
it is certain, sure	مُسَلَم است
am convinced, certain	مُطْمَئِن هستم/ یَقین دارم
am informed that	اِطلاع دارم
know	میدانم
understand	میفهمم
see	میبینم
hear	میشْنَوم
feel	حِس میکنم
deny	اِنْکار میکنم
confirm	تَصْدیق میکنم

پیداست (که) شاگرد خیلی زرنگی است .

It's clear that he is a very clever student.

یقین دارم (که) فارسی خیلی زود یاد میگیرید .

I am sure that you'll learn Persian very fast.

شنیدم (که) خیابانِ لاله زار را بستند .

I hear that they closed Lalezar Street.

b) **Present of fact**

One point needs special attention. When an action or situation is ongoing or exists, i.e. is a fact, and thus <u>present</u>, at the time of speaking, the tense in the subordinate clause describing the fact remains unchanged and '<u>present</u>' or 'present perfect', if a state is described, irrespective of the tense of the main clause (cf. p. 228); e.g.:

معلوم شد (که) ده نفر هستند .

It became clear that they (<u>are</u>) <u>were</u> ten people.

دیدم (که) حسن نشسته است .

I saw that Hassan (<u>is</u>) <u>was</u> sitting there.

مادرش گفت (که) کار میکند .

His mother said that he (<u>is</u>) <u>was</u> working.

3) <u>INDIRECT QUESTIONS (</u> که <u>OPTIONALLY INTRODUCES QUESTION)</u>

Generally the appropriate question word is used.

Note that the question word occurs where the answer will

occur, e.g.:

میپرسد (که) <u>چرا</u> کار نمیکند. He asks why it does not work.

میخواستم ببینم (که) ماشین I wanted to ask where your car is.
تو <u>کجا</u>ست.

میخواستم ببینم (که) این کار I wanted to ask how you do this.
را <u>چطور</u> میکنی.

میخواستم ببینم (که) <u>چکار</u> کردی. I wanted to ask what you did
today.

ببین (که) <u>چه</u> ماشین خوبی See what a nice car it is.
است.

The question word آیا 'whether,' however, is generally omitted.

میدانی (که) (<u>آیا</u>) امروز میآید؟ Do you know <u>whether</u> he comes today?

DRILLS

تمرین

A) Fill in the blanks with the cues given in parentheses and
translate. Decide whether the indicative or the subjunctive
is required:

(to sit)   ۱) میدانستم که جوادمعمولا پهلوی شما ـــــ .

(to write)   ۲) برای او توضیح دادم که این تمرین ها را ـــــ .

(to come)   ۳) برایش نوشتم که هر چه زودتر اینجا ـــــ .

(to close)   ۴) دیروز شنیدم که اتوبان تهران به کَرَج را ـــــ .

(to be tired)   ۵) حس میکردم که کمی ـــــ .

(to lose)   ۶) همین که ته خیابان رسیدم فهمیدم راه را ـــــ .

(to be closed)   ۷) رادیو خبر داده بود که امروز مدرسه ها ـــــ .

(to show)   ۸) از ایشان خواهش کردم که این آدرس را به من ـــــ .

(to study)   ۹) خیلی دوست دارم که اقتصاد ـــــ .

(to be finished)   ۱۰) ممکن است که بلیط برای امشب ـــــ .

(to meet)   ۱۱) قرار است که سر چهار راه همدیگر را ـــــ .

(to take)   ۱۲) لازم نیست که ماشینتان را به این تعمیرگاه ـــــ .

B) Translate the following sentences into Persian:

1). I did not know where Javad usually sits.

2) I did not explain to him how to write this drill.

3) I did not write him when to come here.

4) I did not hear which road they closed.

5) I understood how you felt.

6) I understood what had happened.

7) The radio did not report when they will close the schools.

8) I asked him how to get there.

9) I like what you like.

10) It is necessary for you to know which question to ask.

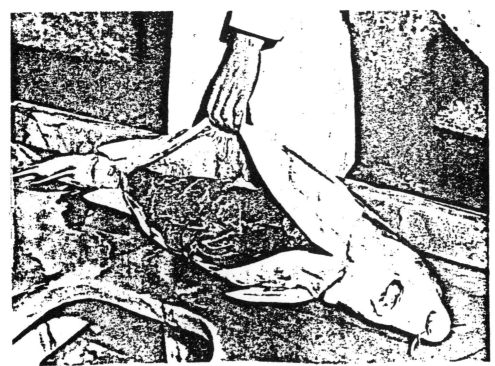

ببینید در شکم
این ماهی خاویار چقدر
تخمهٔ ماهی انباشته شده
است. از این تخمه ها
خاویار تهیه میشود.
خاویار در قوطیهای
بزرگ و کوچک یک
کالای گرانبهاست.

Caviar

DIALOGUE   گفتگو

program   ‫A) امشب تلویزیون چه بَرنامه ای دارد ؟‬

movie   ‫B) درست نمیدانم ولی فکر میکنم فیلم سینمائی داشته باشد .‬

                 ‫A) همین الان ؟‬

news   ‫B) نه ، بعد از اَخبار .‬

sound   ‫A) ممکن است روشنش بکنی ؟ ولی صدایش را کُم کن .‬

                 ‫B) راستی، امروز صبح مُنیژه تلفن کرد .‬

                 ‫A) چی میگفت ؟‬

                 ‫B) هیچی ، میخواست حال مرا بپرسد . گفتم امشب برای شام با شوهرش‬
                 ‫بیایند اینجا .‬

                 ‫A) شوهرش بالاخره کار پیدا کرد؟‬

future,   ‫B) نه ، هنوز بی کار است ولی قرار است از هفتهٔ آیُنده در یک شِرکتی‬
next   ‫کار بکند .‬

                 ‫A) جدی ، کدام شرکت ؟‬

                 ‫B) نپرسیدم .‬

                 ‫A) کِی قرار است بیایند ؟‬

                 ‫B) باید تا یک ساعت دیگر پیدایشان بشود .‬

                 ‫A) برای شام چی درست کردی ؟‬

chicken/   ‫B) دارم خوراکِ مُرغ درست میکنم . یک کمی هم لوْبیا پُلّو درست کردم .‬
rice and beans

                 ‫A) چیزی لازم داری من از بیرون بخرم ؟‬

                 ‫B) نه همه چی خریدم .‬

درس بیست و شش

ADVERBIAL CLAUSES FOLLOWING THE MAIN

CLAUSE

جمله های قَیْدی (بعـــــد از جمـــلهء اَمْلی)

1) زیرا , 2) که , 3) تا 'until,' 4) تا 'so that,' 5) مُگَر ,

6) طوری ... که / آنقدر / ازبُس / چُنان , drills; reading.

---

1) __زیرا '(THIS IS) BECAUSE '__

An explanation __following__ an action or situation is introduced

by زیرا (or چون (که) ، برای اینکه) , e.g.:

بعد دیگر به کلاس برنگشتم زیرا فکر میکردم تعطیل شده بود .	Afterwards I didn't go back to class because I thought it was cancelled.
همه جلوی پمپ بنزین ها صَف کِشیده بودند زیرا میترسیدند بنزین تمام بشود .	Everyone was lined up in front of the gas station because they were afraid the gas would run out.

2) ___ که ___ 'WHEN (ALL OF A SUDDEN)'

An event not preceding but following and interrupting

another action or situation is introduced by که , e.g.:

هنوز به درنرسیده بودم کـه در باز شد .	I hadn't reached the door yet when it opened.
ما داشتیم میرفتیم کـه ناگهان تلفن زنگ زد .	We were about to leave when all of a sudden the phone rang.

3) ___ تا ___ 'UNTIL (A FINAL FACT)'

An action coming to a conclusion after another is introduced

by تا and followed by the preterit, e.g.:

یک ساعت گذشت تا اَحمدنوُکَرم آمد .	The hour passed until (finally) my servant Ahmad came.
در کلاس ماندیم تا درس را تمام کردیم .	We stayed in the class until we had finished the lesson.

4) ___ تا ___ 'SO THAT, IN ORDER TO, UNTIL'

تا describing an objective or goal to be achieved is followed

by the subjunctive. 'So that' may also be expressed by

برای اینکـه , or که , e.g.:

دراز کشیده ام تا / برای اینکه راحت تر بخوابم .	I am lying here so that I can read more at ease.
به او بلیط دادم تا /برای اینکه شکایت نکند .	I gave him a ticket so that he wouldn't complain.
اینجا باش تا / برای اینکه ببینم چه میشود .	Stay here until/so that I see what will happen.

(cf. also lesson 28)

5) ‏مَگَر (اینکه)‏ _____ **'IF NOT, UNLESS'**

An exception made with regard to a preceding action or

situation is introduced by ‏مگر‏ . The verb is generally

in the <u>subjunctive</u>, e.g.:

| ‏ما الان میرویم مگر (اینکه)‏
‏کار دیگری باشد.‏ | We leave now unless there is
something else. |
| ‏بنزین تمام خواهد شد مگر (اینکه)‏
‏کسی یک کاری بکند.‏ | The gas will run out unless
somebody does something. |

6) ‏از بس / آنقدر / طوری ... که‏ _____ **'SO, SUCH...THAT'**

The consequence of an action is expressed by phrases like

e.g.: ‏از بس .... که / آنقدر ... که / طوری ... که,‏

| ‏از بس/ آنقدر/ طوری او را زد‏
‏که افتاد.‏ | He hit him such that he fell. |

With nouns and adjectives, ‏چنان‏ is used, e.g.:

| ‏آن چنان حرفی زد که همه خندیدند.‏ | He said such things that every-
body laughed. |

<u>DRILLS</u>   تمرین

A)   Translate the following sentences into Persian:

1)   I went to Germany to learn German.

2)   We will have a party in the garden unless it rains.

3)   He is coming here in order to see his mother.

4)   I was taking a shower when the water got cold.

5)   This winter it snowed so much that our street was
     blocked (بسته) most of the time.

6)   He sits in the first row so that he hears
     everything well.

7)   I brought you this so that you put it on because
     it is very cold outside.

8)   His/her nose is so long that you don't believe it.

9)   Let's read this together so that we practice the
     (its) pronunciation.

10) I don't agree with it because it takes (میخواهـد)
     a lot of time.

B) Fill in the blanks with مگر (اینکه)، که ، تا ، زیـــــرا

and then translate the sentences into English:

۱) این را هم توضیح میدهم—— برای قسمت بعدی لازم است .

۲) ما داشتیم رانندگی میکردیم—— ناگهان فهمیدیم ماشین پنچر است .

۳) پنج دقیقه بیشتر نگذشته بود—— دیدیم یک کامیون دارد میآید .

۴) یک ساعت گذشت —— ماشینمان درست شد .

۵) مجبوریم امشب اینجا بمانیم—— اینکه کسی بما کمک بکند .

۶) من این روزها رِژیم میگیرم—— لاغر تر بشوم .

۷) آنقدر غذای این رستوران بد بود—— نتوانستیم بخوریم .

۸) لطفا بفرمائید در آن اطاق بنشینید—— آقای دکتر تشریف بیاورند .

۹) ما نمیتوانیم این را به شما بدهیم—— اینکه قبلا مقداری پول بدهید .

۱۰) یک نقشه بخرید—— در شهر گم نشوید .

READING

خواندنی

مارگیر (بقیه)

وقتی به هوش آمدم مثل آن بود که از حوض بیرون آمده باشم ، دزد بالای

سرم نشسته بود و بسر و صورتم آب میزد. گفت :خانم نترس ، خدا مـــرا

فرستاده بود که شما را از دست این مار خلاص کنم ، ببین دستها یم خالی

است ، یک پوش نمیبرم ، ما حق و حساب میدانیم .

چون قوهٔ حرکت نداشتم گفتم:آن کیف را از روی میز بیاور. رفت و آورد.

(cf. p. 177) دہ تومان نشان دادم ، گفت:بخدا، اگر بجای شما مرد بود ،کارش را میساختم .

گفتم به عوض این جوانمردی ، خیر میبینی ، برو، هروقت بی پول شدی،

بیا اینجا .

(ادامه دارد)

account	حِساب	conscience	هوش
power, strength	قُوّه	pool	حَوْض
(guess!)	کارش را میسازم	release	خلاص میکنم
in exchange for	به عَوَضِ	empty	خالی
courage, generosity	جوانّمَرُدی	tiny bit	پوش
be blessed, rewarded	خَیر دیدن	truth	حق

I felt like coming out of a pool	مثل آن بود که ... آمده باشم
God (had) sent me to save you	مرا فرستاده بود که ... خلاص کنم
If instead of you it had been a man, I would have fixed me	اگر به جای شما مرد بود کارش را میساختم
Whenever you run out of money (note شدی)	هر وقت بی پول شدی ...

مار گیر (بقیه)

مار کُشْته را برداشت و گفت:شما که حال ندارید در کوچه را ببندید ،
من بیرون کشیک میکشم تا نوکرتان بیاید ، همهٔ دزد ها که مثلِ من حق و(p.273)
حسابدان نیستند . یک ساعت گذشت تا حسن نوکر آمد ، معلوم شد فراموش
(p.2o9) کرده بوده در را قفل کند . برای اینکه مرا از فحش دادن و فریاد کردن
منصرف کند ، گفت خانم یک مردکه ای آنطرفِ جوب نشسته یک مار دستش است
بقدرِ اژدها .

بعد ها تقریبا هر ماه یکبار دزد جوانمرد میآمد و در میزد ، میگفت:
بخانم عَرْض کنید " مار گیر "است . مبلغی میگرفت و میرفت . اتفاقا یک
روز که آمده بود پول بگیرد،مَجْلِسی دا شتیم ، شوهرم قصه را برای مهمانها
تَعْریف کرد .

guy	مَرْدکه	killed	کُشْته
gutter	جوب	alley	کوچه
dragon	اَژْدِها	guard	کِشیک میکشم/کشیدم
say (polite)	عَرْض میکنم	servant (male)	نَوُکَر
amount (of money)	مَبْلَغ	lock	قُفْل میکنم
get-together, meeting	مَجْلِس	curse	فُحْش دادن
story	قِصه	divert	مُنْصَرَف میکنم از

Notes:

1) compare subjunctive and 'preterit':

کشیک میکشم تا نوکرتان بیاید .

یک ساعت گذشت تا حسن نوکر آمد .

2) note the subjunctives:•• شما که حال ندارید در کوچه را ببندید

فراموش کرده بود در را قفل کند .

برای اینکه مرا ... منصرف کند ...

3) note the habitual past :

هر ماه یکبار میآمد و در میزد و میگفت :

4) note the past perfect, and subjunctive :

یک روز که آمده بود پول بگیرد ...

نوروز

نوروز شد و دوباره دُنیا

شد نرگس و سُنبل و بَنَفشه

نوشد همه جا و خُرَّم و خوش

نوروزِ خُجَسته آمد و باز

رنگین شده دَشت و کوه و صحرا

پُر از گُل و سبزه گشت و زیبا

از آمدنِ بهار پیدا

دارد همهٔ جهان تماشا

« یَمینی شَریف »

world

turned/ beautiful

narcissus/hyacinth/violet

fresh, pleasant

happy, auspicious

درس بیست و هفت

'IF' ، اَگَر

1) Fact, 2) possibility, 3) irreality, counterfactual; drills; reading

---

اگر 'if' describes the conditions, stipulations and
requirements on which an action or situation depends. There
are three different basic types of conditions:

1) FACT

Factual conditions accept a given action or situation as a
fact, and take it from there: 'if this is true, then...'
The verb is in the indicative, e.g.:

اگر مرا دوست‌داری مرا ببوس

If you (really) love me, kiss me.

اگر او را میشناسی مرا به او مُعَرّفی
کن .

If you (really) know him, intro-
duce me to him.

اگر ساعت پنج رفته است تا بحال
رسیده است .

If (it's true that) he has left
at 5, he has arrived by now.

In Persian, verbs which by their nature are often in the indicative are verbs which describe:

1) factual states or situations: ۱) دارد ــ است

2) mental and physical states, e.g.: ۲) میخواهید ــ میتوانید ــ

میدانید ــ میشناسید

3) the result of a change of state, e.g.:

۳) نشسته است ــ خوابیده است ــ ایستاده است

2) POSSIBILITY

Possible conditions describe actions and situations not a fact but quite likely to come about and/or suggested to come about (or not to come about). The verb of the اگر - clause is in the present (incomplete) subjunctive when referring to an event that has not happened yet, and in the perfect (complete) subjunctive when referring to an event that may have happened in the past. The verb of the main clause may be in the present, future, suggestive subjunctive, or imperative. Note that in both cases English uses the <u>indicative</u> present or perfect, e.g.:

اگر برود ، میمیرم .   If he <u>leaves</u>, I'll die.

اگر رفته باشد ، میمیرم .   If <u>he has left</u>, I'll die.

اگر تمرین بکند ، زود یاد میگیرد .   If he <u>works</u>, he'll learn fast.

اگر تمرین کرده باشد در کلاس اول میشود   If <u>he has worked</u>, he'll become the first in his class.

اگر مرا دوست داشته باشی ، مرا میبوسی .   If you <u>like me</u>, you will kiss me.

اگر آنجا <u>باشد</u> به او بگو .   If he <u>is</u> there, tell him.

3) <u>IRREALITY, COUNTERFACTUAL</u>

The irreal condition describes actions and situations which
the speaker sets up and refers to as contrary-to-fact. The
irreal is thus the opposite of the factual conditional.
Both the conditional clause and the main clause are contrary-
to-fact and imply negation of fact.

When referring to an action that has not happened yet the
incomplete irreal is used, which is formally identical with
the incomplete past, i.e. the می -past: (Remember that بود
and داشت do not have می-forms and are thus used for
irreal without می .)

In English, the incomplete irreal is usually expressed by the
past tense in the conditional clause and by 'would' in the
main clause; e.g.:

اگر <u>میرفت</u> ، <u>میمردم</u> .   If he <u>left</u>, I <u>would die</u>.

اگر مرا <u>دوست داشت</u> ، مرا   If he <u>loved</u> me, he <u>would</u> kiss me.
<u>میبوسید</u> .

اگر دوست من <u>بود</u>، <u>نمیرفت</u> .   If he <u>were</u> my friend, he <u>would</u>
<u>not</u> leave me.

(The use of 'were' for 'was' is a last vestige of this mood in
English.)

These sentences imply negation, as mentioned. Thus 'If he left I would die' implies: 'I will not die if he stays'; 'If you loved me, you would kiss me' implies: 'you do not kiss me, so you don't love me'; 'if you were my friend, you would not leave me' implies: 'you are not my friend because you leave me.'

When referring to an action that has already happened, the complete irreal is used, which is formally identical with the past perfect (as in English). Alternatively, the incomplete irreal, i.e. the می past, may also be used, especially in the main clause, e.g.:

اگر رفته بودی / میرفتی ، مُرده بودم / میمُردم .	If you had left, I would have died.
اگر مرا دیده بودی / میدیدی ، مرا بوسیده بودی / میبوسیدی .	If you had seen me, you would have kissed me.
اگر به او گفته بودی / میگفتی ، نرفته بود / نمیرفت .	If you had told him, he would not have left you.

(Note that بود and داشت have no complete irreal forms.)
Compare: the use of the subjunctive vs. the use of the conditional in:

اگر الان بروی سرِ وقت میرسی .	If you go right now you'll get there in time.
اگر الان میرفتی سرِ وقت میرسیدی .	If you went right now you'ld get there in time.

While both imply a possibility, in this context, the subjunctive is more 'positively' assuring, whereas the conditional is more 'hypothetical'.

<u>DRILLS</u>   تمرین

A) Read the following sentences. For each of the three

groups identify which type of   اگر   is used, and then

translate the sentences:

۱) اگر زودتر میآمدی او را میدیدی .

۲) اگر از منشی میپرسیدی او میدانست .

۳) اگر همه‌ٔ پولت را برای خریدن قالی نداده بودی الان میتوانستی

چیزهای دیگری بخری .

۴) اگر من رئیس بودم خوب میدانستم چکار کنم .

۵) اگر لباس گرم پوشیده بودی سرما نمیخوردی .

۶) اگر ماشین را زودتر به تعمیرگاه برده بودی اینطور خراب نمیشد .

---

۱) اگر قبول داشته باشی این کتاب را برای شما میفرستم .

۲) اگر از این خیابان بروید دورتر میشود .

۳) اگر هوا سردتر بشود ماشینم روشن نمیشود .

۴) اگر سیگار نکشید برای <u>سَلامَتی</u> شما بهتر است .   health

۵) اگر اسم رنگها را فراموش کرده باشید بجا است که دوباره یاد بگیرید .

۶) اگر پیراهن شما <u>تَنگ</u> شده باشد معلوم است که چاق شده اید .   tight, narrow

---

۱) اگر این تمرینها برای شما کم است ، لطفا بگوئید .

line, handwriting   ۲) اگر نمیتوانید خَط مرا بخوانید لطفا بگوئید .

۳) اگر نمیخواهید هر روز دیر به کلاس برسید بهتر است کمی زودتر بلند شوید .

۴) اگر آقا تشریف ندارند ، مزاحم نمیشوم .

wind (watch etc.)   ۵) اگر ساعت خوابیده است چرا کوکش نمیکنی ؟

۶) اگر معنی "اگر" را نمیفهمید چرا نمیپرسید ؟

B) Fill in the blanks with the appropriate verb form.

The main verb will give the clue:

۱) اگر زودتر راه افتاده ـــــ به موقع میرسیدی .

۲) اگر خیلی گرمت ـــــ میتوانی پنجره را کمی باز کنی .

۳) اگر از رنگ آبی خوشت نه ـــــ پس چه رنگی را دوست داری ؟

۴) اگر اینجا ایستاده ـــــ حتما با ماشین تَصادُف کرده بودم .

۵) اگر کسی به من تلفن ـــــ لطفا به او بگوئید من در دفتر کارم هستم .

۶) اگر گلویت گرفته ـــــ چرا پیش دکتر نمیروی ؟

۷) اگر شِکَمت درد ـــــ چرا شَرُبَتِ "پپتو بیسمال " نمیخوری ؟

۸) اگر پسر مُؤَدَّبی ـــــ این حرفها را نمیزد .

۹) اگر ماشینت را اینجا پارک ـــــ پلیس آنرا میبرد .

۱۰) اگر الان شروع ـــــ من میروم .

خواندنی

پروانه ها :

نوشتهٔ غُلامْحُسَیْن نَظَری ، ۱۳۴۴ ، (مَجَلّهٔ سُخَن ، جِلدِ پانزدهم ، صَفْحهٔ ۶۷۰)

غافلگیرشان کردم، وارد اطاقی که شدم ، سه تائی نشسته بودند دَوْرِ

کرسی . مادرم از جا پَرید و شاخه های خشک دستهایش را از هم گشود. دوباره

دیدم همان کودک بی پناه و از مدرسه گریخته‌ای هستم که به آغوشش پناه

میبرد. به خودم گفتم :" مرد، تو دیگه بزرگ شده‌ی" ولی من هیچوقت بزرگ

نخواهم شد، هرگز بزرگ نخواهمشد .

با برادرم و خواهرم دست دادم و پیشانی هاشان را بوسیدم و نشستیم.

مادرم چشم از صورتم بر نمیداشت :

" خوب تعریف کن ببینم ."

آب دهانم را فرو دادم : " بگو ببینم ، این دوسال کجا ها بودی.

چه کار ها کردی ؟"

"هیچی."

"خسته ای ؟" جواب ندادم . برادرم نشسته بود روبرویم . پشتِ لبهایش

سیاهی میزد و چشمهایش .... اِنگار چشمهایش را ترسانده بودند. از او

پرسیدم : " تو چکار میکنی ؟"

"هیچی ."

به خواهرم چیزی نگفتم . فقط به یکدیگر نِگاه کردیم ، هر دو ساکت

مثل دو تا عاشق نا امید ، فقط به یکدیگر نگاه کردیم .

(ادامه دارد)

پَرْوانه   moth, butterfly

غافِلْگیر میکنم   take by surprise

all three together (stressed ی)	سه تائی
around	دَوْر
(see note)	کُرْسی
twig, branch	شاخه
dry	خُشْک
open wide	از هم میگُشایم / گُشودم
child	کودَک
without protection	بی پُناه
fled, escaped	گُریْخْته
hug	آغوش میکِشم
pick up	بر میدارم
swallow	فُرو میدهم
show first signs of a beard	سیاهی میزند
it was as if	اِنْگار
frighten	میترسانم / ترساندم
lover	عاشِق
hopeless	نا اُمید

NOTE

کرسی : stool-like frame of wood covered with blankets under
which a fire is placed for heating legs in winter.

Note the complex sentence:

دوباره دیدم	Again I saw
که همان کودکِ	that I was that same child,
بی پناه و (ازمدرسه گریخته) ای هستم	without protection and escaped from school
که بهآغوشش پناه میبرد.	which was seeking protection in her arms.

L E S S O N   T W E N T Y - E I G H T

درس بیست وهـــشت

S U B O R D I N A T E   C L A U S E S   (C O N C L U S I O N)

A D V E R B I A L   C L A U S E S   (C O N C L U S I O N)

تا

1) 'As long as,' 2) 'as soon as,' 'by the time' (present),
3) 'until, before,' 'by the time' (future), 4) until not = unless;
drills, reading.

تا

As a preposition (see Lesson 13 above), تا indicates the
stretch of distance (تا رُم 'until Rome') or time (تا فردا 'until
tomorrow'). As a temporal conjunction, تا likewise indicates
a) the <u>time stretch</u> of an action or a situation ('as long as,
while'), or b) the <u>end point of the stretch itself</u> ('as soon
as, at the time, by the time'), or c) the <u>time stretch with
its conclusion</u> ('until the time').

(for تا see also pp. 318)

1) 'AS LONG AS, (ALL THE) WHILE'

    a) When the action is <u>ongoing</u> and <u>factual</u>, the notion of stretch is usually that of 'as long as' or 'all the while' and the verb is in the indicative present or past in both the تا clause and main clause, e.g.:

تا کار میکند خوشحال <u>است</u> .

    As long as he <u>works/is working</u>, he is happy.

تا کار میکرد خوشحال <u>بود</u> .

    As long as he <u>worked/was working</u>, he was happy.

تا قیمت نفت گران <u>است</u> با اتوبوس <u>میروم</u> .

    As long as the price of gas <u>is</u> so high, I <u>go</u> by bus.

2) 'AS SOON AS, BY THE TIME (PRESENT)'

When the action implies the end of a stretch of an action immediately preceding the other action, تا is usually translated as 'as soon as.' The main verb is usually in the past or past perfect, e.g.:

تا اتوبوس <u>رسید</u> صف دوبرابر <u>شده بود</u> .

    By the time the bus <u>arrived</u>, the line had gotten twice as long.

تا اتوبوس <u>رسید</u> همه بالا <u>پریدند</u> .

    As soon as the bus <u>arrived</u>, everyone jumped on it.

تا موضوع را <u>فهمید</u> لبخند زد.

    As soon as he <u>understood</u> the matter, he began to smile.

3) 'UNTIL/BY THE (FUTURE) TIME, BEFORE (SUBJUNCTIVE)'

When the action preceding the other is not complete and
thus not a fact yet, but regarded as a future possibility, the
verb is in the subjunctive and تا usually has the meaning
of 'until/by (the time)' or 'before.' The main verb is
usually in the suggestive, the present or the future, e.g.:

تا حسن بیاید کمی بازی کنیم .

> Until the time/before Hassan comes, let's play a little.

تا نفت بیشتری پیدا کنیم از زغال اِستِفاده میکنیم .

> Until/before we find more oil, we will use coal.

تا اتوبوس برسد صف دو برابر خواهد بود .

> By the time/before the bus arrives, the line will be twice as long.

تا نامه برسد ما برگشته ایم .

> By the time/before the letter arrives, we will have returned.

4) 'UNTIL (NOT) = UNLESS'

In certain contexts, especially when both the تا clause and
the main clause are negated, the smoothest English equivalent
of تا ... نه is often simply 'until.' As a rule of thumb,
whenever a clause with 'until' can be changed to 'only when,'
use تا ... نه , e.g.:

تا این را یاد نگیرید چیزی
نمیفهمید .

Until you learn it, you won't
understand. =

Only when you learn it,
will you understand.

تا نفت تمام نشود مردم فکرش را
نخواهند کرد .

Until gas runs out, people won't
bother. =

Only when gas runs out,
will people bother.

تا آنرا نخواندم نمیدانستم چقدر
خوب است .

Until I (had) read it, I did not
know how good it is. =

Only when I (had) read it,
did I realize how good it is.

SUMMARY

تا ... میروی / میرفتی

'as long as' - present or past
continuous

تا ... تا آمد

a) 'as soon as' - past/present
b) 'until (final fact)' (p. 318)

تا ... بیاید

a) 'until'/before - subjunctive
b) 'so that, in order to' (p. 318)

تا ... نیاید ... (نه)

'unless, until' - negative
subjunctive

DRILLS

تمرین

A) Read the following sentences. For each of the five groups identify which type of تا is used and then translate the sentences:

۱) تا بچه خوابیده است رادیو را روشن نکن .

۲) تا این قالی فروشی باز است بهتر است چند تا از قالی هایش را ببینیم .

۳) تا کمی از پولمان مانده است یک <u>هدیه</u> برای او بخریم .

۴) تا دارند فیلم تلویزیون را تماشا میکنند کسی نمیتواند حرف بزند .

۵) تا آنها آنجا نشسته اند کسی نمیتواند از آنجا عبور کند .

۶) تا تب داری نباید از خانه بیرون بروید .

gift

---

۱) تا غذا حاضر بشود ما از گرسنگی مرده ایم .

۲) تا سال تمام بشود قیمت نفت دوبرابر خواهد شد .

۳) تا آوازش تمام بشود سالن خالی خواهد شد .

۴) تا شوهرم یک تلویزیون رنگی برای ما بخرد پیر خواهیم شد .

۵) تا همهٔ این تمرین ها را تمام بکنی همه چیز را یاد گرفته ای .

---

۱) تا غذا حاضر بشود بفرمائید کمی قدم بزنیم .

۲) تا اتوبوس برسد میتوانیم یک قهوه با هم بخوریم .

۳) تا وسط خیابان برسیم چراغ راهنما قرمز میشود .

۴) تا گارسون غذا را بیاورد اجازه بدهید من یک تلفن بکنم .

۵) تا دکتر برسد فشار خون شما را میگیرم .

---

۱) تا از چهار راه رد شدم مُتَوَجِه شدم اِشْتِباه آمده ام. aware/(by) mistake.

۲) تا نامهٔ پدرم رسید فورا به او تلفن کردم .

۳) تا ضبط صوت را خاموش کردم همه صدایشان در آمد .

۴) تا درسم را تمام کردم در این اداره مشغول کار شدم .

۵) تا خانواده ام به اینجا آمدند مجبور شدم این آپارتمان را اجاره کنم .

---

۱) تا باران نیایددرخت ها سبز نخواهند شد .

۲) تا این قرص ها را نخورید حال شما بهتر نمیشود .

۳) تا دهانت را باز نکنی نمیتوانم چیزی بشنوم .

۴) تا کاملا توضیح ندهی این موضوع را نمیفهمم .

۵) تا موافق نباشی آنها نمیتوانند در کلاس شرکت کنند .

B) Fill in the blanks with the appropriate verb forms. The main verb at the end will give the clue:

۱) تا از اتوبوس پیاده ـــــ او را دیدم .

۲) تا کار ـــــ همیشه نارحت است .

۳) تا وارد اطاق ـــــ تلفن زنگ زد .

۴) تا این تمرینها را ـــــ چیزی یاد نخواهی گرفت .

۵) تا این عَیْنَک را ـــــ نمیتوانم خوب بخوانم .

۶) تا آخرین گُروه از مهمانها ـــــ اولین گروه حاضر بودند بروند . group

۷) تا خودتان در اینجا رانندگی ـــــ نمیتوانید بفهمید رانندگی در اینجا چقدر سخت است .

۸) تا منزل جَدید ما را ـــــ باوَر نمیکنی چقدر قشنگ است . recent new/believe

۹) تا هواپیما در فرودگاه ـــــ هوا تقریبا تاریک شده بود .

۱۰) تا برف ـــــ مجبوریم در خانه باشیم .

خواندني

پروانه ها (بقیه)

روی کرسی همان چراغ گرد سوز قدیمی میسوخت و چند تا پروانه دَور حباب چرخ میزدند . هیچ چیز تغییر نکرده بود . درها ،دیوارها ،پنجره ها ،پرده ها ، تیرهای سقف . هیچ چیز تغییر نکرده بـود . فقط مادرم فرسوده تر شده بود . و چشمهای برادرم را ترسانده بودند و خواهرم ... خواهرم مثل عروسک قشنگی نشسته بود و چانه اش را تکیه داده بود به لبهٔ کرسی و با چشمهای شیشه ای اَش به شعلهٔ چراغ نگاه میکرد . مادرم گفت :" مگه زبون تو دهنت نیست ؟"

"چی بگم ؟"

"آخه این دوسال کجا بودی ؟ چکار کردی ؟"

"هیچی ."

"خسته ای . پاشم برات چائی درست کنم ."

نه ، هیچ چیز تغییر نکرده بود : درها ، دیوار ها ، پنجره ها ، پرده ها ، تیر های سقف ، همه همان جور مثل سابق بود . فقط گمان کنم که در قَلبِ ها مان چیزی شکسته شده بود . در قلب ها مان چیزی را شکسته بودند . چراغ روی کرسی میسوخت . پروانه ها دیگر نمیچَرخیدند و چسبیده بودند به حباب چراغ . سماور غلغل میکرد ، و سر خواهرم مثل کلهٔ کنده شدهٔ عروسکی افتاده بود گوشهٔ کرسی . شب آهسته میگذشت و ما در اندوهی خاموش به یکدیگر نگاه میکردیم .

oil lamp	چراغِ گِردُ سوز
old (from old times)	قَدیمی
burns	میسوزد / میسوخت
lamp shade	حُباب
circle	چَرْخ میزد / زد
change	تَغْییر میکند
ceiling beam	تیرِ سَقْف
worn out	فَرْسوده
doll	عَروسک
lean against	به ... تِکیه میدهم
edge	لَبه
glass-like	شیشه ای
flame	شُعْله
former	سابِق
I should believe, think	گُمان کنم
(guess from context!)	غُلْغُل
head	کَله
pulled off	کَنْده شُده
corner	گوشه
sadness	اَنْدوه

هیچ چیز	=	هیچی	مگر (cf.p.189)	=	مگه
پا بشوم	=	پاشَم	زبان	=	زبون
برایت	=	برات	چه بگویم	=	چی بِکَم
			آخر after all	=	آخه

A P P E N D I X   I

T H E   G L O T T A L   S T O P

هَمْزه

1) Initial position, 2) medial position, 3) connecting vowels,
3A) words ending with a vowel, 3B) words beginning with a vowel

---

There are two letters for the glottal stop: one is ع which occurs
only in Arabic loanwords. The orthography of this letter is always
the same. The other glottal stop occurs in loanwords, as well, but
it is also used as an <u>orthographic</u> device in Persian to indicate the
connection between two adjacent vowels. This glottal stop is indicated by the diacritic ء (in shape like a small ع). The orthography of this diacritic (not its pronunciation) presents the only
problem of Persian orthography (a problem the Persians willy-nilly
adopted together with the Arabic writing system). Pending on the
vowels that precede and/or follow it, this diacritic is placed over:

أ   ؤ   ئـ

The last letter is, in fact, the letter ـئـ without the two dots.
Just as is the case with the other diacritics, ء is usually omitted
over أ and ؤ , but not with ئـ (since the two dots are omitted,

there must remain some distinctive symbol over the hook).

Alphabetically, أ follows آ ,but ؤ is ordered together with

و ; ئـ follows بـ .

1) <u>INITIAL POSITION</u>

In initial position the diacritic is written over ا . This is

also the case with all initial vowels, as all initial vowels be-

gin with a glottal stop. Thus, e.g., very correct orthography would

write أبر /abr/ 'cloud', or إسم /esm/ 'name'. Generally, how-

ever, neither diacritic is written, thus: اسم – ابر.

2) <u>MEDIAL POSITION</u>

   a) <u>hamze</u> preceded by /o/ is written   ؤ

   b) <u>hamze</u> preceded by /a/ and followed by /a/ is written   أ

   c) <u>hamze</u> preceded by /a/ and followed by /ā/ is generally written   آ

   d) elsewhere <u>hamze</u> is generally written ئـ

a)	o ?	رُؤَسا	سُؤال
b)	a?a	مُتَأسِّف	كأخير
c)	a?ā	بِآثر	مآخذ
d)	e?o a?u	نِئون	مَئول

Note: following more recent trends in orthography ׃ ئـ before

/i/ and /e/ can also be written as   ـيـ , e.g.:

پا ئيز   or   پا ئيز

قا ئِل   or   قا ئِل

3)   <u>CONNECTING VOWELS</u>

3A)   <u>WORDS ENDING IN A VOWEL</u>

The glottal stop is also an <u>orthographic</u> device that occurs when
words ending in a vowel are followed by endings, suffixes, etc.,
which themselves begin with vowels.   There are five main contexts
where the final vowel of a word is bound to 'clash' with the following vowel: a) the verb 'to be' / ام – ای – است /etc.; b) the
verbal endings / م – ی – د /etc.;   c) the possessive suffixes
/ ام – ات – اش / etc.; d) the suffix ی (unstressed); e) the
suffix ی (stressed); f) the connective /e/ of the اضافه .

a)   There is no problem with the <u>verb 'to be'</u>; all forms begin
     with ا , e.g.:

خسته ام	'I am tired', etc.
رفته ام	'I have gone.'

b)   There is no problem with the <u>verbal endings</u>, they follow the
     rule: insert ی /y/ between two vowels, e.g.:

میایم	'I come'

c)   <u>Personal suffixes:</u>

     1) after words ending in /-e/:   ا : خانه اش 'his house'

     2) after other vowels: ب : بابایش 'his daddy'

d) __The unstressed suffix__ ‌ی :

1) after words ending in /-e/: ای   e.g.   خانه ای   'a house'

2) after words ending in /-i/: ∅   e.g.   قالی   'a carpet'

          rarely: ئی   e.g.   قالی ئی   'a carpet'

3) after other vowels: ئی   e.g.   دانشجوئی   'a student'

e) __The stressed suffix__ ی :

1) after words ending in /-e/: گی   e.g.   خستگی   'fatigue'

                                       ئی   e.g.   قهوه ئی   'brown'

2) after other vowels: ئی   e.g.   آمریکائی   'American'

f) __The connective /-e/ of the__ اضافه :

1) after words ending in /-e/ : (ء)   e.g.   خانهٔ من   'my house'

2) after words ending in /-i/: ∅   e.g.   قالی من   'my carpet'

3) after other vowels: ی   e.g.   آقای میلر   'Mr. Miller'

g) __Overview__

The main orthographic rules described above are:

word ends in:	'to be'	endings	suffixes	-i	-í	/-e/
1. /-e/	ام	—	ام	ای	گی / ئی	ء
2. other vowels	ام	یم	یم	ئی	ئی	ی
e.g.	خسته ام / دانشجوای	— / میآیم	خانه ام / با بایش	خانه ای / دانشجوئی	خستگی / آمریکائی	خانهٔ خوب / آقای میلر

Note on ی

The orthographic rules for vowel combination as given above reflect the general rules found today. One occasionally finds some 'older' and some 'modern' orthography for ی :

	اضافه	unstressed ی	'you are'	stressed ی
general	خانهٔ خوب	خانه ای	خسته ای	آمریکائی
modern	خانه‌ی خوب	خانه یی	خسته یی	آمریکایی
older/ other	خانه خوب	خانهٔ	خستهٔ	

3B) WORDS BEGINNING WITH A VOWEL

a) preposition به

The preposition is occasionally linked up with the <u>alef</u> of the following word, e.g.:

بهآن/بان ـ بهاو/باو 'to him, to that'

(note older: به آن = بدان)

b) the prefix به

/be/ → /bi/	before /ā/ e.g.:		بیابد	'may he come'
/bi/	before /a/ e.g.:		بیأرزد	'may it be worth'
/bi/	before /o/ e.g.:		بیأفتد	'may it fall'
/be/ → /be/	before /i/ e.g.:		بأیستد	'may he stand up'

APPENDIX II

SOME BASIC NOTES ON ARABIC IN PERSIAN

1) اَل, 2) number and gender, 3) Arabic tri-literal roots, 4) derived stems

---

Arabic loans are quite numerous in Persian. These include single words as well as phrases. The following is a summary of some major points of Arabic grammar in Persian.

1) اَل

The Arabic definite article ال, found in certain phrases and personal names in Persian, is assimilated to a following dental and palatal, the so-called حروف شمسی 'sun letters' (ش representing the group); these letters are:

ن ر ط ص ش س ث ت

ل ظ ض ز ذ د

e.g.:

رُكْنُ آلدّين	rokno-d-din
قَوامُ آلسَّلطنه	qawāmo-s-saltane
مَلِكُ آلشُّعَرا	maleko-š-šoʔarā
ذوآلنّور	zo-n-nur

2) <u>NUMBER AND GENDER</u>

    a) The <u>dual ending</u> indicating 'two' occurs with a few words, e.g.:

                v$\bar{a}$led<u>eyn</u>   'parents'

                والِدَيْن

                hazrat<u>eyn</u>   'highnesses (king and queen)'

                حَضْرَتَيْن

                taraf<u>eyn</u>   'both parties' (sides)

                طَرَفَيْن

b) Gender-plural

    1) The Arabic <u>feminine ending</u> appears in Persian as <u>e</u> or <u>at</u>;

    for both the plural is <u>-$\bar{a}$t</u>, e.g.:

        emk$\bar{a}$n - emkan$\bar{a}$t   'possibility/-ies'

    امكانات ـ امكان

        ed$\bar{a}$re - ed$\bar{a}$r$\bar{a}$t   'office/-s'

    ادارات ـ اداره

        em$\bar{a}$rat - em$\bar{a}$r$\bar{a}$t   'building/-s'

    عمارات ـ عمارت

But in most cases the Persian plural ها is appropriate. Note that the '<u>feminine</u>' plural -$\bar{a}$t is the usual ending for plurals of abstract nouns, as امكانات . Even a few Persian words have sometimes the <u>feminine</u> plural ending -$\bar{a}$t, e.g.:

        deh-$\bar{a}$t   دهات   'villages'

        sabzij$\bar{a}$t سبزيجات 'greenery, vegetables'

c) <u>Masculine plurals</u> in Arabic loans are either <u>-un</u>, or more frequently <u>-in</u>, e.g.:

moslem - moslem<u>in</u> 'Moslem'

مسلمین ــ مسلم

mosāfer - mosāfer<u>in</u> 'traveler'

، مسافرین ــ مسافر

Such plurals are increasingly replaced by ها .

<u>OVERVIEW</u>

	singular	dual	plural
masc.			-un/-in
fem.	-e/-at	-eyn	-āt

3) ARABIC TRI-LITERAL ROOTS

Most Arabic words are based on a tri-literal root, i.e., three consonants which give the basic meaning. Changes in the vowel pattern, prefixes and suffixes identify more specific meanings. E.g., compare the nouns on the right with their roots on the left:

root		sample derivation			
سلم	'be safe'	سَلام	'peace'	اِسْلام	'Islam'
درس	'learn/teach'	تَدْریس	'instruction'	مَدْرَسه	'school'
علم	'know'	تَعْلیم	'teaching'	مُعَلِم	'teacher'
قبل	'receive'	اِسْتِقْبال	'reception'	قَبول	'accepted'
مكن	'be able'	اِمْكان	'possibility'	مُمْكِن	'possible'
عذر	'forgive'	مَعْذِرَت	'forgiveness'	عُذْر	'forgiveness'
وقع	'fall, happen'	مَوْقِع	'moment'	واقِع	'located'
عجب	'wonder'	تَعَجُب	'surprise'	عَجیب	'strange'

a) Thus, irregular plurals are formed by changes in vowel patterns; the most frequently found patterns in Persian are:

CoCoC	e.g.:	ketāb ➡ kotob	'books'	کتاب ـ کتب
CoCuC	e.g.:	haqq ➡ hoquq	'wages'	حق ـ حقوق
CoCaCā	e.g.:	vazir ➡ vozarā	'vezirs'	وزیر ـ وزرا
aCCāC	e.g.:	taraf ➡ atrāf	'sides, directions'	طرف ـ اطراف
		vaqt ➡ ovqāt*	'times'	وقت ـ اوقات

*Note that av- changes to ov-.

b) <u>Root-nouns and adjectives</u> are created by various vowel patterns, e.g. (root H - R - M):

CaCaC	e.g.:	haram	'forbidden (place), harem'
		حرم	
CaC̄aC	e.g.:	harām	'forbidden (by law)'
		حرام	
CoCC-at	e.g.:	horm-at	'honor, esteem, interdiction'
		حرمت	

c) <u>Place</u> is marked by the prefix /ma-/; <u>instrument</u> by the prefix /me-/; e.g.:

place:	ma-CCaC	e.g.:	ma-xzan	'magazine, storage'
			مخزن	XZN
	ma-CCaCe	e.g.:	ma-dras-e	'school'
			مدرسه	DRS
occupation:	CaC-C-āC	e.g.:	kaffāš	'shoemaker'
			كفاش	KFŠ

d) The basic <u>active participle</u> has the pattern C̄aCeC; the basic <u>'passive' participle</u> has the pattern ma-CCuC; e.g.:

active:	C̄aCeC	e.g.:	ʔālem	'knowing, wise'
			عالم	ʕLM
passive:	ma-CCuC	e.g.:	ma-ʔlum	'known, evident'
			معلوم	

4) <u>DERIVED STEMS</u>

The patterns mentioned so far are derived from the basic stem of
the Arabic verb. There are ten and more derived stems, each of
which modifies the basic verbal meaning. There are thus ten or
more 'modified-basic' meanings involved. The pattern of these
derivations is quite regular and systematic. Since 99% of the
Arabic loan words in Persian are participles and verbal nouns,
only those are given in the following chart. As can, of course,
be expected, no one root has all derivations. For the sake of
this overview the root <u>h-r-m</u> is played through <u>eight</u> derivations.
The approximate modified-basic meanings of each of the stems is
indicated at the bottom.

Tentative abstracted base elements of Arabic

(Root H - R - M)

		<u>Cause</u>	<u>For</u>
1.	Partc.	mo-hrem	mo-n-harem
		محرم	منحرم
	Noun	e-hrām	en-herām
		احرام	انحرام
2.	Partc.	mo-harrem	mo-hārem
		محرم	محارم
	Noun	ta-hrim	mo-hāreme/herām
		تخريم	محارمه/حرام
3.	Partc.	mo-ta-harrem	mo-ta-hārem
		متحرم	متحارم
	Noun	ta-harrom	ta-hārom
		تحرم	تحارم
4.	Partc.	mo-sta-hrem	mo-h-t-arem
		مستحرم	محترم
	Noun	este-hrām	e-h-t-erām
		استحرام	احترام

	<u>'Causing'</u>	<u>'Doing for'</u>
1.	'make (like)'	'become (like)'
2.	'cause other'	'do for/with other'
3.	'cause self'	'do for/with each other'
4.	'cause other do for self'	'do for self/other'

Note:

The participles given above are active participles.

'Passive' participles are distinguished only by the final vowel,

which is /-a-/; e.g.:

active: /moharr<u>e</u>m/;   'passive': /moharr<u>a</u>m/

مُحَرِّم   مُحَرَّم

APPENDIX III

HANDWRITING

1) Base lines, 2) diacritic dots, 3) ک 4) س 5) smooth connections
to ر and د and final ه 6) ه—ها 7) connecting from above, 8) م
9) connecting from below, 10) some elegant slants, 11) the traditional way.

1) **Base lines**

There are a main and a minor base line: groups of connected letters
begin above the main base line, but the last letter ends up on the
main base line somewhat like this:

Isolated letters, too, sit on the line. The slanting should not be
too much.

2) **Diacritic dots**

Reduce ‑‑‑‑‑ ‑‑‑‑ to ‑‑‑ ‑‑‑ e.g.: ب — پ / ش — ش

and ‑‑‑‑ ‑‑‑‑ to ‑‑‑ ‑‑‑ e.g.: ت — ت / ي — ي

3) a. ا and ک are linked as ﮔ (also: ﮔ)

 b. ل and ک are linked as کل (also: کل)

 (c. ا and ل are linked as لا)

4) **س**

The three hooks of س are simplified to ⌣ with the letter
beginning slanted (never vertically). This is especially helpful
when the three hooks of س are preceded or followed by letters whose
basic shape is a hook, too, e.g.:

شش — ش — ش / بس — بس — بس

355

a. The single hook is directly connected to س but begins vertically to distinguish it from single س , thus:

$$ \text{بس ــ بس / س ــ س ــ س} $$

b. When more letters precede, the middle hook appears as a roof, e.g.:

$$ \text{تنش ــ تنش / بینیش ــ بینیش} $$

c. س is directly connected to a following hook and other letters, e.g.:

$$ \text{شکت ــ شکست / نسبت ــ نسبت} $$

d. Bothersome sequences can thus be quite simplified, e.g.:

$$ \text{نشت / نشت ــ نشت / نیت ــ نیت} $$

5) <u>Smooth connecting to ر and د and final ه</u>

a. ر : نظر ــ نظر / کر ــ کر / سر ــ سر / بر ــ بر

b. د : چقدر ــ چقدر / نبد ــ نبد / سد ــ سد / بد ــ بد

c. ه : که ــ که / تنه ــ تنه / سه ــ سه / به ــ به

<u>Note</u>: The smoothened د and ه end on the baseline while ر reaches under the base line.

$$ \text{سر ــ سر ــ سر / کر ــ کد ــ کر / بر ــ بد ــ به} $$

6) a. <u>ه or ﮭ</u> : Optionally, initial ه is written quite differently:

$$ \text{همه ــ همه / هر ــ هر} $$

b. <u>ها or ٔ</u> : The plural marker is frequently not written as ها
but as ٔ (which is a merged form of: ه + ا ــ ٔ)

$$ \text{یا ٔ ــ یاها / خانهٔ ــ خانهها} $$

7) Connecting from above

Four letters are generally connected from above thereby making the connection more fluent.

a) medial and final ح

hooks: رنج — رنج / پنج — ينج / شجره — شجره

others: حج — حج / کج — کج / محمد — محمد

b) medial ه (ﻬ)

hooks: بهر — بهر / تنها — تنها / شهید — شهید

others: ظهر — ظهر / مهر — مهر / لحاف — لحاف

c) final ی

hooks: بی — بی / ابی — ابی / سی — سی

others: کی — کی / اکی — اکی / می — می

d) medial or final م

hooks: بم — بم / بیم — بیم / سم — سم

others: لم — لم / کمک — کمک / صمیمی — صمیمی

8) م at the beginning of the sequence after ک

ملک — ملک / مکان — مکان / میکنم — میکنم

9) <u>Connecting from below</u>

a.

b.

c. Similarly, but with less swing:

10) <u>Some elegant slants</u>

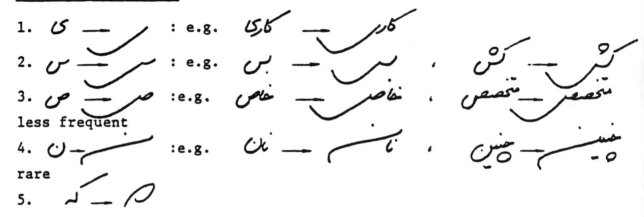

1.   : e.g.

2.   : e.g.

3.   :e.g.

less frequent

4.   :e.g.

rare

5.

and a good number more

11) <u>The traditional way</u>

The relative sizes of the letters are indicated in the accompanying Persian guide. The small rhombi there indicate the size of the tip of the reed-pen, which is cut in a slant. The size of the tip thus defines the size of the letters (the ballpoint pen makes things a little more difficult, especially since it does not allow for the beautiful variation of breadth of the strokes.

انتهای هر پنج نقطه باید اندازه از سر دو نقطه شبیه و قیمت ... باید میزو رستی از ۹ نقطه بدون اینکه باید زده و نوشته شود

که گذاره، با راست مینه نقطه و کشیده، و دسته‌ای نقطه تورت مریم در بعضی آ ابلای زیبا، زیرش کشیده، سه نقطه مینه دارد

سرس و سرط، با به طوری نوشته شود با هم تفاوت داشته باشد بهتر، سرسر و سرط باندازه هر نقطه سرازیر باشد

میم بامیه نقطه باید بهتر و طرای ... در چنانچه مسکو سرکاه دارد بامی و شکل داد و شود

طریقه تراش و صفات و بدست گرفتن قلم :

قلم را باید در میان انگشت شست و سبابه قرار داد و به انگشت وسطی تکیه کرد .

قلم باید رسیده و خوش شکرنگ و راست و متناسب باریزی و درشتی خط باشد

طول تراش قلم باندازه قطر و فاق کاملا و سط قرار گیرد .

A P P E N D I X   IV

M O R E   O N   P R O N U N C I A T I O N

1) Syllables, 2) stress, 3) consonants in word-final position

---

1) SYLLABLES

In English there is a tendency to drop short unstressed vowles,
e.g.: classificatory may become /klasfktori/; political may become /plit(i)kl/. Unlike English, in Persian syllables are pronounced with roughly the same length. Especially in the begin-
ing, the learner should speak slowly, syllable by syllable. Short
vowels are never dropped.

2) STRESS

a) nominal words and noun-phrases

Nominal stress is progressive: i.e., it is placed on the
final syllable in nominal words and on the final syllable
of the final word in noun-phrases.

Suffixes, endings, connectives and prefixes are unstressed.

Nominal words

The stress in nominal words, i.e., nouns, adjectives, adverbs,
numbers, as well as verbal nouns and participles, is on the

<u>final</u> syllable, e.g.: /xāné/ 'house', /bozórg/ 'big', /pahlú/ 'beside', /hezār/ '1000', /didán/ 'visit(ing)', /rafté/ 'gone'.

Similarly, <u>derivative nominals</u> have final stress, the derivative suffix attracting the stress, e.g.: /didan-í/ 'worth seeing', /ketāb-cé/ 'booklet'.

<u>Plural endings</u> are also stressed, e.g.: /ketāb-hā/ 'books', /xub-ān/ 'the good (people)', /deh-āt/ 'villages'.

Noun-phrases

Noun-phrase stress supersedes nominal stress, e.g.: /ketāb-e xùb-e moʔallèm-e fārsí/ 'the good book of the Persian teacher'. Given their semantics, the following usually, but not always, attract stress:

1) question words:	/kodām mašìn/	'which car'
2) demonstratives:	/ín mašìn/	'this car'
always stress:	/hám-in/ /hám-ān/	'this/that very ____/'
3) 'each':	/hár mašìn/	'each car'
'not (any)':	/híc mašìn/	'not any car'
4) numbers:	/pánj tā mašìn/	'five cars'
'many':	/xéyli mašìn/	'many cars'
'some; few'	/báʔzi; kám mašìn/	'some; few cars'

b) <u>Verb form and verbal stress</u>

Verbal stress <u>is</u> <u>regressive</u>: it falls normally on the last syllable of the verb stem in past and perfect forms, and with the infinitive.

/oftád-am/	'I fell'
/šekást-am/	'I broke'
/avordé am/	'I have brought'
/nešasté am/	'I have sat'
/xordán/	'to eat'
/ferestādán/	'to send'

The prefixes /mi/ and /be/ supercede normal verb stress.

/mí. ferestam/	'I am sending'
/bé šekanam/	'I am breaking'

Compound verbs with prepositions or adverbs take the stress on those particles wherever they occur, superseding the stresses above.

/dár āvordam/	'I took off'
/dár miāram/	'I take off'
/raftam jelów/	'I went forward'

Nouns used in the generic sense are stressed when they precede verbs, and the stress on these nouns supercedes other stresses above.

/šír mirizam/	'I pour milk'
/lebás biyār/	'bring clothes'

In the case of generic nouns used with compound nouns, stress may be either on the separable particle <u>or</u> on the generic noun.

/lebás dàr miāram/   'I take off (my) clothes'

<u>or</u> /lebàs dár miāram/

Primary stress <u>always</u> falls on the negative particle /na/ which supercedes all other verb stress.

/šir némirizam/   'I am not pouring/will not pour milk

/lebas dar némiāram/   'I am not taking off/will not take off (my) clothes

To summarize, verb stress occurs according to the following hierarchy: 1) /na/, 2) generic nouns and separable particles, 3) /mi/ and /be/, 4) final syllable of verb stem.

c) <u>Others</u>

Initial stress is always placed on:

/xéyli/ 'many', /bá?zi/ 'some', /?áyā/ '?', /?ámmā/ 'however'.

/váli/ 'but', /háttā/ 'even', /yá?ni/ 'i.e.', /hánuz/ 'yet, still'.

/bale/ 'yes' may have as many stress and intonation patterns as English 'yes': /bále/ 'yes!', /balé/ 'yes?', etc.

/agár/ 'if': /ágar/ 'if (it is so that)', /magár/ '...unless': /mágar/ 'do you mean that ...?'

d) <u>Vocative</u>

Similar to English, the stress-pitch of the vocative may be on the first or the last syllable, e.g.:

/táhere/ 'Táhere! (come!)': /taheré/ 'Taheré ('your turn' or 'where are you', 'and you?', etc.)'

3) <u>CONSONANTS IN WORD-FINAL POSITION</u>

The pronunciation of consonants differs as to their position in a word, i.e. whether they occur word initially, between vowels, before or after other consonats, and/or at the end of a word. This latter word-final position needs the learner's attention, at least initially: voiceless stops /p-t-c-k/ and voiceless fricatives /f-s-š-x/ are quite audible; but initially the learner may find it difficult to clearly identify the other consonants, especially the voiced stops /b-d-j-g/. This is because these consonants tend to be 'stopped' in word-final position; the consonant is articulated in the mouth but stopped from being released. Final /d/ sometimes sounds like /t/, final /b/ like /p/, etc. However, the difference between /p-b/ or /t-d/ in final position is quite easily determined: the voiceless stops tend to be followed by slight aspiration, but the voiced stops not: thus,

$$/p^h{:}B/, \quad /t^h{:}D/, \quad /c^h{:}J/, \quad /k^h{;}G/.$$

(Here the capital letters symbolize the unreleased consonants.)

Such 'non-release' is especially observable after other consonants, e.g. /hokM/ 'order', /hefZ/ 'retaining', /satL/ 'bucket', /sabR/ 'patience'. (As mentioned above, /h/ and /?/ tend not to be pronounced word-finally; see also p. 24.)

A P P E N D I X   V

FORMAL TO INFORMAL PERSIAN

In informal pronunciation certain distinctions made in formal pronunciation are dropped or merge with others.

These changes from formal to informal are predictable. The inverse,
informal to formal, is somewhat less predictable.

To give an example: formal /ān/ changes to /un/ in informal. This
is predictable. But /un/ in colloquial therefore may correspond to
either /ān/ or /un/, e.g.:

colloquial /cune/ ⎡——— /cāne/ 'chin'
                  ⎣——— /cune/ 'cake of dough'

Unless one already knows the formal pronunciation, one cannot predict
which of the two formal pronunciations is the correct one. There
will be few contexts where the meaning maybe both 'chin' and
'cake of dough'.

There is no standardized way of representing colloquial Persian
in Arabic script. Modern writers have developed certain orthographic
conventions, but these vary.

For the purpose of this textbook, specifically for the dialogues,
some colloquial pronunciations are represented in the writing and
some are not.

Note the following special orthographic signs used in transcription:

⌣ - slight up-down intonation

: - lengthening (for /a/, /e/, /o/)

1. آ م / آ ن ← آم / اون / اوم ← ān/ām → un/um

تموم ← تمام   اون ← آن

اومد ← آمد   ایشون ← ایشان

میخونم ← میخوانم

کتابمون ← کتابمان

کتابتون ← کتابتان

کتابشون ← کتابشان

This change is generally not found with 'formal' words such as:

<u>proper names</u>

ساسان ‐ مهران ‐ نظامی ‐ بهرامی

<u>words related to officialdom, etc.</u>

دانشجو ، دانشگاه : دانش ‐

گذرنامه ، روزنامه ،نامه : ‐ نامه

الان ‐ آماده ‐ راننده ‐ اعلان

<u>loan words</u>

آپارتمان ‐ رمان 'novel' ‐ مبلمان 'furnishings'

2. را ← و (ر) ← rā → /(r)o/ ‐‐‐‐‐‐

/ro/ after vowels: آقارو /āqā-ro/

/e-ro/ ‐‐ /a-ro/:   خونه رو /xuna-ro/

/o/ after consonant: کتابو /ketāb-o/

note: مرا /ma-rā/:   منو /man-o/

note: /rā-ham/ often is reduced to /-am/, e.g.:

/kifetān-rā-ham/ → /kifetun-am/

3. /ar/ → /e/

اکر ← اکه   دیکر ← دیگه

مکر ← مگه   آخر ← آخه

Note that /r/ also is often dropped after a consonant, e.g.:

/fekr/ → /fek/; /sabr/ → /sab/; /ceqadr/ → /ceqad/.

This loss is **not** represented in writing here.

4. بر ← ور / باز ← وا   bar → var/ bāz → vā (preverbs)

بردار ← وردار / بازایستاد ← وایستاد

5. **numbers**

a. یک ← یه   before consonant, including glottal stop, e.g.:

یک وقتی ← به وقتی   /yek vaqti/ → /ye vaqti/

یک آقائی ← به آقائی   /yek ʔāqāʔi/ → /ye ʔāqāʔi/

b. **other changes**

هفده ← هیوده   پانزده ← پونزده

هجده ← هیژده   پانصد ← پونصد

شش ← شیش   شانزده ← شونزده

6. <u>personal suffixes after vowels</u>

The glide ـی inserted in formal Persian between a vowel and the /-e/
of the ezafe does not appear in colloquial, e.g.:

پایم ⟵ پام

پایت ⟵ پات

پایش ⟵ پاش

پایمان ⟵ پامون

پایتان ⟵ پاتون

پایشان ⟵ پاشون

پارتیات ⟵ پارتیت   برایت ⟵ برات   کتابهایم ⟵ کتابهایم

پالتوت ⟵ پالتوت   رویش ⟵ روش   کجایش ⟵ کجاش

note 1: final /-e/:

خانه اش ⟵ خونه اش   /xāne-y-aš/ ⟶ /xuna-š/

(Change not represented in writing.)

note 2: /aš/ and /at/ tend to be pronounced /eš/, /et/, e.g.:

/ketāb-aš/ ⟶ /ketāb-eš/

7. <u>verbs</u>

    a. 3rd person singular ending

        <u>/-ad/ ⟶ /d/ after /a/ in:</u>

               میاد ⟵ میآید   /miāyad/ ⟶ /miā-d/

            میخواد ⟵ میخواهد   /mixāhad/ ⟶ /mixād/

        <u>/-ad/ ⟶ /e/ elsewhere</u>

           میکنه ⟵ میکند   میبینه ⟵ میبیند

           میپرسه ⟵ میپرسد   میسازه ⟵ میسازد

    b. 2nd and 3rd person plural endings (optional)

        <u>/-id/ ⟶ /in/; /-and/ ⟶ /-an/ (optional)</u>

           گوش کنید   ⟶   گوش کنین

           گوش نمیکنند ⟶ گوش نمیکنن

     کجا پیدایش کردید ؟ ⟵ کجا پیدایش کردین ؟

   نامه رو کی فرستادید؟ ⟵ نامه رو کی فرستادن ؟

    8. <u>verbs contracted</u>

        a. /mi-<u>nešin</u>-ad/ ⟶ /mi-<u>nšin</u>-e/ ⟶ /mi-<u>šin</u>-e/ (bi-šin!)

            /mi-<u>nevis</u>-ad/ ⟶ /mi-<u>nvis</u>-e/

            /mi-<u>andāz</u>-ad/ ⟶ /mi-<u>ndāz</u>-e/

            /mi-<u>gozār</u>-ad/ ⟶ /mi-<u>gzār</u>-e/ ⟶ /mi-<u>zār</u>-e/

        b. /mi-<u>āvar</u>-ad/ ⟶ /mi-<u>ār</u>-e/ (biār!)

            /mi-<u>dav</u>-ad/ ⟶ /mi-do-e/ (bodo!)

            /mi-<u>tavān</u>-ad/ ⟶ /mi-tun-e/

c. /mi-xāh-ad/ ⟶ /mi-xā-d/

    /mi-ā-y-ad/ ⟶ /mi-ā-d/ (biā!)

d. /mi-deh-ad/ ⟶ /mi-d-e/ (be-de!)

    /mi-rav-ad/ ⟶ /mi-r-e/ (bo-ro!)

    /mi-šav-ad/ ⟶ /mi-š-e/ (bo-šo!)

    /mi-guy-ad/ ⟶ /mi-g-e/ (bo-gu!)

Note the assimilation of /be-/ to the following vowels:

/bi-šin/; /bo-ro/; /bo-gu/; also /bo-kon/.

9. /ast/ ⟶ /e/ (except after /ā/, /e/)

جوونه ⟵ جوان است   /javān-ast/ ⟶ /javun-e/

درسته ⟵ درست است   /dorost-ast/ ⟶ /dorost-e/

چیه ⟵ چه است   /ce-ast/ ⟶ /ci-e/

Note that است is dropped in the perfect:

رفته ⟵ رفته است   /rafte-ast/ ⟶ /rafte-e/ ⟶ /rafte/

خوابیده ⟵ خوابیده است   /xābide-ast/ ⟶ /xābide-e/ ⟶ /xābide

After /ā/, /e/ ⟶ /-st/

کجاست ⟵ کجا است   /kojā-ast/ ⟶ /kojā-st/ (or /-s/)

خسته‌ست ⟵ خسته است   /xāste-ast/ ⟶ /xāsta-st/ (or /-s/)

Note change of /é-as(t)/ ⟶ /á-s(t)/ (not represented in writing)

10. /q/ (غ - ق) before voiceless stop ➞ /x/

وقت ➞ va<u>x</u>t   رقص ➞ ra<u>x</u>s

11. The /e/ of the اضافه is often dropped especially after vowels:

توی کلاس ➞ tu_kelās

خانهٔ بزرگ ➞ xune_bozorg

12. Loss of /r/ after consonants such as in

فکر ➞ /fek/;   صبر ➞ /sab/;   قدر ➞ /qad/

13a. /h/ (ح - ه)

   a. replaced by lengthening of vowel before <u>consonant</u>

      شهر ➞ ša:r

   b. dropped <u>after consonant</u>:

      صبح ➞ sob_   خوشحال ➞ xošāl

   c. softened <u>between vowels</u>

      بهار ➞ ba͡ar

b. ها ➞ /ā/,   هم ➞ /am/

   کتابها ➞ ketābā   من هم ➞ man-am

   اینجا ها ➞ injā͡a   اینجا هم ➞ injā-m

   after /e/: بچه ها هم ➞ bac͡ā   بچه ها ➞ bacā-m

14. <u>glottal stop</u> (ٔ - ع) (same as /h/)

a. معلوم ➝ ma:lum   تعریف ➝ ta:rif   تأخیر ➝ ta:xir

b. ربع ➝ rob_   دفعه ➝ daf_e   وزرا (ﻉ) ➝ vozarā

c. ساعت ➝ sā~at   اطلاعات ➝ etelā~at   متاسف ➝ mota~asef

15. <u>Note on hamza</u>

The glottal stop between final vowels and endings is not pronounced:

a. stressed ی : قهوه ای /qahve-i/

         آمریکائی /āmrikā-i/

b. unstressed ی : خانه ای /xune-i/

         رادیوئی /rādio-i/

c. personal suffix after /-e/:

     خانه ام /xāne-y- / ➝ /xuna-m/

     خانه ات   /xuna-t/

     خانه اش   /xuna-š/

     خانه امان   /xuna-mun/

     خانه اتان   /xuna-tun/

     خانه اشان   /xuna-šun/

d. <u>'to be' after /-e/</u>

     خسته ام /xaste-am/ ➝ /xastá-m/

     خسته ای   /xasté-i/

     خسته ایت   /xastá-st/(or /-s/)

     خسته ایم   /xasté-im/

     خسته اید   /xasté-id/ (or /-in/)

     خسته اند   /xastá-nd/ (or /-an/)

e. <u>perfect endings</u>: a slight up-down curve (˜) is added to the final vowel. Stress is placed at the beginning of the curve.

رفته ام /raftãm/

رفته ای /raftĩ/

رفته است /raftẽ/

رفته ایم /raftĩm/

رفته اید /raftĩd/ (or /ĩn/)

رفته اند /raftãnd/ (or /ãn/)

Colloquial constructions

16. اش

a. is often added to the past, e.g.:

گفتش <u>goft-eš</u> he said; رفتش <u>raft-eš</u> he left

b. is often used to refer back to a preceding statement, e.g.:

بعدش bá:d-eš 'afterwards, after that'

آن وقتش un váxt-eš 'at that time'

آن تویش un tú-š 'in there'

اینطوریش into(w)rí-š 'in this way'

همه اش hamá-š 'all of it, totally'

کوشش kú-š-eš 'where is he?'

17. <u>Referential /-é/</u>

In Persian colloquial, there is an equivalent of American colloquial 'this', 'them' as in 'This clown comes here and wants to...', i.e., the clown I was talking about. The ending is stressed /-é/. After vowels, this is added with up-down intonation (⌣). In writing colloquial Persian referential /-e/ is represented as ه , e.g.:

a. <u>singular</u>

این پسره اومد گفت /in pesār-é umad goft/ 'this guy came and said'

Note: after /e/: بچه هه /bace‿é/ 'this kid'

<u>with adjectives</u>: (/-e-/ of the اضافه may be omitted)

پسر کوچولوهه /(in) pesar_kutule-‿é/ 'this tiny guy'

b. <u>plural</u>

This /e/ is absorbed by the plural ending and only

noticeable by a drawl on the plural ending:

پسرا ← پسره ها /pesar‿ā/

پسر کوچیکه ها /pesar_kucik‿ā/

18. واسه /vāse/ 'for'; هی /hey/ 'on and on'

واسه چی اومدید؟ ── برای چه آمدید؟

هی میآمد و میرفت

19. <u>prepositions and personal suffixes</u>

ازم ── از من /azam/

باش ── با او /bāš/

بهاش ── به او /beš/

20. <u>exclamations</u>

ده /de!/ - exclamation of disbelief and surprise

اِ /e!/ - exclamation of objection

ای وای /ey vāi/ - alas!

به به /bah bah!/ - exclamation of approval and praise

آخ /āx/ - exclamation of strong feeling or emotion
often with pain

اوخ /ox/ - ouch!

آ /ā‿/ (at end of sentence) - exclamation of
remonstration